Penguin Education
The Social Psychology of Mental Disorder

G000166928

The Social Psychology of Mental Disorder

Jim Orford

Penguin Education

To Jack and Margaret Orford

Penguin Books Ltd,
Harmondsworth, Middlesex, England
Penguin Books,
625 Madison Avenue, New York, New York 10022, U.S.A.
Penguin Books Australia Ltd,
Ringwood, Victoria, Australia
Penguin Books Canada Ltd,
41 Steelcase Road West, Markham, Ontario, Canada
Penguin Books (N.Z.) Ltd,
182–190 Wairau Road, Auckland 10, New Zealand

First published 1976
Copyright © Jim Orford, 1976

Made and printed in Great Britain by
Cox & Wyman Ltd,
London, Reading and Fakenham
Set in Monotype Times

Contents

Preface

This book is about the bringing together of the discipline of social psychology, on the one hand, and the many problems and issues surrounding mental disorder, on the other hand. Abnormal psychology and social psychology have long existed side by side, but separately, and there has never really been a coherent *abnormal social psychology*. My main purpose has therefore been to stimulate an interest in this new field, and to try and get the reader to share with me the excitement that I feel about this union. The psychology which has been applied, in the past, to the problems of mental disorder has very largely been an *individual* psychology. Clinical psychology has been dominated by interests in cognitive and intellectual testing and processes, and in learning theory. And yet it seems to me that so many of the problems surrounding mental disorder are so obviously *social* in nature.

The field which could be covered in a book with this title is, of course, potentially quite vast, and I have necessarily had to be highly selective. Needless to say, I have exercised a personal choice. This means that there are things which some readers will expect to find here which they will be disappointed not to find. Some of the gaps of which I am aware include: the topic of social stress, life events and related matters; the related area of community psychology concerning the physical environment, work, etc.; and the whole area of sexual behaviour. There must be many other gaps of which I am unaware. The result of my choice is really six essays, each of them representing a broad area for the application of social psychology to an issue, or a set of issues, surrounding mental disorder.

Within each of these areas I have not attempted anything like a complete review, as I felt that this would not serve the main purpose of stimulating interest. Rather I have tried to illustrate what I consider to be some of the more interesting developments, and sometimes to illustrate a few of the dangers and blind alleys as well. The approach varies somewhat from chapter to chapter depending upon the state of knowledge in that area, and the type of research which has been done. For example, Chapter 1 represents an area where the amount of research which has been done is vast, but where the quality of research has generally been poor. As a result, few facts are known despite all the activity. For this reason, more of this chapter than of any other is taken up with voicing misgivings, and warning of the pitfalls in doing, and interpreting, research. Chapter 4, in some respects, represents the opposite extreme. The area it covers has scarcely yet been identified as an area for social psychological study and the amount of research is small. That being the case, it seemed more useful to provoke and speculate, rather than to be overly critical. Chapters 1, 3, and 5 represent traditional areas of investigation, built around study of the parent–child, husband–wife, and therapist–client relationships. Chapter 6, concerning the wider treatment milieu, is scarcely traditional yet, but has in recent years excited a great deal of interest. Chapters 2 and 4 are built more around interpersonal processes than around specific types of relationship or traditional 'problem areas'. They represent a different sort of challenge to the social psychologist, and could conceivably be the areas of greatest growth in the not too distant future.

Acknowledgements

I should like to register the debt of gratitude which I owe to colleagues at the Institute of Psychiatry for the support and stimulation I have received from them. In particular I should like to thank my psychiatrist colleague, Griffith Edwards, who, over a number of years of collaboration, has been the person most instrumental in pointing me in the direction of areas of concern to the practicing clinician, which are ripe for the application of social psychology. My warmest thanks are also due to Joyce Oliphant whose good nature and typing proficiency have helped to bring this book to a conclusion.

Acknowledgements for permission to reproduce Figures and Tables are due to The American Psychological Association (for Fig. 1 and Tables 6 and 8); E. Schaefer (Fig. 1); Academic Press, London, and F. Fransella (Fig. 4); The British Journal of Psychiatry (Figs. 5 and 7); A. Ryle (Fig. 5); N. Kreitman (Fig. 7); The William Alanson White Psychiatric Foundation (Figs. 6 and 9 and Table 10); Academic Press, New York, and E. Jones (Fig. 8); G. Fairweather (Fig. 10 and Table 11); The Nuffield Foundation (Table 1); The Editor, British Journal of Preventive and Social Medicine, G. Brown, E. Monck, M. Carstairs and J. Wing (Table 3); The Society for the Psychological Study for Social Issues, and M. Radke-Yarrow (Tables 4 and 5); E. Siegelman (Table 6); F. Fiedler (Table 8) and the Aldine Publishing Company (Table 9). Thanks are also due to S. Hirsch and J. P. Leff who allowed me to see relevant chapters of their book in manuscript form.

Chapter 1

Parents and Children: The Early Environment

Introduction

The view is widely held that mental disorder can be at least partly attributed to childhood experiences, particularly those occurring in the family. Unfortunately, however, problems of theory and research method are such that proving the influence of early family life is quite another matter.

In the past the dominant theoretical approach to this field has been that of the psychoanalysts. Modern views on the validity of psychoanalytic theory differ markedly, from the views of those such as Kline (1972) who believes that hypotheses have received a large measure of support, to others (e.g. O'Connor and Franks, 1960; Eysenck and Wilson, 1973) who believe that they have been largely invalidated. Quite apart from that controversy, it is the case that Freud's original ideas, and later work which has stemmed from them, have much more to say about *individual* psychology (the relationships between perceptual, cognitive, and emotional processes) than about *social* psychology. Even Kline (1972) admits that there is only extremely scanty support for the sort of association between infant–parent interaction and later personality that would be predicted on the basis of Freudian theory. One of the few positive findings (Goldman-Eisler, 1951), an association between early weaning from the breast and a later detached, unhappy personality, could be explained in terms of a more general influence of parental personality upon child personality, and need not imply a specific effect due to weaning experience.

Of course the association discovered by Goldman-Eisler could be totally explained in terms of the genetic determinants of both mother behaviour and child personality (Eysenck and Wilson, 1973). Indeed whenever social explanations are offered for mental disorder, the possibility has to be faced that the latter phenomena are so largely determined by genetic, interuterine, or birth-related factors that little room is left for the influence of interpersonal events. This possibility has to be seriously faced and is one to which this chapter will return.

It is evident, therefore, that no single theory of sufficient generality or power exists in the family life and mental disorder field, and the result is a current plethora of overlapping, and in many cases ill-defined, terms, many of which have a lay or common sense rather than theoretical basis (e.g. love, warmth, rejection). We may be in a better position at the end of this chapter to judge whether any satisfactory alternative to psychoanalysis is beginning to emerge.

The difficulties of research method are equally great. To date the main source of data about relevant childhood events has been the recollections of individuals, usually adults, who have *already* developed a mental illness and who are undergoing some form of treatment for it. This is, quite obviously, because the problem of mental illness does not become a 'visible' one, and therefore available for study, until people make contact with medical or other helping agencies. By that time the events of childhood are usually beyond the reach of objective study or unbiased recall, particularly if the matters referred to are relatively abstract (e.g. parental 'strictness'), or when events are relatively remote.

'Distant' Family Life Variables

One of the problems with the hodge-podge of ideas which at present takes the place of a coherent theoretical approach concerns the many different 'levels' of analysis to which reference is made. It is possible to invent credible theories linking mental illness with the way the ill person has come to *think* of his childhood past, with aspects of the *actual* caretaking he received, with the attitudes of his parents towards child-rearing in general, with the degree of marital harmony or disharmony between his parents, with the intactness of his home in childhood, with his age and sex in relation to that of his siblings, with aspects of his parents' personalities or even with elements of the upbringing his parents received when *they* were children. Hoffman and Lippitt (1960) discuss these various possible inroads into the problem in terms of a 'causal sequence schema'. Some of these variables are 'causally closer' to the fact of mental illness, others are causally 'more distant'. The latter type of variable, of which the parents' *own* childhood backgrounds or the mentally ill person's birth order in his family are examples, is relatively 'remote' conceptually from the behaviour (mental disorder) with which the theorist expects it to be linked. No one seriously expects to find that all mentally ill people were first-born in their families, for example. If there was a link between a certain birth order and a certain type of mental illness then it would probably be a weak one and as soon as such a link were established we would almost certainly want to offer some explanation for it, at a less 'distant' level, in terms of an intervening social psychological process.

Parental loss as an example of a 'distant' family life variable

The idea that temporary or permanent separation of child from parent (particularly early separation, e.g. Bowlby, 1961) is an important factor in the etiology of adult mental illness is no longer *uncritically* accepted. Munro (1969) has concluded that there is a case for linking separation with suicide, attempted suicide and 'personality disorder', but that the evidence is inconclusive regarding neurosis, schizophrenia and even depression where Bowlby and others had proposed a specific link in terms of a chronic 'bereavement reaction'.

The association between early parental death and psychiatric hospital admission in Scotland has recently been examined by Birtchnell (1970). The incidence of early parental death was no higher for patients with a diagnosis of depression than for control non-psychiatric patients but it was significantly higher in those patients with *severe* depression. However it is to be noted that percentage differences were small (37 per cent for severe depression versus 24 for controls) and were not consistent across all sex-of-patient/sex-of-parent/age-at-death-of-parent groups. The strongest association existed when parental death had occurred before the age of five, and Birtchnell suggests that previous investigations which have found stronger associations have done so because they concentrated on the question of parental death in this early age group.

It does however appear to be fairly well established that broken homes and *delinquency* are related (Wootton, 1959; Koller and Castanos, 1970). But even here Koller and Castanos make the important point that there are a host of factors which should be taken into account if the circumstances of parental loss are to be adequately described. Their list, which could so easily be expanded, includes the age at which parental loss occurred, whether one or both parents were lost, the sex of the lost parent if only one was lost, the cause of loss, and the nature of the subsequent child-rearing environment. The crudity of the concept of a 'broken home' and its 'distance' from the fact of mental disorder, is demonstrated by as simple a procedure as dividing broken homes into those caused by the death of a parent and those caused by divorce or separation. Several studies have shown the latter to be much more predictive of delinquency than the former. Koller and Castanos (1970) report that parental loss, when it occurred in their non-delinquent control group, was more usually due to death, illness or factors extraneous to the family (e.g. war service) whilst amongst prisoners causes mentioned were more likely to reflect some degree of breakdown in interpersonal relationships. Furthermore prisoners who had lost parents were more often placed subsequently in a foster home or institution than were non-delinquents who lost parents.

Ainsworth (1962) pointed out some time ago that the term 'deprivation' has been used to cover three broad categories of conditions to which children may be exposed and which themselves subsume a range of greatly varying circumstances. The three categories are: *insufficiency* of interaction; *distortion* in the quality of interaction; and *discontinuity* of interaction through separation.

Discontinuity on the one hand, and the sufficiency or quality of relationships on the other, are hard to separate. For one thing separation from one parent is often complicated by some degree of separation from the other parent and separation from one parent alone may in some cases be related to aspects of the remaining parent's behaviour. Others have been unable to isolate maternal separation from a 'bad psychological climate' in the home and

Rutter (1972), who has reviewed at length the evidence for both long-term effects (mental retardation, dwarfism, delinquency, 'affectionless psychopathy', depression?) and short-term effects concludes that these probably have more to do with *distortion* of relationships before, during and after separation than with the fact of separation itself.

Even in the very short term the immediate reactions of infants separated from their mothers are known to vary widely (Maccoby and Masters, 1970, pp. 134–7) and some of the factors accounting for this variation may well lie in the health of the existing mother–infant relationship. In work with monkeys (Hinde and Spencer-Booth, 1970) one finding was that greater 'distress' followed separation when the infant–mother relationship, prior to separation, was characterized by the greater initiative of the infant in making contact with its mother, who tended to reject the infant's contact-making attempts.

Birth order as a further example

Even a variable as apparently straightforward as birth order turns out to be deceptively complex (Clausen, 1966). Are only children equivalent to other first-born children, for example? In addition factors such as the spacing between siblings and the sex of older and younger siblings must be assumed to modify the effects of birth order but are in practice rarely controlled for. Research scarcely even approaches the standard set by Koch (1956) whose sample consisted of 384 first and second-born children of approximately the same age with equal representation from each of the eight possible birth order/sex/sex of sibling combinations. Within each subgroup were equal numbers of children representing three different sibling-age-spacing levels (less than two years between subject and sibling; two to four years; four to six years). (See p. 39 below, for some results obtained from this sample.)

Nonetheless there is evidence that alcoholism is more common amongst men who were the last born in their families (Blane and Barry, 1973) and that different types of childhood psychological problem predominate in eldest and youngest children. For example Rutter *et al.* (1970), in a survey of a representative sample of children on the Isle of Wight, find 'neurotic' disturbances more frequently in eldest children and less often in youngest. The effect was reversed for 'socialized anti-social' disorder.

Theories of the Family Interior

Factors to do with the basic structure of a family seem not to take us very far. Relationships with mental disorder are hard to establish, are at best weak, and even when they are established the 'causal nexus' remains unexplored. We have to face up to the need to examine what the editor of one book has called 'the psychosocial interior of the family' (Handel, 1968). Although it has taken us some time to reach this conclusion which we might have adopted at the outset, the course of the discussion so far is justified by the amount of discussion and research which has been devoted over the years to the relationship between mental disorder and superficial characteristics of families.

It is in the study of schizophrenia that some of the most interesting attempts have been made to formulate concepts with which to handle intra-family abnormalities of interpersonal functioning. A number of research groups have adopted the very necessary strategy of studying intensively a relatively small number of families, each containing two parents and at least one child of adolescent or early adult age who has been diagnosed as schizophrenic. Well known amongst these groups have been three US teams, those working at the National Institute of Mental Health (NIMH), Yale, and Palo Alto, associated particularly with the names of Wynne, Lidz and Bateson respectively. However, the concepts and conclusions emerging from these studies have been dissimilar and opinions differ concerning the ease with which they can be integrated.

It is also important to realize that the studies of these three groups which will be cited were not intended to test hypotheses systematically, but rather to generate fresh ideas on the basis of a close examination of families involving many hours of observation of family interaction. On occasions several members of the same family were brought into hospital for the purpose. For one thing, control groups were lacking in these studies. They have also been criticized for the general bias of their samples towards higher socio-economic status groups. In addition, diagnostic details are rarely given, and this is crucial if it is to be supposed that the processes described are specifically linked with schizophrenia. Studies are now showing that the diagnostic habits of psychiatrists in different countries are quite dissimilar. For example US psychiatrists diagnose schizophrenia almost twice as often as UK psychiatrists (Kendell *et al.*, 1971). There may be agreement in severe cases but there is much less agreement for milder cases and the terminology (e.g. 'schizophreniform psychosis', 'borderline psychosis', 'pseudoneurotic schizophrenia') is varied and confusing.

Double binds

The Palo Alto group introduced the concept of the 'double bind' to describe certain features of the patterns of communication witnessed in families undergoing conjoint family treatment. Briefly, it refers to situations in which one person (typically the child) receives contradictory messages from someone with whom he is involved in an intense emotional relationship (typically a parent). One message is usually conveyed by verbal content (e.g. 'go to bed, you are very tired, I want you to get your sleep'), the other by non-verbal signals conveyed by facial expression, gesture, posture, or tone of voice (e.g. said in a tone of voice implying 'get out of my sight, you make me sick'). Repeated exposure to such situations is thought to be especially damaging if the recipient cannot escape from the situation, is forced to respond to the more abstract, usually the verbal, 'primary injunction' and is punished if he attempts to point out the contradiction. Conformity to these conditions is said to encourage a style of interpersonal perception and behaviour involving the consistent ignoring of certain aspects of social communications (Bateson *et al.*, 1956).

Recent reviewers (e.g. Schuham, 1967) have faulted the double bind notion for its indefiniteness, pointing out that the concept has lately been broadened to include almost any apparent contradiction to which an individual is exposed in the context of an important emotional relationship. Furthermore, the concept has been applied to conditions or deviant behaviours other than schizophrenia, such as delinquency, as well as to situations usually thought of as outside the scope of abnormal psychology altogether, such as art, humour and play.

The most telling criticism is the lack, so far, of empirical support for the relationship with schizophrenia or even for the unequivocal existence of the phenomenon at all. However, the methodological difficulties in arranging suitable conditions under which aspects of interpersonal communication at such a 'micro' level can be isolated and counted are considerable. Several studies have provided an inadequate test, for example, by asking patients suffering from schizophrenia to recall typical statements made by their mothers, by asking parents and children to agree on the meaning of proverbs which have two equally correct meanings, and by observing how evasive mothers of schizophrenic patients are in the course of an interview with a third person. Particularly challenging have been Ringuette and Kennedy's (1966) findings. They asked a number of groups, including a group of research workers who were involved in the initial formulations of the double bind concept and a group of clinicians trained in the concept, to identify double binds in letters written by parents to their hospitalized schizophrenic children (such letters providing one of the contexts originally giving rise to the concept). The level of agreement between the raters turned out to be very low.

Multi-channel studies of emotional communication

One recent attempt to make a more objective 'micro-analysis' of inter-channel communication discrepancies of the double bind type was made by Bugental *et al.* (1971) who made video-tape recordings of twenty children, who had been referred for behavioural or emotional problems, while they interacted with their parents. They compared them with similar recordings of ten normal children and their parents. Verbal, vocal and visual aspects of interaction were analysed separately by examining scripts, content-filtered sound recordings and visual recordings separately, and significantly more inter-channel conflict was found to be displayed by mothers of the referred children than by mothers of controls when delivering *evaluative* messages. Typically, a message with a negative verbal content, such as a reprimand, would be spoken to the child in a positive tone of voice. The results show that the phenomenon is certainly not confined to mothers with children who receive a diagnosis of schizophrenia. In a similar study, Beakel and Mehrabian (1969) compared video-taped recordings of severely and mildly disturbed adolescents and their parents. They could find no differences in terms of *conflict* between communication levels but observed a higher incidence of communication of negative feelings in the severely disturbed group.

Argyle *et al.* (1970, 1971) conveyed messages to their (normal, well) subjects which were ambiguous with regard to the degree of dominance or of warmth which they displayed. The presence or absence of indications of dominance or warmth were systematically, and *independently*, varied both in terms of verbal content and non-verbal signals. The receivers of these messages then rated the degree of dominance or warmth conveyed by the message as a whole. The results showed that, at least in these experiments, when verbal message and non-verbal signals (facial expression, head posture, tone of voice etc.), differed, they relied very much more upon non-verbal aspects than upon verbal content. Ambiguity over warmth and hostility appeared to be more disturbing to subjects than ambiguity over dominance and submissiveness. Of course these last-mentioned experiments do not contain the supposedly important double bind elements of strong emotional relationship and lack of opportunity for escape or comment.

It can fairly be said then that the concept of the double bind is an intriguing one which links the applied field with experimental social psychology, but its significance for mental disorder, and for schizophrenia in particular, is at the moment quite unclear.

Pseudo-mutuality, family myths and values

Research at the NIMH has particularly drawn attention to role relationships between members of families which might provide the antecedent conditions for 'thought disorder'. Relationships in families from which young adult schizophrenics are drawn are said to be characterized by a rigid 'pseudo-mutuality' in which adherence to a fixed set of ideas concerning how the family should function is rewarded (e.g. that the parents love each other and make sacrifices for the children) and an accurate perception of elements of individual and group functioning which are discrepant with this stereotype is discouraged, or meets with denial or reinterpretation (Wynne *et al.*, 1958). The growth of a true individual 'personal identity', as opposed to an identity as merely part of a rigid group structure, is said to be stunted by such a system. Notions of family 'myths' (Jackson, 1957) and family 'axis values' (Scott and Ashworth, 1965), in defence of which spontaneity and individuality are sacrificed, are closely related ideas.

Psychopathology in family members, marital schism and marital skew

The Yale group suggest, among other things, that the incidence of previous *treatment* for mental illness gives a gross underestimate of the true rate of psychopathology and personality abnormality in both *parents* and *siblings* of index patients. Upon closer study, siblings can be described as either clearly 'disturbed' or 'constricted' personalities, or alternatively as having escaped family influence by separating themselves or by minimizing family contact at an early age. In addition they view the marital relationship of these patients' parents as being of one of two types; 'schismatic' or 'skewed'. In the former type strife and disharmony between the parents is open and obvious; in the latter type open discord is less apparent but the influence on the home atmosphere of the more disturbed parent is dominant and inadequately compensated for by the more healthy but less assertive parent (Lidz *et al.*, 1957).

The Transmission of Disorder

Many other investigators besides Lidz *et al.* (1957) have noted the 'psychopathology' of other members of the families of the mentally ill, and have been lead to think in terms of some form of environmental transmission of disorder from parents to children.

One important conclusion from several studies is that distinctions between mental and physical illness, both for parents and children, are not very useful when the coincidence of illness in different members of the same family is being considered. Rutter's (1966) study is typical in finding a relatively high rate of recurrent or chronic *physical* illness, as well as a relatively high rate of psychiatric illness, amongst parents of child guidance clinic attenders.

In a series of large-scale Scandinavian clinical studies, Alanen and his colleagues (e.g. 1966) have examined the standing of the parents and siblings of schizophrenics, neurotics, and well controls on a five- or six-point 'severity of disturbance' rating scale. They find that parents (and to a lesser degree siblings also) of patients with a diagnosis of schizophrenia are relatively unlikely to be rated at the normal end of the continuum. However for the most part they are not to be found at the other end of the continuum, in the psychotic or borderline psychotic categories, either. The majority occupy an intermediate position in a 'severe neurosis' or 'personality disorder' group and are described as typically 'schizoid', aggressive, emotionally constricted and lacking in understanding of, and respect for, the patient. Muntz and Power (1970) find that the more psychiatric patients show 'thought disorder', the more their parents do too.

Twin and sibling studies

Not all children in the same family develop a mental disorder of the same type or of the same degree of severity, and there have been many suggested explanations of sibling and twin differences along environmental lines. Studies of identical twins discordant for schizophrenia (i.e. one twin is diagnosed schizophrenic, the other is not) (e.g. Mosher *et al.*, 1971; Pollin *et al.*, 1965) provide a particularly important source of data on the role of social psychological factors in etiology as many of the major contaminating factors (e.g. genetic, ethnic, socio-economic and sibling age differences), which normally make inferences about social factors impossible, are automatically controlled.

Both Mosher *et al.* (1971) and Pollin *et al.* (1965) note the lighter birth weight of most of the schizophrenic twins and hypothesize that they were 'selected', perhaps on the basis of this or other physical differences, as a special focus for parental concern and attention, particularly from the less healthy parent. Their greater vulnerability, it is suggested, derives from a combination of organic and social psychological sources. The non-schizophrenic twin may be afforded 'protection' by closer association with the healthier parent. A very similar type of explanation has been put forward to explain discordance for affective illness (i.e. a condition characterized by excessive depression or elation).

Transmission by contagion

Although some of the conditions under which mental ill health may be found in both parents and children have been suggested above, the mechanisms through which illness may be transmitted from parents to children are rarely more than hinted at. For the most part however, possible mechanisms fall into one or other of two main classes, those that posit family 'tension' or some other form of abnormal family 'climate' responsible for the link between parental illness and child illness, and those that suppose a much more specific form of transmission in terms of imitation or 'identification' of child with parent.

Amongst proposals of the latter type is Ehrenwald's (1963) 'contagion', a term which he uses to describe a pattern of inter-personal relationships within the family whereby neurotic disorders in particular are spread from one member to another. Ehrenwald provides the 'Obscomp family' (a fictitious name for a real family) as an illustration. Thirteen out of fourteen members of this family, spanning three generations, suffered from obsessional and/or compulsive symptoms. This family gave the impression of a 'veritable epidemic of obsessional-compulsive neurosis, handed down from one generation to the next with very little variation on the basic themes of control and compliance, dominance and submission, compulsion and doubt' (Ehrenwald, 1963, p. 80). He speaks of both *homonymic* contagion, when identical or similar symptoms occur in two family members, and of *heteronymic* contagion, when symptoms are different but interpersonal influence, via processes such as rebellion or 'negative identification', is still apparent.

What is transmitted from one family member to another may

take the form of chronic 'frustration-hostility-aggression' states (Thorne, 1957), disparaging attitudes (Cleveland and Longaker, 1957), irrationality (Lidz *et al.*, 1958), fears and phobias (Marks, 1969, pp. 64–5), preoccupation with food and weight (Amdur *et al.*, 1969) or simply a characteristic family atmosphere associated with a variety of deviant behaviours (Fisher and Mendell, 1956).

Clearly related is the clinically described phenomenon of *folie à deux*, or 'psychosis of association', in which a close associate, often but not necessarily a family member, comes to share a person's symptom, usually a psychotic delusion. Observers of this phenomenon have stressed the *isolation* of the pair from the wider community, as well as the presence in the dyad of one partner who is superior or dominant in terms of age, intelligence, education or temperament, and a relatively submissive partner whose symptoms are dependent upon the continued presence of the former. Nor need the relationship be confined to two people. Waltzer (1963) has described what he considers to be a case of *folie à douze* in a single family. Both parents and five of ten children were diagnosed paranoid schizophrenic and the remaining five children were described as suffering a 'paranoid reaction' with delusions of similar content.

Imitation

Experiments demonstrating the effects of simply *observing* another person's behaviour (e.g. children who witness aggressive behaviour model their own behaviour in a more aggressive direction) have been influential in the growing acceptance of the importance of imitation as a mechanism producing learning. Under what conditions is 'modelling' most effective? In relation to the principal of contagion, Ehrenwald (1963) suggests the simple, but nonetheless very important, principle that influences may be accumulative, so that a neurotic mother, by virtue of her more intense and longer association with her child, will have more influence than a neurotic teacher or a neurotic baby-sitter. Most children are likely to have more contact over a period of years, simply in terms of number of hours together, with parents, than with anyone else. Parents are therefore likely to be well ahead of anyone else in influencing their children, if influences are accumulative in this way.

Another suggested principle, governing the relative influence of different models, concerns the *exclusiveness* of influence, or the degree to which an individual is isolated from alternative influences. The importance of this principle is suggested by many clinical reports and theories. The theory of the double bind for example has, as an important element, the rule that the individual exposed must be unable to *escape* from this source of influence. Writings on *folie à deux* have stressed the closeness of the relationship between the dominant and submissive partners, as a necessary condition, and 'protection' by the less deviant parent as an explanation of twin or sibling differences has already been referred to. In addition there are many reports of the isolation of families containing a member who subsequently becomes ill with a diagnosis of schizophrenia. In particular the isolation of the child from peer group social contacts has been referred to (e.g. Rosenthal, 1963). Classic studies in social psychology have discovered the importance of support from other people in resisting group pressure towards deviant norm formation, and studies of attitude change and brainwashing have suggested that isolation from 'normal' influences is an important ingredient.

Many formulations of 'identification' have stressed the need for a strong emotional tie, 'bond', or 'attachment' to the source of influence, and although this quality of a relationship is rarely well defined, experiments on imitation or 'observational learning' do suggest that influence is more likely the more a model is a 'loved or prestigeful person'. Experiments suggest that imitative responses are more likely when the model is relatively nurturant or rewarding or when the model is someone who has power and control over valued resources (Bandura, 1971). It is probably correct to think of these as 'facilitating' rather than essential conditions for imitation.

Gewirtz (1969), presenting an admittedly fairly extreme view, considers the concept of imitation to be unnecessary. His argument is that responses that appear to be imitated are likely to be the same responses which, when emitted by the child, are rewarded by the socializing agent. The principle of 'operant conditioning' (reward and punishment training) could be sufficient to account for identification. Parents may most readily convey their standards, as opposed to their actual behaviour, by differential reward and punishment of the child's behaviour but as the popular saying, 'don't do as I do, do as I say', suggests, the two may not always coincide.

Interaction Studies

The last ten to fifteen years have witnessed a spate of investigations involving *direct* observation of the joint interaction of families containing a mentally ill child (usually diagnosed schizophrenic) who is typically of late adolescent or early adult age. Sometimes the predictions tested in these studies concern male patients only and sometimes they only concern those male patients with a history of an abnormally constricted social and sexual life even prior to the onset of their illness (sometimes termed 'poor pre-morbid personality').

The techniques used to obtain a sample of family interactive behaviour have frequently been based upon the Revealed Differences Technique (RDT) introduced by Strodtbeck (1954). As originally described by Strodtbeck the technique required father, mother and son to answer a number of questions about hypothetical decisions or issues of relevance to adolescents or their families (but not particularly relevant to psychological problems), and particular questions about which family members disagreed were then chosen for joint family discussion. Some chosen items were those upon which father and mother disagreed with son but agreed with each other, others put father in the odd-man-out role, and yet others put mother in that position. The triad was asked to talk over each of these chosen questions in turn, to try and come to an understanding of why each participant made his or her prior individual response, and if possible to reach a consensus. The subsequent interactions were recorded and various interaction indices derived.

While many investigations use the RDT, others require participants to discuss issues without regard to prior agreement, and most employ issues for discussion which are more relevant to family conflict or problems (e.g. how to deal with situations in which children of various ages are cheeky to parents; what to do when children want to take jobs which are thought not to be in their best interest). Sometimes only father and mother are included, sometimes it is a threesome, and in some investigations a well or problem-free sibling is included to make a family tetrad.

Dominance and conflict

Two major hypotheses which have been tested concern an expected relative dominance of mothers in comparison with fathers, and an expected high level of marital conflict or disharmony.

The following interaction indices are fairly typical of those that have been used:

Dominance indices (Farina and Holzberg, 1967, p. 383)

1. Number of times spoken: the number of times each parent spoke first, second or last.
2. Total time spoken: the length of time in seconds each parent spoke.
3. Passive acceptance: the number of times that each parent accepted the resolution offered by another family member by agreeing without further elaboration.
4. Total yielding: a scale score indicating the relative movement of each parent from his/her initial position on an issue to the joint resolution of the issue.

Conflict indices (Farina and Holzberg, 1968, p. 115)

1. Frequency of simultaneous speech: the number of times in the interview during which two, or all three, members spoke concurrently.
2. Failure to reach agreement: the number of hypothetical problems for which the family members failed to arrive at a mutually satisfactory solution.
3. Interruptions: the number of times during the interview that a family member interrupted another.
4. Disagreements and aggressions: the number of times one of the family members disagreed with or displayed aggressive behaviour towards another.

Fontana (1966), and more recently Hirsch and Leff (1975), have reviewed much of this work. Only a minority of studies were found to be free of major weaknesses in method such as failure to match groups on age, social class and hospitalization experience. However, these reviewers are in agreement that certain tentative conclusions are possible on the basis of the more satisfactory studies. In general they fail to confirm the existence of an unusually large 'marital skew' or 'dominance discrepancy' between parents of schizophrenic children but they do in general support the idea that the relationship between such parents is likely to be characterized by higher levels of hostility and conflict than are to be found in 'normal' groups. It is not clear, however, that this finding is peculiar to groups in which the children have a diagnosis of schizophrenia as opposed to some alternative psychiatric diagnosis, and the results are clearest for the families of patients with 'poor pre-morbid personality' and for those who are chronically hospitalized by the time they and their families are studied.

Knowing that parents have a disharmonious relationship tells us little, however, about parental behaviour towards children or how the link with mental disorder in a child may be explained. Once again, it is a matter of the two variables (parental marital discord and child mental illness) being conceptually too 'distant' and the intervening mechanisms remaining unexplored. Hoffman and Lippitt (1960) suggest a number of alternative theories to explain a link between marital tension and child maladjustment. Does the child become insecure as a result of perceiving the marital tension? Does a tense relationship with the spouse lead a parent to reject or scapegoat a child, perhaps because the child is perceived as being like the disliked spouse, or as taking the latter's side, or because the child is seen as a barrier to dissolving the marriage? Does the lack of a satisfactory relationship with the spouse lead a parent to over-invest in his/her relationship with a child? Does marital disharmony lead parents to neglect their child-caretaking role? Or is there a third factor, to do with the personality of one or both parent(s), which contributes to both marital disharmony and maladjustment in a child?

Decision-making and choice fulfilment

The nature of family disharmony has been pursued still further in the course of a programme of research conducted by Ferreira and Winter and their colleagues (e.g. Ferreira and Winter, 1965, 1968) on the subject of family decision-making. Families were required to discuss amongst themselves and come to a joint decision 'as a family' concerning certain preferences, for example preferred countries in which to live if a year were to be spent abroad, preferred films to be viewed, preferred food to be chosen in a restaurant, and so on. Prior to the family interaction and decision-making session each family member separately had completed the same preference questionnaire but individual preferences were not openly revealed to others unless individual members chose to reveal their preferences in the course of interaction.

There were three main indices of family functioning in these investigations. Spontaneous Agreement (SA) was the number of likes and dislikes which family members shared prior to interaction. Decision Time (DT) was the time taken by the family to complete their joint questionnaire, and Choice Fulfilment (CF) was the number of joint family preferences which coincided with prior individual preferences.

The major finding was that 'abnormal' families, that is families with at least one member (usually the adolescent or young adult child) having a known emotional or delinquency problem, were significantly lower on SA and CF and had significantly longer DTs than matched groups of 'normal' families. The problem-specificity of these effects has been examined by comparing families with a schizophrenic child, families with a delinquent child and families with a 'maladjusted' child (Ferreira and Winter, 1965). Interestingly enough these three groups were equally deviant in terms of SA and DT but the families containing a schizophrenic child were significantly lower than others on CF and produced significantly more joint family responses which these researchers termed 'chaotic' because they represented joint family preferences which did not coincide with *unanimous* prior individual preferences. This suggests that certain aspects of disharmony may be common to a number of abnormalities but that interaction in families with a schizophrenic member may have an additional 'irrational' element.

Lerner (1965), using the RDT, reports a further aspect of 'irrationality' in the communication of parents of male schizophrenic patients. Parents in these studies frequently failed to reach agreement on a topic but 'denied' this failure by continuing to act as if they had reached agreement ('failure to reach agreement, with distortion'). They also displayed a high frequency of agreeing without acknowledging that this agreement contradicted a previous expression of opinion ('masking'). These reactions were more frequently found amongst parents who themselves showed relatively greater degrees of schizophrenia-like 'thought disorder'.

A family pathology cycle

In later studies (Ferreira, Winter and Poindexter, 1966; Ferreira and Winter, 1968) two further indices were examined, namely 'silence proportion' and 'information exchanged'. In comparison with 'normal' families, families containing either a schizophrenic or a delinquent member spent more of the time in silence when set the task of making up a story together or when attempting to reach agreement over certain issues. In addition, during discussions of issues they displayed fewer instances of clear and explicit communication between one member and the rest of the family. These and other findings lead Ferreira and Winter (1968) to propose the idea of a 'family pathology cycle' of self-perpetuating events which once started leads the family into greater and greater pathology of communication. Less information exchanged and more silence leads, they suggest, to a state in which less information is shared about each other and in which there is less spontaneous agreement, less individual choice fulfilment, and in which it takes longer to reach decisions. This state produces further dissatisfaction and frustration in family members which tends to lower information exchanged and increase silence still further.

Channels of communication

A somewhat different approach was adopted by Lennard and Bernstein (1969) who analysed the results of forty-five minutes of mother–father–son discussion. They were more concerned with the overall form of interaction than with its content. A small group of ten families, each with a son aged nine to fourteen who had been diagnosed schizophrenic, borderline schizophrenic or psychotic, differed in two ways from an even smaller group of control families. Firstly, the communication 'channel' between son and father was relatively under-utilized and that between son and mother tended (but not significantly) to be relatively over-utilized.

Secondly, it was noted that there were differences in patterns of initiation and control of interaction. Average lengths of dyadic sequences (i.e. an interaction sequence during which only two family members spoke, to each other, without the intervention of the third) were longer for 'schizophrenic families'; sons in these families made fewer attempts than sons in control families to intrude upon mother–father sequences; and all members in such families were significantly less likely than their counterparts in control families to be successful in getting a response from one of the others when they did make such 'intrusion attempts'. Sons themselves were particularly unsuccessful in this regard.

Haley (1964), using a similar approach to that of Lennard and Bernstein, found a greater deviation from randomness in the sequencing of speakers in abnormal three-member families than in normal families. For example, in the case of sequences of two speakers (either FM, MF, CF, FC, CM, or MC) there was a relative imbalance in the abnormal families with some of the possible sequences being displayed much more frequently than others. Similarly some of the sequences of three speakers (FMC, FMF, MFC, MFM, etc.) occurred much more frequently than others and the same was true for longer sequences.

The Structure of Parental Behaviour
The circumplex

A simplification of our conceptual framework regarding the behaviour of parents towards their children would be of undoubted value provided it did sufficient justice to the complexity of real life events. Schaefer (1959) has suggested that the relationships between maternal behaviour variables obey a law of circular, or 'circumplex', ordering as shown in Figure 1. Individual aspects of

Figure 1 Schaefer's Hypothetical Circumplex Model for Maternal Behaviour

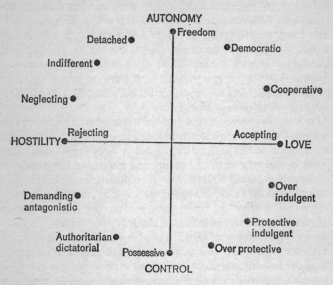

(Taken from Schaefer, 1959, p. 232, Figure 4)

behaviour are positively associated with other aspects shown at *neighbouring* points on the circle, are negatively associated with those shown on the opposite side of the circle and are relatively independent of those at intermediate distances around the circumference. For summary purposes maternal behaviour can be described in terms of two bipolar dimensions which Schaefer labels *autonomy versus control* and *love versus hostility*. Evidence for this structure comes from ratings of notes made during observations of mothers with their infant children as well as from ratings made from notes following home interviews with mothers of children aged between nine and fourteen years. It is similar to schemes suggested by earlier researchers and has recently been shown to provide an adequate fit to parental behaviour data collected in Holland (Renson *et al.*, 1968).

Goldin (1969) has reviewed studies of children's reports of their parents' behaviour. Two major factor analytic studies, supported by others, suggest three rather than two independent factors, one concerned with acceptance or love and their opposites, the other two concerned with styles of control and discipline. In addition to a factor of control versus autonomy, the studies of children's perception suggest an additional dimension of *firm versus lax control* showing that it is possible for children to perceive parents as firm but allowing autonomy, or lax but controlling, in addition to the more obvious combinations.

It is an attractive idea that parental behaviour can be reduced to a limited number of dimensions or to a structure as elegant as the circumplex and indeed, at the present state of knowledge, these frameworks may serve to organize and integrate a large body of ideas and empirical findings. However, these schemes seem bound to represent only a crude approximation. For one thing, the data upon which they are based mainly takes the form of global observer or interviewer ratings or children's perceptions. Furthermore, there is no way of knowing to what extent the list of variables included in an analysis is exhaustive. These proposed structures may conceivably, therefore, have more to do with the structure of people's (parents', children's, interviewers', research workers') *impressions* of other people's behaviour than with the structure of behaviour as it actually occurs. In other words, the circular 'map' may really be the map which most people, knowingly or unknowingly, have in their heads for construing or judging the behaviour of others. This 'universal conceptual bias' (Baumrind and Black, 1967) may have some basis in fact and may be an adequate approximation for its primary task, namely enabling individuals to roughly categorize and predict other people's social behaviour in the course of their everyday lives, but may be too approximate as the basis for scientific study.

Maternal over-protection

The variables representing the control end of Schaefer's (1959) autonomy versus control dimension include mother anxiety, intrusiveness, concern about health, achievement demand, excessive contact, fostering dependency, and emotional involvement. This list corresponds quite well with the description of over-protective maternal behaviour provided by Levy (1970) based upon clinical observation. Levy thought of maternal over-protection as an unusually intense exaggeration of normal maternal protective and nurturant behaviour characterized particularly by excessive contact with the child. It could include age-appropriate but quantitatively excessive contacts as well as age-inappropriate behaviours such as prolonged breast feeding or sleeping with the child until the latter was of unusually advanced age. However, Levy distinguished two forms of this behaviour; a 'dominant' and an 'indulgent' form. The former is characterized by excessive maternal control, with submissiveness on the child's part, whilst the latter involves an unusual *lack* of maternal control which is exploited by the child.

Restrictiveness and power assertion

A number of studies of the child-rearing *attitudes* of mothers with schizophrenic children suggest that some such mothers (fathers have been less studied) may be predisposed to behave towards children in an unusual way. For example, in one of the earlier studies of this kind, Mark (1953) found mothers of schizophrenic children to be more restrictive and controlling in attitude than mothers of children with no psychiatric illness. McGhee (1961) found that more than a quarter of the items in a child-rearing questionnaire differentiated mothers of hospitalized schizophrenics from both mothers of non-hospitalized patients with neurosis and mothers of children (in all three groups the 'children' were mostly in their twenties and thirties) with no psychiatric illness. These items seem to reflect two general tendencies: one towards over-restrictive control (e.g. 'a child should not plan to enter an occupation of which his parents do not approve', 'a good mother should shelter her child from life's difficulties'); and secondly, a preoccupation with the adverse effects of knowledge about, and experimentation with, sex (e.g. 'children who take part in sex play may become sex criminals when they grow up', 'it is not the duty of parents to teach the child about sex').

Hoffman (1960) had this to say about the parent–child relationship:

> ... the parent, by virtue of his greater physical strength, his complete control over the child's material and emotional supplies, and the existence of little external restraint, has a great deal of power (potential for compelling another to behave in a certain way) in all areas of the child's life (p. 141).

From detailed accounts of the previous day's events, he recorded the frequency with which each parent without qualification demanded immediate compliance from their child ('unqualified power assertion' or UPA). Observations of the children's nursery school behaviour showed that certain types of maternal UPA were associated with greater child hostility, 'power needs' and 'autonomy strivings', particularly directed towards other children.

Lewin *et al.* (1939, a social psychology classic) found that the introduction of either authoritarian or *laissez-faire* leadership, in contrast to 'democratic' leadership, led to marked irritability and aggressiveness between members of a club for eleven-year old boys and led to dissatisfaction with club activities. Subsequent studies have for the most part confirmed this finding although ages and activities have varied (Secord and Backman, 1964, pp. 389–90).

The accusation that parents may have abused their position of power is not confined to discussions of *mental* disorder, but crops up repeatedly in writings on psychosomatic illnesses. To give but one example, Harburg *et al.* (1969) formulated the idea, based upon previous findings, that rheumatoid arthritis was promoted, precipitated or exacerbated by feelings of 'chronic resentment' traceable to the exercise of parental 'arbitrary authority'.

The Choice of Criterion

Objective studies of family characteristics not infrequently discover significant differences between ill and well groups but are unable to distinguish between criterion groups which differ in psychiatric diagnosis (Frank, 1965; Hirsch and Leff, 1975) or even sometimes between ill and delinquent groups (e.g. Ferreira and Winter,

1968). Although the traditional psychiatric diagnostic groupings are readily available, the division of the psychiatrically ill into these groupings is not based on social psychological theory and their exclusive use as criteria may hinder progress.

Socialized and unsocialized disorders

Examples of what might be achieved if variables or categories are appropriately chosen come from studies of childhood maladjustment. Both Hewitt and Jenkins (1946) and later Lewis (1954) and Hetherington *et al.* (1971) found a significant degree of association between the particular form taken by abnormal child behaviour and the type of family environment. Table 1 shows the association

Table 1 Child's Pattern of Disturbed Behaviour at Reception Related to Background Pattern

Background pattern	Unsocialized Aggression (destructiveness, defiance, etc.) (52 children)	Socialized Delinquency (offences committed with other children, etc.) (57 children)	Inhibited, Neurotic (fearful, shy, etc.) (80 children)
Rejection	39	23	27
Neglect and bad company	5	43	5
Constraint	28	21	50

(Adapted from Lewis, 1954, p. 69, Table 38. Note that column totals exceed the number of children represented in each column as a child might have been exposed to more than one background pattern.)

found by Lewis in her war-time study of children admitted to a Reception Centre. That constraint should lead to inhibition, rejection to defiance, and neglect to associating in the street rather than in the home, are suggestions that are highly intelligible in social psychological terms but certain distinctions, such as that between the 'socialized' and 'unsocialized' delinquent patterns (Hewitt and Jenkins, 1946) had to be grasped before such relationships could be discovered. Such useful distinctions may not always be reflected in medical or legal systems of nomenclature which were designed for quite other purposes. (Although Lewis's study is exemplary in this major respect it has to be admitted that the diagnoses of background and child behaviour patterns involved may not have been made perfectly independently, and the effects of home background upon behaviour which were demonstrated were short-term at best).

Some of the conclusions of Goldin's (1969) review of studies of children's perceptions of their parents' caretaking behaviour are also relevant to this discussion of specificity. Whilst those in the general category 'problem children' tend to perceive their parents as relatively low on the *acceptance* dimension, those whose problems have come to light because of delinquent conduct perceive their parents disciplinary or control practices rather differently from those whose problems have come to light through attendance at a guidance clinic or as a result of nominations as 'maladjusted' by teachers, other adults or peers. The former are more likely to describe their parents' behaviour towards them as low on psychological *control* whilst the latter see their parents as relatively high on the *demanding* or *firmness* dimension.

Alternatives to illness or disorder as outcome criteria

To pursue further the argument about appropriate criteria of disorder or maladjustment, it has to be admitted that most of the research upon which this chapter has drawn has employed illness, or even hospitalization for illness, as a criterion against which to judge the importance of differences in social experience. This practice can be justifiably criticized in view of the many factors, some quite irrelevant to the processes which the research attempts to understand, which determine whether a person with a certain degree of mental disability gets referred to a mental health specialist, is diagnosed as mentally ill, or is hospitalized for mental illness (see Chapter 4). There is an obvious need for research to take account of differences between notified and unnotified mental illness in much the same way as criminological research has had to face up to the existence of both official and unofficial delinquency.

But the matter can be taken still further. Overt mental illness itself may not always be the most useful criterion. This would certainly be the case if there were causes of overt disorder additional to causes of disorder *proneness*. In this case trying to predict illness itself would prove to be difficult and the operation of at least two more fundamental processes would be obscured. Looked at in this light much work which tries to predict not illness or disorder itself, but personality characteristics presumed to be associated with illness, becomes very relevant to our concerns. Amongst relevant personality characteristics which have been studied in this way are self-esteem (Coopersmith, 1967; Rosenberg, 1962), social competence in children (Baumrind and Black,1967) and decrements in perceptual-motor task performance under stress (Heilbrun *et al.*, 1967 a & b).

Coopersmith concluded, on the basis of interviews with predominantly middle-class high-school students and their mothers in one part of the US, that relatively high self-esteem is associated with a combination of parental warmth and support, 'firm, clear and demanding' parental behaviour and a belief in democratic practices on the mother's part. Parents with high self-esteem children used a greater number of rules and regulations in exercising control, but at the same time were more likely to *disagree* with attitude statements such as, 'a child should be seen and not heard' and 'the child should not question the thinking of the parents', and to *agree* with such statements as, 'a child has a right to his own point of view and ought to be allowed to express it'. Both Coopersmith (1967) and Rosenberg (1962), who conducted a similar study, found a relationship with birth order, first and only children being more likely to have a relatively high degree of self-esteem.

Baumrind and Black's (1967) report is notable for its account of their attempt to record objectively the details of naturally occurring behaviour in the home using a method which they term 'Home Visit Sequence Analysis'. The outcome of each attempt by a child to control a parent, and of each parental attempt to control a child, during a period of time extending from just before the evening meal until just after the children's bedtime, was noted. Data obtained by these means were supplemented by verbal parent reports of behaviour and feelings, and were correlated with the children's nursery school behaviour rated by a number of independent observers. As well as finding differences in parental behaviour depending on the sex of the child (parents being on the whole stricter and more demanding in certain ways with girls) the authors of this report draw conclusions somewhat similar to those of Coopersmith (1967) despite differences in age group and criterion variables. They conclude that consistent discipline and enforced demands coupled with the granting of independence and the allowance of verbal 'give and take' are associated with stable and assertive infant behaviour. It has to be stressed, however, that these much over-simplified conclusions only very roughly do justice to the complexity of the results.

Heilbrun has conducted a series of experiments with student subjects. Using the Parent Attitude Research Instrument (PARI) (Schaefer and Bell, 1958) and the Parent–Child Interaction Rating Scales (Heilbrun, 1964) subjects' perceptions of their parents' behaviour were elicited, and accordingly subjects were divided into four groups on the basis of 'control' (high or low) and 'nurturance' (high or low) received. Some of the results suggested the particular vulnerability of those subjects whose perceptions of parental behaviour indicated that they might have been relatively 'rejected' (i.e. they fell in the HCLN, or high control and low nurturance, category).

Male HCLN subjects obtained higher scores on a number of questionnaire measures of psychological disorder (Heilbrun, 1968) and female HCLN (from father) subjects experienced the greatest disruption in perceptual-motor task performance (e.g. substituting symbols for digits as rapidly as possible) when under stress (Heilbrun et al., 1967a). Both male and female HCLN subjects lost more confidence than other subjects under similar circumstances (Heilbrun et al., 1967b). In a further experiment the performance of LN male subjects proved to be more dependent, than that of HN subjects, upon the experience of fellow subjects (i.e. LNs were more responsive to 'vicarious reinforcement') (Heilbrun, 1970).

It is difficult to draw overall conclusions from a small number of such diverse studies but certainly they point towards the importance of care-taking behaviours which can be subsumed under the generic headings: nurturance; granting of autonomy; firm guidance.

Early Non-Parental Social Influences
Siblings

Parents of course are not the only sources of social influence in childhood although they may be the most crucial in most cases. Certainly the emphasis in research and clinical writings on the role of early experience in mental disorder has been upon parent-child relationships almost to the exclusion of any consideration of others. The imbalance badly needs correcting. For a start there is good reason to suppose that siblings influence one another in important ways. An interesting demonstration of this in young monkeys is provided by Suomi *et al.* (1970) who showed that monkeys of similar age could, to some degree, be substitutes for mothers when the young were reared away from their mothers but in the company of other young. When their peer partners were removed 'protest' and 'despair' reactions were shown similar to those shown by normally reared monkey and human young when separated at certain ages from their mothers (Maccoby and Masters, 1970, pp. 104–5).

Brim's (1958) reanalysis of Koch's (1956) data showed that, at least in two-child families, children's sex-role behaviour was influenced by the sex of their sibling and that the effect acted more strongly upon the second born. Five- and six-year-olds had more traits usually associated with the opposite sex ascribed to them (e.g. girls were rated 'aggressive' and boys 'kind') by teachers when they had an opposite sex sibling, particularly when the sibling was older.

Sutton-Smith and Rosenberg (1970) attempted to account for the link between birth order and type of childhood problem (see p. 15, above) in terms of a 'sibling dominance hierarchy'. Their research suggested that first-born children used 'high-power tactics' to influence their younger sibs and were seen both by themselves and by second borns as more 'bossy'. Younger born children tended to make more use of 'low-power procedures' such as appealing to others for help, crying, pouting, sulking or threatening to tell tales.

It remains to be seen whether or not the influences that siblings have upon one another have implications, directly or indirectly, for mental health and disorder.

Multi-generational influence

Although the direct influence of grandparents has rarely been considered, their indirect influence, through the parents, has been the subject of much speculation. Social workers in close contact with families are often left in no doubt that interpersonal attitudes and patterns of behaviour with implications for mental health can be passed on, through environmental mechanisms, over more than a single generation gap. It often looks, for example, as if the harsh treatment received by some children can be traced back at least as far as the harsh treatment meted out by their maternal grandparents to the child's mother, or that a daughter's choice of husband is related to the attitude towards men prevailing amongst the female members of the same family over a number of generations.

There have been numerous suggestions regarding the importance of such multi-generation influence for mental illness. Ehrenwald's (1963) example of the Obscomp family has already been referred to (p. 22) and Alanen (1966) is another author who writes of 'a train of disturbed emotional relationships proceeding from generation to generation' (p. 193).

Fascinating anecdotal accounts of two four-generation families with repeated 'chronic frustration-hostility-aggression states' is provided by Thorne (1957). In both cases the 'source' was identified in the person of a difficult dominant individual who provoked a state of chronic anger, directly in at least one member of the immediately following generation, and indirectly in subsequent generations via the influence of his children and grandchildren. Clinically these 'anger states', which Thorne considered to be analogous to the better publicised 'anxiety states', were manifested as paranoid psychoses, alcoholism, neurotic invalidism, ulcers and behaviour disorders in children. Steele (1970) describes the low self-esteem and feelings of unworthiness which are frequently found clinically amongst parents of 'battered' or 'tormented' children and suggests a multi-generational transmission, the parents themselves having been subjected as children, if not to battering or tormenting, at least to recurrent criticism. Highly relevant too are observations of the abnormal maternal behaviour displayed, at least towards their first offspring, by monkey mothers deprived in childhood of normal maternal comforting (Harlow *et al.*, 1966).

Appealing and credible though such propositions are, objective evidence for their validity with humans has scarcely been forthcoming, but it is also true that attempts to demonstrate their validity have been few and far between, and that the methodological problems in so doing are even greater than usual. Several researchers have attempted to trace patterns of behaviour across three generations with little conclusive success.

Ingersoll (1948) did find that subjects tended to report congruence between the parental and grandparental generations in terms of which marital partner was the more 'controlling'. When subjects described two controlling grandmothers, they nearly always described a controlling mother, and the same was true of grandfathers and fathers. Unfortunately this interesting piece of work suffered inevitably from being based upon written histories provided by single informants, and involved a large measure of inference in making ratings from the histories.

Beyond the family

In comparison with the family of origin, other potentially harmful social systems to which an individual with a mental illness may have belonged have received remarkably little attention. The harmful effects of certain extreme situations such as war-time evacuation (Freud and Burlingham, 1943), racial and political persecution (Haefner, 1967) and civil disunity (Fraser, 1973) have been described although these clearly represent situations which are abnormal in many instances, not just in the social psychological sphere.

More normal social systems organized around 'school' and 'work' are surely candidates for closer scrutiny. (See Morrison and McIntyre, 1971, pp. 106–24, and Cowen, 1973, for summaries of relevant work on school systems.) Regarding work, Aronson and Polgar (1962) report their impressions following group and individual, tape-recorded and subsequently transcribed, interviews with 185 individuals at a number of army posts. Their data scarcely concern *early* social influence but their results are interesting and their methods applicable to other settings. All these individuals knew personally one of thirteen soldiers who had developed overt psychotic symptoms after at least one year's service and had been mentioned, either by the ill soldier himself or by a relative as a 'significant other'. In some cases they were the subjects of the ill man's paranoid delusions and in some, but not all cases, they were superior officers. The impression formed from these interviews was that the patient's level of work performance and the development of symptoms depended upon the type of relationship established with these other figures. Three types of relationship were described depending on the combination of acceptance, support, and expectations for conforming behaviour, shown towards the individual. Support alone ('pseudotherapeutic') or the rigid setting of expectations without emotional support ('contratherapeutic') appeared to be associated with breakdown whilst a combination of the two ('quasitherapeutic') was associated with adequate work functioning. In the latter cases breakdown seemed to occur when the relationship was broken, for example by a change of posting for either party concerned. The source of data for this study was excellent but the analysis admittedly highly inferential, and as most of the men concerned had had previous overt psychotic episodes the study is really one of relapse rather than illness onset. Kornhauser (1965) provides evidence of the importance for mental health of job status and job satisfaction in a more conventional work setting. Brown (1954, pp. 265–72) summarizes other relevant studies on work and mental health.

Although relationships in the family, at school, and at work are likely to constitute early sources of influence with greatest implications for subsequent mental health, there are obviously others. Quite apart from the importance of mate choice and marriage, which is the subject of a later chapter, non-family friendships must be supposed to have an important bearing particularly upon the acquisition of habitual behaviour patterns in the areas of sexual preference and behaviour, and alcohol, tobacco and other drug use.

Are There Social Causes of Mental Disorder?

It may seem as though much of this chapter has been written under the assumption that there *are* social causes of mental disorder and indeed the author should admit his bias towards believing that there are. Nonetheless, it has to be admitted that despite all the clinical and research activity in this area, there is as yet little incontrovertible proof of it. The little soundly based and relevant knowledge which has been acquired is out of all proportion to the immensity of the literature and it is only right that this chapter should end with a consideration of the main pitfalls awaiting the over-enthusiastic student or research worker.

Validity of measurement techniques

In many examples of the research mentioned in this chapter there remains the important question of validity. Do the techniques employed really measure what they are assumed to measure? For example, can the conditions of family life be reproduced using the RDT or some variant of it? And if they can, is it clear how 'long decision times' or 'choice fulfilment', for example, are to be interpreted?

Inconsistency in behaviour

Just as fundamental is the question of the reliability or stability of indices of behaviour. When more than one index of a supposedly unitary attribute is used, inter-index correlations frequently fail to be significant. For example, when Yarrow *et al.* (1968) compared results from three different indices of child dependency ('attention wanted', 'closeness wanted', and 'separation anxiety') and from two different sets of informants (teachers versus mothers), there was little agreement about who were the children who were high and low on dependency.

These criticisms apply equally of course to supposedly consequent variables (e.g. child behaviour) and antecedent variables
(e.g. parent behaviour) and are a reflection of a wider problem
affecting much of that part of psychology concerned with individual differences (Mischel, 1968; Hutt and Hutt, 1970).

Over-generalization

Yarrow *et al.* (1968) also point out the danger of generalizing from
the small restricted samples (mostly white kindergarten children
and their professional, North American, suburban parents) that
are usually employed in child-rearing studies and, even more
seriously still, they note the tendency of reviewers to ignore the
reservations of the original research workers. Indeed they go so far
as to liken the process whereby these research findings are conveyed through reviews and text-books to the process whereby
rumours are spread, an analogy that would be humorous if it were
not so true and alarming. For example, results established for one
sex only, or within a limited age range, are reported as general
findings with much wider applicability; results based upon a single
unvalidated measure of an attribute, such as 'aggression' or
'anxiety', are reported as generalized findings; and relationships
which are statistically significant but slight, in terms of percentage
differences between groups or in terms of absolute sizes of correlation coefficients, are uncritically reported without mention of
magnitude, or worse are misreported as evidence of a strong
relationship. These sins are extremely common in a field where
favoured theories rarely receive more than marginal support and
no doubt this author has been guilty of committing them from
place to place in this book.

Many warnings about the dangers of generalizing results could
be cited from studies of mental disorder. For example, Myers and
Roberts (1959) found that families containing a schizophrenic
member were equally disturbed, but in different ways, in two social
status groups. Family disorganization and lack of parental
empathy took a more aggressive form in the lower status group and
anxious over-protection was more obvious in the higher status
group.

The general importance of some of the findings of studies of family interaction is seriously called into question by Lennard and Bernstein's (1969) own results with German families in Cologne. The median percentage of 'intrusion attempts' by clinic-attending sons in the German families was abnormally low, to an extent even greater than that of the American schizophrenic sons whom they studied, even though it appeared that the former were less disturbed. German fathers, unlike their American counterparts, had the highest rate of intrusion attempts. Although other interpretations are possible these cross-cultural results strongly suggest that differences in family patterns of communication between different cultures may be large enough to swamp differences between families with and without disturbed children. It is certainly only to be expected that relationships, established with subjects in one culture or sub-culture, will not generalize readily to cultures or sub-cultures with different structures and customs.

Lack of evidence of long-term effects

Then there is the issue of the long-term, as opposed to merely short-term, effects on child behaviour. The absence of prospective follow-up studies to test assumptions about long-term effects is as much a feature of the general literature on child rearing and child behaviour as it is of the more specialized literature on the child-rearing correlates of mental disorder. A recent exception is Sears (1970) who has provided data on a follow-up of children whose mothers were interviewed when the children were five years old as part of the well known *Patterns of Child Rearing* study (Sears *et al.*, 1957). The self-esteem of twelve-year-old boys and girls in this middle-class sample was significantly related to measures of maternal and paternal warmth obtained seven years earlier, as well as to smallness of family size, early ordinal position in the family and higher current attainments in basic school subjects.

Rousell and Edwards (1971) report on some antecedents of psychopathology (as measured by the much-used MMPI, or Minnesota Multiphasic Personality Inventory) amongst sixty-four twenty to twenty-two year olds from the same study. For males only, scores on several clinical scales were negatively correlated with the degree of rated 'warmth' in the mother–child relationship seventeen years earlier, whilst for females only there were a number of unexpected but significant positive correlations with 'permissiveness'.

Siegelman *et al.* (1970) compared men and women in their mid-thirties who had been described by two or three psychologists in terms suggestive of optimal adjustment, with others who were described in opposite terms. (For a discussion of this criterion of 'adjustment' see Chapter 4, pp. 142–4, below.) Childhood data was available for these subjects who were part of a longitudinal cohort studied since infancy. The parents of the better adjusted men and women had more frequently been rated as well-adjusted sexually. Mothers of well-adjusted *men* had been rated more accurate and rapid in thinking, and as less talkative, and mothers of well-adjusted *women* had been rated more intelligent, openminded, curious and cooperative over the study itself, and less restless and worrisome. They were even rated as more poised, and as having relatively pleasant voices and facial expressions. Fathers of well-adjusted *men* had been rated as responding more openly and directly to conflict.

The 'third factor'

In this field of inquiry, as in any other, a link discovered between two variables can be misleading because of the association of both with an unmeasured third variable, even when the two linked variables were measured at very different points in time. Observed parental abnormalities could give rise to similar deviant behaviour in children, either directly through processes such as modelling or social conditioning, or less directly via an unfavourable climate in the home. However, they could equally well be an indication that parents who do not develop the full condition themselves nonetheless carry the genes that can give rise to it and themselves have a milder, partial, form of the same condition. Even if parents are found to be, and even if they always were, hostile and conflict-ridden, this need not imply that these conditions *caused* the onset of any disorder which develops in their children. The true cause may lie in a third factor associated with both the parental relationship and the disorder. In the case of the disorders grouped under the term schizophrenia an as yet unspecified genetic factor is presumably amongst the most likely candidates.

The likelihood of there being a 'third factor', possibly genetic in origin, linked to both parental and child abnormalities and explaining the connection between the two, seems on the face of it even more possible when the parental abnormality takes a form which is similar to aspects of the child's disorder (see the discussion of parental mental illness, pp. 20–21). The point is that hereditary and environmental influences which might be responsible for the transmission of disorder nearly always coincide. Studies of children separated early in life from their biological parents (e.g. Heston and Denney, 1968) leave no doubt that there is a large genetic factor in the etiology of schizophrenia, but on the other hand recent studies of twins show considerably lower concordance rates for monozygotic twins (e.g. Tienari, 1963), than were found in the course of earlier studies which employed more select samples. Plenty of room is therefore left for the operation of environmental influences.

Rosenthal and his colleagues (1963) at the US National Institute of Mental Health, took advantage of the extremely rare event of quadruplets all of whom became mentally ill and were diagnosed as having schizophrenia. Although careful testing for zygosity suggested that the quads were indeed monozygotic (there remains a possibility that Hester, the most severely ill, may have come from a separate zygote) their illnesses were dissimilar in severity and duration. Hester was continually hospitalized for several years whilst Myra, the least severely ill, recovered completely after brief episodes and subsequently married. The quads' history was meticulously reconstructed from over fifty informant sources and the result is a classic multiple case history. In addition all members of the family were extensively tested and were observed together over a period of time when the whole family lived at the Institute and at other times when the parents visited their children there. It would appear that all four children were subjected to the same parental restrictiveness, a heavy-drinking, punitive and suspicious father, and a dominant mother. Parental responses to the Parent Attitude Research Inventory (PARI) tended to confirm this impression. The case history material also provides many examples of parental interference with, and disapproval of, any social life which the girls attempted to make for themselves in adolescence, and instances of rejection and cruelty were recounted.

However convincing the case history may seem, it clearly does not constitute any sort of proof of a social contribution to etiology, particularly as electro-encephalogram (EEG) testing revealed abnormalities in the girls similar to an abnormality shown by their father in whose family there was a recent history of mental illness. Nonetheless there is evidence that the individual quads were treated differently from an early age. Hester, subsequently the most severely and chronically ill, was the last delivered and the smallest at birth. She was considered by her parents to be 'babyish' and was subsequently victimized particularly over the subject of masturbation. At the other extreme, Myra, who was the least severely ill and showed the most complete recovery, was apparently always chosen as favourite by the least disturbed parent, the mother, and appeared to have been given a degree of affection and responsibility which Hester, at least, was not.

Of course these are impressions rather than facts and are organized around crude abstractions which attempt to summarize years of social interaction in a family with six members (and hence fifteen dyadic relationships). Exceptional though the case history is, it remains merely a retrospectively reconstructed case history, but nevertheless one which offers a rich source of very credible ideas on the influence of family factors in modifying the form of a serious mental disorder.

Really there is no conflict here. Behaviour has both genetic and environmental, social and non-social, determinants and the only fault lies in totally discounting the possibility of influence from one of these sources. Even when the basic etiology of a condition can be explained in genetic terms, social psychological factors may still play an important role in modifying the form and course of the condition. Mattsson and Gross (1966), to give but one example, suggest that the poor adjustment of some children with haemophilia, a condition with a known genetic transmission of a recessive sex-linked type, could be largely attributed to their mothers' over-solicitous and over-protective behaviour.

The influence of children on parents

There is an increasing trend in the literature to admit the possibility that children may influence their caretakers as well as vice versa. This development seems to coincide with the increasing popularity of explanations which attribute causes to the *joint* operation of heredity and environment, as well as with an extension of the concept of socialization which formerly referred almost solely to the process whereby children were induced to behave in accordance with adult expectations. The term socialization is now used with reference to processes of adaptation, by adults as well as children, to new situations, institutions, or roles of many kinds. If we can talk of socialization for parenthood it is only a short further step to consider the role of the child as one of the agents in the socialization of his or her parents.

One of the staunchest advocates of this perspective has been Bell (e.g. 1968) who argues that most positive findings from the child socialization research literature, usually interpreted as indicating the influence of parents upon children, could equally well be reinterpreted as indicating the influence upon parents of children who differ congenitally or as a result of inter-uterine or birth experiences. Given the early existence of such individual differences it is not hard to conceive that some children may invite what Bell calls 'parent upper-limit control behaviour'. Such parental behaviour is designed to reduce the degree or frequency of child behaviours which go beyond what is acceptable. Other children, those who are most inactive, may invite contrasting 'lower-limit control behaviour'; a response to child behaviour which falls below acceptable limits. Bell speculates that the hostile and control extremes of the two dimensions of parent behaviour identified by Schaefer (1959) may represent upper- and lower-limit control behaviours respectively and that Schaefer's system may therefore represent a system of *effects* of children upon parents. As Walters and Stinnett (1971) write in the course of reviewing the literature of the 1960s on parent–child relationships,

... [there is] a distrust of simplistic explanations concerning the direction of causality in explaining the nature of parent–child relationships. The era of viewing children as solely products of their parents' influence is past, for it is recognized that children themselves exert powerful influences upon parent–child relationships (pp. 100–101).

Many of the relationships referred to in the course of this chapter could be reinterpreted from this perspective. An unusually high degree of conflict or hostility between parents of a child hospitalized with a diagnosis of schizophrenia would seem to be readily interpretable as a *reaction* to a serious, complex, and still stigmatized condition. Neither an explanation in terms of parent-to-child influence nor one in terms of child-to-parent influence would seem to have obvious priority. Nor does it seem particularly useful to try and find a single source of the 'family pathology cycle' described by Ferreira and Winter (1968). Such cycles are probably to be found in families in association with all manner of 'problems' including the problem of a family having to look after an aged and infirm relative. It would obviously be ridiculous to think of family characteristics 'producing' old age and infirmity but presumably it is equally incorrect to think of old age and infirmity being responsible in themselves for producing family pathology.

Conclusions

What does it all add up to? Is there convincing evidence that caretaking conditions during childhood have the implications for later mental health or ill-health that are so widely supposed? It probably has to be admitted that the evidence is suggestive but by no means conclusive. For example, links, not usually strong, have been established between certain structural features of family life (e.g. the intactness of the home, and birth order in the family) and certain child or adult behaviours or conditions. Pseudo-naturalistic family interaction studies show a relatively high level of conflict, lack of consensus between family members, problems in decision-making, and peculiarities in the sequencing of interactions, in families with a problem or disordered adolescent child. There is evidence for a degree of association between parental and child mental ill-health and both studies with a prospective design, and others with a retrospective design, suggest that caretaking behaviour which combines relatively high levels of warmth or affection with a degree of firmness which does not prevent the granting of autonomy may be generally facilitative of mental health.

However, inevitably, because of the fragmentation in this area of study, findings are inconsistent and often impossible to compare because of differing samples and methods. Furthermore, the difficulties of establishing that social events in childhood are truly influential, in the causal sense, are such that those who would favour a genetic or biological explanation need not feel compelled to alter their favoured position.

Nor can it be said that an alternative to psychoanalysis has yet emerged on the theoretical front. Varieties of 'social learning theory', including notions of imitation, modelling or contagion, may offer some hope in this direction. The widening of the concept of socialization and the breakdown of an exclusive preoccupation with parents as shapers of personality are also encouraging. Studies of sibling relationships, of peer-group influence, and of social events in educational institutions and places of work, for example, may bring a more general and theoretical 'social systems' approach to the whole subject.

Chapter 2

Eccentricity:
Disordered Interpersonal Processes

Introduction

Not surprisingly symptoms and disabilities have been the main traditional concerns of mental illness specialists. There are however a number of reasons why a major area for the potential application of social psychology concerns not symptoms themselves but rather matters under the general heading of 'personality'.

For one thing, 'symptoms' and more enduring personal characteristics may not always be easily separable and the process of becoming ill is an insidious one in many instances. Foulds (1965) argues for making a clear distinction between signs and symptoms of 'personal illness' and aspects of personality, but in practice the distinction is not always easy to draw. There are many borderline cases where the definition of 'illness' will depend upon the amount of personal distress caused by behaviour, feelings or thoughts, and also upon the tolerance of other people. Furthermore, enduring traits can be distressing in themselves and can occasion referral to a specialist. The large category of the 'personality disorders' to be found within most psychiatric taxonomies is witness to that. As Foulds points out there are many confusions of terminology. The terms 'obsessional', 'hysteric' and 'paranoid', for example, are used to describe character types, symptom complexes, or single symptoms, or are used as terms of abuse.

A further reason for the concern of this chapter lies in the point made in the previous chapter about the difficulty of establishing antecedent-consequent links between characteristics of social situations or systems on the one hand and symptoms of, or treatment for, disorder on the other. The gap to be jumped is often too great but might be filled by intervening variables that have something to do with pre-illness behaviour or 'pre-morbid personality'.

Abnormal Self-Attitudes
Self-attitudes and mental health

In her authoritative review of concepts that were then (and mostly still are) current about 'positive mental health', Jahoda (1958) devoted much space to considering criteria under the heading of 'attitudes of an individual toward his own self'. There have been many suggestions concerning the importance of self-attitudes for mental health. 'Self-awareness' (knowing oneself fully, and being unself-consciously oneself), 'self-objectivity' (being able to see oneself *as other people do*), 'self-acceptance' or 'positive self-regard' and integration or clarity of the self-concept have all been stressed from time to time.

On the basis of previous views on the subject, particularly those of the post-Freudian psychoanalysts (e.g. Adler 1929; Horney, 1951; Sullivan 1953), Coopersmith (1967) speculated that there were four major sources of self-esteem: a feeling of *significance* based upon acceptance, attention and the affection of other people; an awareness of personal *competence* based on past and present achievements; a sense of *power* rooted in the ability to influence and control other people; and a sense of *virtue* derived from adherence to one's own moral and ethical standards.

Adolescent boys in Coopersmith's study who indicated by their responses to a questionnaire that their self-esteem was relatively low, and who in addition were rated by their teachers as low in self-confidence, reported that they found it harder than others to make friends, that they were more frequently 'listeners' than 'talkers' in groups, that they were more self-conscious in public, that they were too concerned with inner problems to be worried about broader problems of the world and that they were relatively sensitive to criticism. In addition, they proved to be more conforming to group pressure on a line-length judgement task (a situation much used to study conformity processes). Tests of creativity showed subjective self-esteem to be positively related to creativity also. Coopersmith writes of the 'self-trust required for social independence and creative expression' (p. 58).

As a damper on over-enthusiastic environmentalism it is important to point out that self-esteem may, at least partly, have a biological basis. Amongst the post-Freudians, Adler's views (1929) place much emphasis upon biological differences such as size, strength, physical attractiveness and the presence or absence of disfigurements and handicaps as factors influencing social comparison processes. Furthermore, there is now much evidence that self-attitudes may be related to individual differences in nervous system functioning (Eysenck, 1967) as well as to externally visible attributes.

Low self-esteem and anxiety

The importance of self-esteem for mental health is illustrated by Rosenberg's (1962) demonstration of a strong association between self-esteem and anxiety amongst a large sample of high school students in New York State. Self-esteem was assessed by means of a ten-item scale which included items such as: 'on the whole, I am satisfied with myself'; 'at times I think I am no good at all'; and 'I feel that I have a number of good qualities'. Anxiety was assessed by means of self-reports of fourteen psychosomatic symptoms including: trouble in getting to sleep and staying asleep; trembling; nervousness; heart beating hard; pressures or pains in the head; fingernail biting, etc. Rosenberg also examined a number of factors which it was felt might explain the link between self-esteem and anxiety. It was found that *instability* of self-image (e.g. 'does your opinion of yourself tend to change a good deal or does it always continue to remain the same?'), the presentation of a *false front* or face to the world (e.g. 'I often find myself putting on an act to impress people'), vulnerability or *sensitivity to criticism* (e.g. 'criticism or scolding hurts me terribly'), *feelings of isolation* ('do you think most people know the kind of person you really are, or do you feel that most people do not know what really goes on underneath?') as well as feelings of *loneliness*, all showed a strong relationship both with overall self-esteem and with anxiety.

Social sensitivity

These various associations demonstrate the *social* nature of self-esteem and at the same time provide a link with concepts derived in the clinical field. It has, for example, been noted that many psychiatric patients have 'insecure personalities' and suffer from high levels of self-uncertainty, self-blame, guilt, and feelings of inadequacy and inferiority (Schneider, 1958). It has been suggested that such personalities are particularly prone to suffer from sexual conflicts. Whilst many people who receive help for a psychological problem are *generally* fearful of other people and places where other people are met, Marks (1970) has described a group of *specific* 'social phobias' including fears of eating, drinking, speaking or writing in public and fears of the possibility of shaking, blushing or even vomiting in the presence of other people.

Not surprisingly, sensitivities about aspects of the body are sometimes extreme and sometimes have little objective basis. Hay (1970a) has reported an investigation of forty-five patients each of whom was concerned about what was felt to be an imperfection of his or her nose. Some of these patients had originally been referred to psychiatrists but others had originally been referred for plastic surgery. By comparing the patients' own judgements of the degree of imperfection with judgements made, from photographs of the patients' noses, by six independent raters, it was possible to arrange the patients into those whose sensitivity was relatively 'reasonable' and those whose sensitivities did not seem to be based upon objective evidence. The term 'dysmorphophobia' has been used when such complaints have no objective reality and Hay (1970b) has described an additional series of seventeen patients who were complaining, apparently without objective cause, about some aspect of mouth and smile, breasts, lines under the eyes, buttocks, arms, legs, eyebrows, stomach or chin. Hay notes that six of these patients had a psychiatric diagnosis of a psychotic type and that all the remainder had personalities characterized by a severe degree of over-sensitivity and insecurity.

The phenomenon of social sensitivity seems otherwise to have received little attention although Argyle and Williams (1969) have adopted the interesting tactic of asking people to rate the degree to which they felt 'mainly observed' or 'mainly observer' in a number of social situations. The degree to which people feel observed appears to be a function of both the situation and the individual's personality. Situational determinants include the sex and the relative age of 'the other'. Normal subjects, particularly if they are adolescents, tend to feel observed by older people, and women tend to feel observed by men who are of the same age or older than themselves. Feeling observed in many situations correlated positively with scores on a scale of insecurity and negatively with scores on a scale of dominance. There is some indication that popularity may be inversely related to the degree of social anxiety.

Positive self-regard

Rogers' (e.g. 1959) views on the importance of 'positive self-regard' have been highly influential. He proposed that psychological disorder in general is associated with relatively high discrepancies between a person's view of himself and his idea of how he would ideally like to be. A reduction in this *real-self/ideal-self discrepancy* has been used as a measure of favourable outcome following psychotherapy. Although there is evidence that many people with psychological problems view themselves as falling short of their ideals this appealingly simple idea has to be corrected in a number of respects. For example, it has been suggested that high discrepancies are only associated with disorders of a neurotic type and that the theory is less applicable in cases where the diagnosis is one of psychosis. This has been confirmed; patients with a diagnosis of schizophrenia (Hillson and Worchel, 1957) or paranoid schizophrenia (Friedman, 1955) display discrepancies markedly lower than those with a diagnosis of neurosis and are in fact scarcely different from groups of non-patients in this respect.

Miskimins *et al.* (1971) have examined the relationship between the discrepancy and the presence of individual symptoms. Whereas large discrepancies are more likely amongst patients displaying such symptoms as depression and anxiety, they are significantly less likely for patients with delusional thoughts or inappropriate behaviour for example. These latter symptoms are, however, associated with a different sort of discrepancy, namely a discrepancy between the patient's own view of him/herself and the view of him/herself attributed by the patient to other people. Patients with these symptoms are particularly likely to think that other people have a lower opinion of them than they have of themselves.

Block and Thomas (1955) suggested a curvilinear relationship between real-self/ideal-self discrepancy and psychological adjustment. Although they presented no direct evidence of such a relationship they did find evidence, amongst their student subjects, for an association between small discrepancies and 'denial'. Their own view is that small discrepancies indicate an unhealthy tendency towards extreme self-satisfaction and defensive over-control.

On the basis of another study of students, some of whom had dropped out of their studies and were under treatment, Silber and Tippett (1965) suggest that the matter is even more complex. As well as patterns indicating low self-esteem they identified patterns of self-esteem which were 'non-defensive-high' as well as those which were 'defensive-high', 'inconsistent' and 'ineffective-defensive'.

Self-deception

Unfortunately many of these studies have relied exclusively on rather simple self-report procedures and have been naive in a number of other respects. Most of them show considerably less ingenuity than that of Frenkel-Brunswik (1939) who studied some 'mechanisms of self-deception' amongst a number of advanced psychology students who were well known at an institute where they had worked for several years. They described themselves, their ideals, and their views on how the institute at which they worked should change, in open-ended form, and in addition a number of colleagues described *them*. The crudest of the mechanisms of self-deception or 'auto-illusions' was 'distortion into the opposite' i.e. a subject described himself in terms opposite to those used by his colleagues in describing him. The more a subject displayed this particular mechanism the more he was likely to be described by others in a manner suggesting 'social incorrectness', for example making intrigues, rejection by the community of the institute, being described as having notoriously neurotic traits. Other mechanisms included omission, justification (for example, a very aggressive subject saying 'I don't let myself be intimidated'), and a shift in emphasis (for example giving little place to a trait to which colleagues gave prominence in describing the subject). In addition there were a number of interesting discrepancies between subjects' statements of ideals and the descriptions of them provided by colleagues. For example, there was a significant *negative* correlation between mentions of 'sincerity' as an ideal and mentions of sincerity in descriptions by colleagues. Furthermore mentioning a relatively large number of ideals was correlated with being rejected by the institute community!

Levels of the self-concept

Many (e.g. Friedman, 1955; Leary, 1957) are critical of concepts of 'self' confined to the self-report level. Leary (1957) argues that at least four levels need to be described: publicly visible self-presentation; conscious self-description; private symbolization (only produced in fantasies, by indirect assessment or by prolonged interviews in depth); the unexpressed unconscious (only displayed by consistent *avoidance*, of hostility for example, at each of the three previous levels). Although the idea that the self-concept exists on a variety of levels varying in the degree to which they are public or private and in the degree to which they require indirect means for their elicitation is highly attractive, there has sadly been little development of these ideas, owing largely it seems to a failure to develop satisfactory techniques for assessment at the more private levels.

Structural variability (across levels) is of course only one source of variability in the self-concept; different situations and time itself being other major sources (Leary, 1957). Regarding stability over time there is some suggestion that self-esteem is amongst the *least* stable of characteristics over a period of years (Tuddenham, 1959).

Styles of coping with identity crises

A further, relatively sophisticated, variation is based upon Erikson's (1956) ideas and has been developed more recently by Marcia (1967). The notion is that in late adolescence people face the problem of developing an identity in terms, for example, of occupational choice and religious and political views. Amongst the styles of coping with this problem are said to be 'identity achievement' (following a crisis period a firm commitment is made), 'moratorium' (continued engagement in decision-making with no firm commitment), 'foreclosure' (firm commitments, often determined by parental example, with no crisis or struggle), and 'identity diffusion' (no commitments, but no apparent struggle either).

Marcia claims to be able to pigeonhole young people into one or other of these categories after a half-hour interview and finds, amongst other things, that 'moratorium' subjects are most self-admittedly anxious and 'foreclosure' subjects least anxious and most authoritarian.

This approach seems, to this writer at least, to have a ring of truth about it, but the idea could be much extended. Commitment to marriage and family would seem to be an important missing area which may be of greater importance than occupation, religion and politics for most people; and identity crises are surely not confined to late adolescence, although identity crises later in life may be more likely to be associated with manifest psychological disorder and some breakdown in functioning.

Abnormal Social Perception
Projection

Amongst the classic Freudian defence mechanisms is that of 'projection'. The notion contains the important idea that the characteristics a person attributes to others bear a predictable relationship to the person's own personality or self-concept. A relatively early objective study of the phenomenon (Sears, 1936) involved students living in joint accommodation who rated themselves and each other for degrees of 'stinginess', 'obstinacy', 'disorderliness', and 'bashfulness'. Sears claimed to have demonstrated that the projection of a subject's own traits (i.e. those traits which fellow-students rated him as having) on to others mainly occurred when a subject lacked insight about his own possession of those traits. For insightful subjects the opposite effect occurred, a phenomenon which Sears refers to as 'contrast-formation'. There are, however, a number of serious possibilities of artefacts occurring in studies of this kind, which will be discussed more fully later (see Chapter 3, pp. 103–7), and it may be partly for this reason that the phenomenon of projection has received relatively little objective study since.

There have however been a number of experimental studies which have served both to demonstrate the situational determinants of projection and also the highly complicated nature of the processes involved. For example, it has been shown that subjects experiencing pain or fright are likely to attribute more fear to a film character especially when the latter is of similar age and sex to themselves (Feshbach, 1970). Bramel (1969) has conducted a series of complex experiments in which a subject whose self-esteem had been artificially inflated or deflated by the false feedback of psychological test results, or who alternatively had been led to believe that he had displayed a high or low level of homosexual interest, had the opportunity to attribute greater or lesser homosexual interest to another person of varying attributes. In one experiment subjects whose self-esteem had been inflated were found to be more likely to attribute homosexual interest than were subjects whose self-esteem had been deflated (but only under conditions in which the other person was evaluated highly). In a further experiment subjects who had been led to believe that they had shown a relatively high level of homosexual interest were more likely to attribute this interest to another person if they thought the other person was a student than if they thought the other person was a 'criminal'. It seems that there are likely to be complex interactions between subject characteristics, characteristics of 'the other', and the nature of the characteristics which could be projected.

A generalization which is frequently made, and which would be of extreme importance were it true, is that the degree of self-acceptance an individual shows corresponds to the degree of acceptance shown by him towards other people. Shrauger and Altrocchi (1964) conclude that the evidence generally supports this hypothesis although relationships are not strong and the evidence is sometimes rather indirect.

Evaluative tone and social perception

A further related suggestion is that social attitudes, or perceptions, whether or not they refer to aspects of the self, have a generally favourable or unfavourable 'colouring' or 'tone'. Long *et al.* (1970) have suggested that children and adolescents with behaviour problems, and adult psychiatric patients, are particularly likely to share a 'triadic pattern' of self–other perceptions which consists of *low self-esteem*, a *low level of social interests* and concerns, and a *high degree of egocentricity* or self-centrality. They used the word 'alienation' to describe this pattern, a term which serves to link this area with a large body of research and thinking in social psychology and sociology. Unfortunately the method which they used in their own research, which involved the manipulation of geometric symbols representing people, is of doubtful validity.

Bhagat and Fraser (1970) believed they had demonstrated that young Scottish offenders had a 'negative colouring to their apparent social perception (ASP) . . . an adverse view of self and environs . . . social malperception' (p. 385). In comparison with control non-delinquents they evaluated each of a variety of concepts (self, ideal self, mother, father, home, work, teachers, neighbourhood, friend, Glasgow, etc.) more negatively. Teasdale *et al.* (1971) found that drug users were distinguished from controls in terms of a variety of questionnaire items which represented a mixture of admissions of anti-social behaviours and negative social perceptions including negative parental perceptions.

Hearn and Seeman (1971) compared male students who had a reputation for 'personality integration' with others whose reputation was only average in that regard. Each subject was shown a series of photographs each depicting one or more persons of either sex, of various ages and in different poses, and was asked to write a short paragraph about each telling what was happening. Subjects with reputations for high levels of personality integration were more likely to describe persons in the pictures as relating to, or interacting with, one another, or desiring to do so. They also expressed more relationships in terms of 'toward', 'with', or 'for' vectors, used more affect terms (whether positive or negative), and in particular used more terms indicative of positive affect.

The foregoing represents a very small selection of the many, methodologically very varied, studies which suggest the existence of a link between mental health and a positive evaluative tone to social perception. Whether differences in social perception have their antecedents in 'adverse experience and inadequate social intercourse', as Bhagat and Fraser (1970, p. 386) assume, is another question and one which takes us back to the substance of Chapter 1. It is however notable that in their study delinquents differed most markedly from controls in their negative perceptions of the concept 'neighbourhood'.

Whatever their origins, negative social perceptions seem bound to have important consequences. For one thing there is abundant experimental and other evidence that social liking and attraction is reciprocated (Bramel, 1969) which suggests that a diminished tendency for spontaneous liking for others might delay friendship formation and in extreme cases might contribute to a vicious circle of increasing estrangement from others. That such individual differences may be detected fairly early in life is suggested by the study of Durojaiye (1970) in the course of which differences in the social perceptions of popular and unpopular eleven-year-old school boys were examined by means of a projective technique. Amongst a number of differences the responses of popular boys suggested a higher level of 'concern for others'.

Related to the above are a number of 'personal orientations' with probable, but at present unclear, implications for mental ill-health. Amongst these is the variable of 'internal versus external locus of control' (a belief that one's behaviour is controlled personally, or internally, versus the belief that one's behaviour is largely determined by external people and events; Rotter, 1966); and the variable of 'interpersonal trust' (Rotter, 1967). The content of the scale which Rotter proposes for measuring the latter variable represents a mixture of items, some of which make reference to relationships of which the person completing the scale must have had *past* experience (e.g. 'parents can usually be relied upon to keep their promises') and items suggesting individual differences in the manner of approaching *future* relationships (e.g. 'in dealing with strangers one is better off to be cautious until they have provided evidence that they are trustworthy'). This illustrates yet again the difficulty of disentangling past experience from present and future reaction.

Socially Unskilled Behaviour
The norms of social performance

One totally different approach to the study of the social behaviour associated with mental disorder is that suggested by the term 'social skills'. According to this approach normal social behaviour can usefully be thought of as a complex set of skills acquired, like perceptual-motor skills, by a combination of coaching, example, and experience. The work of establishing objectively the norms of social interaction has only recently begun (Argyle and Kendon, 1967; Argyle, 1969). Many of these norms are taken for granted most of the time and we only become aware of them when they are violated.

Amongst the elements of social performance which have been examined to date are 'looking' and 'eye contact'. Studies in England, Denmark and the USA have established that it is normal in these countries for each of two relative strangers in conversation with one another to look in the direction of the other's face for much of the time, but by no means all of the time. Continuous gazing at the other is normally broken once every few seconds. Furthermore, 'looking' is synchronized both with the other's 'looking' and with the speech pattern of each participant. Accordingly eye-contact (simultaneous looking) is appropriately regulated in accordance with the circumstances and with the intimacy of the relationship. For strangers it is likely to take place rather less than one third of their time together. Kendon (1967) has particularly focused upon the functions of this attention and synchrony in maintaining conversation between two people. By examining films of discussions, frame by frame, it becomes clear that the person who for the moment is the listener is by no means passive whilst waiting his turn to speak, but rather provides a continuous, largely non-verbal, 'commentary' on the speaker's performance. He is likely to grunt, nod his head, smile and otherwise make body movements, gestures and facial expressions at appropriate points, sometimes even copying gestures and expressions made by the speaker. The reinforcement value, to the speaker, of these non-verbal responses has been recognized by psychologists for some time and it can scarcely be doubted that they play a major part in establishing and maintaining satisfactory and rewarding relationships.

A small start has been made in examining mental disorder from this perspective. Hinchliffe *et al.* (1970) have recorded that less 'eye-contact' than normal occurs during the course of interviews with patients suffering from depression and Rutter and Stephenson (1972) have recorded reduced 'looking' on the part of both depressed and schizophrenic patients. In addition, patients with the latter diagnosis 'looked' in glances of abnormally short duration. Hutt and Ounsted (1966) have revealed the abnormal preference of autistic children for animal or blank faces as opposed to human faces.

Quite apart from these specific abnormalities of visual attention, it seems likely that a whole range of signs and symptoms of psychological disorder must be associated with major or minor violations of the norms of social behaviour. Symptoms which contribute to psychiatric diagnoses range widely from the specific and frankly social 'swearing in public' of the rare Gilles de la Tourette's syndrome to the commoner 'inappropriate affect' of schizophrenia, the abnormally raised or lowered moods of the affective disorders (depression, hypomania and related conditions), and the agitation and restlessness of the anxiety states. Argyle (1969) has considered a range of disorders and has listed a number of areas of socially unskilled behaviour which cut across the traditional psychiatric diagnoses. Some of these abnormalities, such as excessive self-reference, or the adopting of an 'interrogator' role by asking an unusually large number of questions, concern the *content* of speech, whilst other abnormalities concern *non-content* aspects of interaction such as 'looking' and gestural aspects. The majority of abnormalities, such as excessive dominance or its opposite, or unusual difficulty in opening and closing conversations, involve both verbal and non-verbal aspects.

Whether aspects of unskilled social behaviour are primary or secondary, of etiological importance or not, they, like negative social perceptions, seem bound to have important social consequences. Foulds (1965) has gone so far as to state that a degree of 'egocentricity' is associated with all mental disorder (the more severe the disorder the greater the egocentricity) and Argyle (1969) suggests that all varieties of mental disorder have in common the fact that those who suffer from them are more than usually likely to create social relationships and encounters which are 'unrewarding' to the participants.

Self-disclosure, interpersonal attraction and intimacy

That social skills and interpersonal attractiveness are intimately related is suggested by a number of experiments, summarized by Argyle (1969), showing that people display a higher level of 'looking' when interacting with someone who is liked. Amongst other factors which it may be supposed contribute to higher levels of intimacy in interaction, is the *topic* of conversation, and particularly the degree of 'self-disclosure'. Not surprisingly, disclosures about matters such as one's sex life, body, feelings about one's own family, and details of financial affairs are likely to indicate a fairly high level of intimacy (Taylor and Altman, 1966). As one might suppose, self-disclosure is also related to friendship or liking (e.g. Jourard, 1959; Worthy *et al.*, 1969).

One hardly surprising, but nonetheless very important, finding is that married subjects reported higher levels of self-disclosure to their spouses than towards any other 'target' person (including parents and friends) and these self-disclosure-to-spouse levels were higher than any levels reported by unmarried subjects (Jourard and Lasakow, 1958). This illustrates the importance of sexual relationships for social as well as sexual intimacy.

Although a connection between non-rewarding social contacts, or lack of opportunity for intimate contacts, and mental disorder has often been suggested, there has been little objective study of this possibility. Mayo (1968) asked three groups of women to report on both the level of their own disclosures to 'the person to whom they felt closest' and the level of reciprocated disclosure from the same person. (The women were in-patients diagnosed as having a neurotic disorder; women who had received no treatment and sought no help for mental disorder but whose answers to a questionnaire measure of 'personal illness' suggested neurosis; and women who were neither hospitalized nor replied to the questionnaire in a way suggesting neurosis.) Reported levels of self-disclosure were significantly higher for the third group of women (women with no evidence of neurosis by either criterion) than for either of the other two groups. Self- and other-disclosure were positively correlated for each group but women in the first group (in-patients) thought they 'gave' more than they 'got'.

The Circumplex Ordering of Interpersonal Behaviour
The Leary system

An introduction to the circular (or circumplex) ordering of inter-personal behaviour was made in Chapter 1 when reference was made to the work of Schaefer (1959) on parental behaviour. In fact there is considerable evidence that non-parental adult inter-personal behaviour can be ordered in the same way. The most comprehensive framework which has so far been suggested is that of Leary (1957), summarized in Figure 2.

A feature of the system, and of the adjective check-list derived from it, is that no part of the circle should represent behaviour which is necessarily any more acceptable or 'socially desirable' than behaviour in other parts of the circle. It was proposed, in theory at least, that behaviour categorized in the 'aggressive-sadistic' octant, to take one example, could take the form of appropriately frank, forthright, firm and critical action when the *occasion* demanded it. On the other hand, unpleasant, unfriendly, punitive and unkind actions would also be categorized in the same octant. Similarly, helpful and supportive behaviour belongs in the 'responsible-hypernormal' part of the circle but so too does behaviour which is pitying, soft-hearted and 'compulsively' hyper-normal. Although there is some doubt about this independence from social desirability, there is substantial evidence that some of the aspects of interpersonal behaviour appearing in Leary's scheme are prominent aspects of social behaviour across a variety of situations and that the circular ordering is appropriate. Much of this evidence has been reviewed by Carson (1969, pp. 98–107).

Lorr and McNair (1965) have also presented evidence for the

Figure 2 The Interpersonal Behaviour Circle

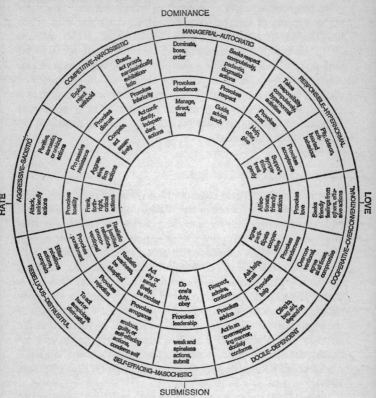

(Taken from Carson, 1969, p. 108, Figure 4.1)

circular ordering of fifteen variables which bear a close resemblance to the Leary variables (in clockwise order around the circle these are: dominance; exhibition; sociability; affection; nurturance; agreeableness; deference; abasement; succorance; submissiveness; inhibition; detachment; mistrust; aggression; competition).

Reservations about such systematized views of interpersonal behaviour have already been voiced in Chapter 1, when parental behaviour was discussed. However, greater confidence may be placed in such schemes as a result of recent evidence that non-verbal aspects of interpersonal behaviour can also, with some justification, be summarized in not dissimilar terms (Mehrabian, 1971). Liking-affiliation is indicated by a variety of vocal, facial and gestural cues including pleasantness of facial expression, amount of eye-contact and frequency of head-nodding; potency or status is indicated by postural signs of greater relaxation such as a sideways lean of the body and asymmetry of limb positions; activation or responsiveness (whether positive or negative) by speech rate and volume etc.

Eccentric interpersonal behaviour

The importance of these ideas on the ordering of aspects of inter-personal behaviour for our present discussion lies in the suggestion which is explicitly made by Leary and Carson, and less systematic-ally and explicitly made by a wide variety of writers on mental disorder, that what appears to an observer to be an individual's distinctive 'personality' consists of social behaviour which is eccentric (in the literal sense) and that much mental disorder is closely associated with such eccentricities. In other words, many people show a notable preference for behaviour in a limited part of the interpersonal behaviour circle. It is further suggested that the stronger this preference, the more rigid, inappropriate and in-flexible the behaviour becomes, the greater the degree of 'sickness' a patient is likely to display (Leary, 1957; White, 1964; Carson, 1969).

White (1964) suggests that feelings such as fatigue, tension and chronic dissatisfaction may be among the *consequences* of these extreme preferences, a proposal which is quite explicit in its sug-gestion that these forms of psychological distress may in part follow from, rather than merely be associated with, aspects of personality. Again, Weinstein (1969) suggests that an important element in 'interpersonal competence' is the possession of a large and *varied* repertoire of 'lines of action' coupled with the posses-sion of resources to employ 'tactics' appropriate to different social situations.

These ideas on the organization of interpersonal behaviour and its implications for mental disorder have their roots primarily in neo-Freudian thought (Adler, 1929; Horney, 1951; Sullivan, 1953) but they, or ideas like them, are widely prevalent amongst mental health specialists whatever their training. Unlike many of the classic psychoanalytic ideas associated with Freud, these ideas are genuinely social, have an appeal to common sense, and have been systematized (particularly by Leary, 1957) in such a way that they could be objectively confirmed, modified or rejected. Hypotheses worthy of test concern the general association of interpersonal rigidity or inflexibility and psychological disorder, and the association of particular types of inflexibility with particular types of disorder and with differential tendencies to seek help.

A Dynamic Model of Abnormal Social Behaviour

The models presented so far for organizing what is known about abnormal social behaviour are somewhat 'static' in nature. They assume either areas of unskilled behaviour, or else rigid adherence to particular forms of social behaviour, in either case showing some constancy from situation to situation. Even more important is the assumption that these abnormalities are to a fair degree independent of who the other person(s) (O or Os) is/are and how they behave. Such a view is of course in accord with an individual diagnostic and treatment approach. If a professional helper has access only to a single individual, artificially extracted from his everyday social relationships, then it is scarcely surprising that there will be a bias towards formulating 'the problem' in terms of something that is wrong with the individual. The realities of social behaviour may be quite otherwise.

The diagram in Figure 3 represents a highly simplified scheme to help try and understand the complex dynamics of social relationships. A number of very similar models have been proposed by others (e.g. Warr and Knapper, 1968; Marlowe and Gergen, 1969). In common with these other models, the one in Figure 3 contains 'feedback' elements. If the model were a simple one-way, stimulus →response one, all the arrows would be going in one direction, from the top of the diagram to the bottom. Indeed simple

Figure 3 A Feedback Model of Social Behaviour

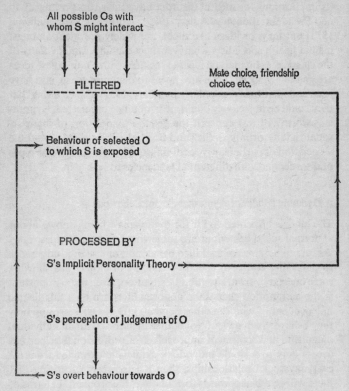

unidirectional models, without feedback, are the ones on which most traditional experimental psychology is based. In the necessarily artificial setting of laboratory research, the stimulus (the independent variable) is manipulated under the control of the experimenter and whilst the subject's response (the dependent variable) is carefully monitored, it is not allowed to act back upon and modify the stimulus (Marlowe and Gergen, 1969). Figure 3, on the contrary, shows the subject (S) and 'the other' (O) acting as both stimulus and response for one another. Hence the circles are endless with no obvious beginning or end, and traditional notions of one thing causing another become difficult to apply to say the least. As Watzlawick *et al.* (1968) point out, 'interpersonal systems – stranger groups, marital couples, families, psychotherapeutic and even international relationships – may be viewed as feedback loops, since the behaviour of each person affects and is affected by the behaviour of each other person' (p. 31).

The eliciting function of interpersonal behaviour

Despite the ring of truth which such a statement possesses, there has been a remarkable absence of objective study of the effects of one person's behaviour upon that of another, in the context of psychological disorder. Once again Leary (1957) has put forward a highly systematic set of hypotheses. He considers that, 'The reflex manner in which human beings *react* to others and *train* others to respond to them in selected ways is . . . the most important single aspect of personality' (this author's emphases). The proposal is that social behaviour belonging in a particular part of the interpersonal behaviour circle 'elicits' or 'prompts' complementary behaviour in other people. There is the additional (at the present state of knowledge unnecessary) assumption that this behaviour is in some way 'purposive', and serves to enhance or maintain the individual's security. In general it is proposed that complementarity operates through *reciprocity* along vertical axes of the interpersonal behaviour circle (e.g. dominance elicits submissiveness and vice versa) and through *correspondence* along horizontal axes (hate induces hate and love induces love) (Carson, 1969). For example, it is proposed that distrustful behaviour 'pulls' irritated rejection from others, respectful conforming behaviour elicits strong, helpful, nurturant leadership from others, over-conventional behaviour encourages liking and so on. Relationships might be similar on the level of brief encounter and on the level of long-term relationships (e.g. tears may have a strong chance of provoking sympathy in the short-term and dependence may foster succorance in the longer term).

Game models of abnormal behaviour

Kelley and Stahelski (1970) have summarized the results from a number of experiments using 'game' analogues of social inter-action (e.g. the 'prisoner's dilemma' game). They conclude that the tendency of individuals to adopt either a cooperative or competi-tive strategy is a fairly stable preference but that cooperators are more likely to modify their strategy in accordance with the behaviour of the other player. Whereas those who prefer a com-petitive strategy are likely to pursue this preference irrespective of their partner's behaviour, those who prefer cooperation are often induced to compete when playing against an O who prefers competition.

Despite the contrived nature of such 'games', they do have a respectable background in game theory or exchange theory models of social interaction (Thibaut and Kelley, 1959; Homans, 1961) which stress the importance of 'costs', 'pay-offs', 'risks' and so on. An attempt to apply this perspective to disordered behaviour has been made by a number of writers, including Berne (1968) and Carson (1969). Carson speaks of 'disordered interpersonal contracts' which appear to serve the function of maximizing cer-tain rewards for each of the participants whilst incurring the costs inherent in repeated performance of self-injurious or deviant behaviour by at least one participant. Many of these disordered contract situations correspond to the unfunny *Games People Play* described by Berne (1968), most of which Carson (1969) considers to be everyday familiarities in the professional work of psycho-therapists. At least one of these games ('alcoholic') corresponds in its title with a psychiatric diagnosis. The pay-off for the person who plays the part of the alcoholic in this game lies, so it is said, in the opportunity the role provides to adopt a submissive and help-less role complementary to the roles of judge–critic and sympathetic helper. These latter parts bring their own pay-off for the wives, social workers and others who play them.

These sorts of formulations are over-simple and at the same time unnecessarily complex. There is over-simplification involved in assuming that a person's behaviour can be summarized in terms of a rounded-off 'role' or 'part' but at the same time it is intro-ducing unnecessary extras to propose that certain outcomes are purposively pursued and provide 'pay-off'. Although it is unclear at this stage how profitable game models will be for an understanding of abnormal social behaviour, the complementariness of different forms of social behaviour represents a series of questions which are likely to receive increasing scientific attention (e.g. Shannon and Guerney, 1973).

Non-verbal aspects as affective symbols

Leary (1957) is amongst the many who have stressed the importance of the non-verbal aspects of social behaviour. In his view, tone of voice, gesture and physical appearance may be amongst the more important aspects of *public* behaviour for provoking reactions from other people. An important attribute of much *non-verbal* behaviour is that it may be produced in a reflex-like fashion, S therefore may be unaware of it and of its effects upon Os, and it may therefore create an impression quite contrary to S's view of the self. Watzlawick *et al.* (1968) suggest the important principle that the nature of relationships between people (hostile, affectionate, superior-inferior etc.) are rarely defined deliberately or in full awareness and depend particularly on non-verbal aspects of communication.

Similar views were put forward several years earlier under the heading of 'affective symbolism'. A quotation summarizes this view:

An affective symbol communicates feeling, while a cognitive symbol communicates information ... an affective symbol may be a tone of voice, a facial expression, a gesture of the hand, or even a meaningful silence ... An affective symbol does not have to be cognitively recognized, at least at the conscious level, in order to communicate its meaning. Its actual method of communication seems to be the arousing in the recipient of the feeling tone similar to, or complementary to, that which is felt by the person who originates the symbol (Cumming and Cumming, 1956, p. 78).

The work of Argyle *et al.* (1970; 1971), already cited in Chapter 1, lends support to these various views on the relative importance of non-verbal elements of interactive behaviour for defining the nature of relationships.

Implicit Personality Theories and Mental Disorder

The scheme depicted in Figure 3 is not simply a behavioural scheme. The analysis of the social behaviour of the mentally ill could conceivably proceed by making reference only to the *overt* behaviour of the participants in a social interaction without any consideration of the attitudes which the participants hold towards one another or towards the world in general. Indeed many would argue that the scientific analysis of the social behaviour of the mentally ill would proceed more effectively without reference to such relatively hidden, or covert, factors. Nonetheless the scheme I have chosen to present shows, as a central element, S's 'implicit personality theory' intervening between the stimuli which S receives from O, and S's responses. The term 'implicit personality theory' refers to the whole array of social and interpersonal attitudes and beliefs held by S.

Kelly's personal construct theory

Essentially the IPT is the 'theory' which S holds about the social world, about other people, and about himself in relation to other people. In that sense there is a very real analogy between S's everyday theorizing and the theorizing indulged in by a social psychologist as part of his or her job. Indeed Kelly (1955) has suggested a view of man 'as a scientist' who tests the validity of his theory by seeing how well it fits the real world in the same way as a good scientist should test and modify his theory in the light of objective facts. According to Kelly, man's most important tools, as an everyday scientist, are the 'personal constructs' in terms of which he judges or construes other people. These constructs take the form of dimensions defined by the polar opposites which serve to label the two extreme ends of the dimension. 'Happy-unhappy', 'considerate-inconsiderate', 'attractive to women-unattractive to women', 'likes me-doesn't like me', could all be examples of constructs in terms of which one person construes the behaviour or personality of others.

An important point made by Kelly, one which we have come across already in several different forms, is that the nature and organization of constructs which a person uses, as well as being derived from *past* experience, also influence *present* and *future* behaviour. Kelly argues that constructs develop from a person's experience in the social world and indeed may often take a 'symbolic' form at first, being defined in terms of specific other people rather than in terms of more abstract qualities or attributes. Examples of symbolic constructs would be 'like my mother-unlike my mother', 'like my brother-unlike my brother'.

Level bias in the IPT

A person's implicit personality theory can be examined from a number of perspectives. Firstly, there is the question of 'level bias'. Even though S may use a construct, similar to constructs used by other people, he may show an individual bias in the level, in terms of that construct or dimension, at which he places the majority of Os he meets. There may be important individual differences in the levels of warmth, friendliness, dominance, hostility, and so on, which different Ss ascribe to others (Marlowe and Gergen, 1969). We have already met this notion earlier in this chapter when considering the possibility that a distinctive 'colouring' or 'tone' to social perceptions might be related to low levels of 'self-acceptance' and to mental disorder in general. On the basis of their review of research using the prisoner's dilemma game, Kelley and Stahelski (1970) suggest a 'triangle hypothesis' concerning the beliefs players hold about other players' orientations towards the game. They believe there is some evidence that those whose preferences are for cooperation believe the orientations of others to be heterogeneous – some preferring cooperation, some preferring competition. They suggest that competitors, on the other hand, believe others to be uniformly like themselves, with a preference for competition. (There is evidence too that Ss high in 'authoritarianism' tend to think that others are uniformly similar to themselves.)

Raush (1965) has suggested the importance of level bias in his account of the differences in interactions amongst a group of hyperaggressive boys and interactions amongst a matched group of socially adjusted children. In both groups an unfriendly act tended to be followed by a further unfriendly act on the part of the recipient. The greater aggressiveness of the hyperaggressive boys when interacting appeared to be attributable to a differential reaction to *friendly* acts. Whereas the socially adjusted children tended to reciprocate with friendly responses, the disturbed children more often responded, 'as though such acts had hostile meaning' (Raush, 1965, p. 498).

Hearn and Seeman (1971) have suggested that a major distinction between psychologically 'integrated' people and others lies in the tendency of the former to perceive relationships as close and non-conflictual, or to anticipate that they will be so.

Construct implications and repertory grid methods

A second focus of concern in the implicit personality theory consists of the nature and strengths of the *associations between constructs*. Categorization of O at a particular level on one construct may have implications for the placement of this same O upon other constructs or dimensions. These implications represent further assumptions about the nature of people. Some of these assumptions about the way attributes are related may be very idiosyncratic (e.g. 'stutterers' are likely to be 'considerate' and 'nonstutterers' are likely to be 'inconsiderate' [Fransella, 1972]), whereas others may be fairly generally shared (e.g. the assumption that people who are 'warm' are likely to be 'sociable' and 'humorous' [Asch, 1946]; or the assumption that 'people who wear glasses' are likely to be more 'intelligent' [Argyle and McHenry, 1971]).

It is this association aspect of the implicit personality theory that Kelly (1955), and the repertory grid methods derived from his theory, particularly focus upon. Unlike some more recent 'direct implication' methods (see Rosenberg and Sedlak, 1972) which require that S states directly the associations which he expects between constructs (e.g. 'If O is extremely kind where is he most likely to lie on a scale ranging from "extremely happy" to "extremely unhappy"?'), most repertory grid methods adopt an *indirect* and inferential approach to the discovery of S's associational assumptions. There are a variety of forms of repertory grid method (Kelly, 1955; Bannister and Mair, 1968; Fransella, 1972), but a commonly used variant takes the following form:

1. S is asked to name a series of Os who have fulfilled a number of particular roles in S's life. Some are relatively straightforward nominations for most people (e.g. S's mother or the person who has played the part of a mother in S's life) whilst others may be more difficult (e.g. an employer whom S found it hard to get along with, or the person whom S would most like to be of help to). In one version of the procedure proposed by Kelly there were twenty-four such roles to be ascribed.
2. S is then asked to consider these people in groups of three. For example S might be asked to consider as a group, a teacher whom S liked, his wife or present girlfriend, and a girl he got on well with when at school. S is required to consider a number of such triads and in each case is asked, 'In what important way are two of them alike but different from the third?' The answer is recorded as one of S's constructs.
3. When the prearranged triads have all been presented, or when S's constructs are becoming repetitive, the construct-eliciting stage in the procedure is concluded and S is then asked to judge each of the nominated Os (the 'elements') in terms of each of his constructs. This may be done in a number of ways (simply yes or no; ranking; rating, etc.).
4. In the analysis of the data each construct is compared with each of the others in turn to see how similarly constructs have been applied to elements and the similarity is expressed in terms of some form of agreement, contingency or correlation coefficient. As well as examining individual inter-construct correlations, construct 'factors' or components can be examined if some form of multivariate statistical analysis, such as factor analysis or principal component analysis, is performed on the data.

Rigidity and construct systems

As was the case with the interpersonal behaviour circle, suggestions have been made within the personal construct framework that mental disorder is associated with rigidity or inflexibility. Kelly (1955) himself suggested that neurosis and psychosis were associated with withdrawal into a more and more 'predictable' social world and that the circumstances which militate against change include being faced with threatening events or circumstances, being preoccupied with old events, people and relationships out of which S's present construct system grew, and having no opportunities to experiment with new relationships or new attitudes towards people.

Fransella (1972) has suggested the application of construct theory to long-standing behavioural complaints such as stuttering and obesity. Of the latter, for example, she writes:

Take the overweight woman. Overweight clearly has meaning for her. People relate to her as a fat person. She is subsumed under such stereotypes as 'a fat person who is a jolly person'. Supposing she was suddenly to lose weight, surely she would need to develop a very different conception of herself. If she is young, she might find out that young men find her attractive and make advances to her, whereas before they had remained companions. She could well be expected to experience anxiety at this turn of events ... (p. 237).

The difficulty lies in predicting when a construct system will show rigidity and when flexibility (i.e. when man will behave like a bad scientist and when like a good one). Kelly and others have made a number of interesting suggestions regarding features of construct systems which are likely to make them more resistant to change. For example the presence of 'impermeable' constructs (those that cannot easily embrace new elements), 'pre-emptive' constructs (where positive instances are totally defined by being positives and can be nothing else) and 'constellatory' constructs (if O is A then he *must* also be B and non-C etc.; in other words there is a constellation or 'complex' of strongly linked constructs) may make change more difficult.

Despite the popularity of Kelly's theory and the grid methods in recent years there has been a surprising absence of systematic study in the field of mental disorder using this approach. Other than the application of the method to a number of stutterers by Fransella (1972) and reports of individual cases, such as that of an arsonist (Fransella and Adams, 1966) and that of a woman seeking a sex-change operation (Bannister and Mair, 1968) there have been few published applications.

Figure 4 Pictorial Representation of a Few of the Statistically Significant Relationships between Constructs in a Grid of One Stutterer

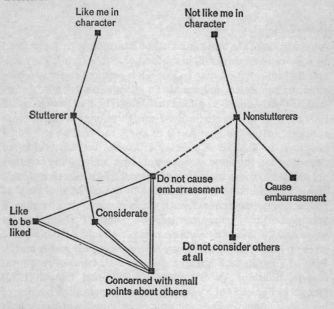

Strong positive relationship
Moderate positive relationship
Negative relationship

(Taken from Fransella, 1972, p. 86, Figure 8)

As an example of the sort of result which the grid method may produce in an individual case, Figure 4, taken from Fransella's book on stuttering, shows a graphic summary of some of the construct relations produced by a stutterer who said that he did not find his stuttering troublesome and that he had been persuaded to come for treatment by other people. He subsequently opted out of treatment. The figure suggests that he sees stutterers, who tend to be like himself in character, in favourable terms, and unlike non-stutterers, who tend to be seen in unfavourable terms. Intuitively, at least, this man's lack of interest in treatment can be understood.

Dyad grids

An extension of the basic grid method has recently been proposed by Ryle and Lunghi (1970) in the form of a 'dyad grid'. They suggest that information may be lost if S is required to apply a construct to an element in general. To ask whether John is 'understanding' may miss S's opinion that John is understanding to Gill but not to his mother. In the dyad grid, therefore, the elements are relationships of the type A→B or B→A rather than individual people A or B. The relationships between constructs may be determined in the same way as before by examining the way they are applied to the elements but additional information is available about S's perception of relationships by examining the 'map' of relationships between elements. Each element (representing a relationship) may be represented by a point in two-dimensional space and the line joining the elements A→B and B→A therefore gives an indication of the *reciprocal role relationship* of A and B. Parallel lines on such a map indicate similar types of reciprocal role relationship. An example from Ryle and Lunghi (1970) (shown in Figure 5) of a young woman who consulted because of her unease about her impending marriage, provides an example. It can be seen that in this case S construed her relationship with each of four successive boyfriends in a manner very similar to the way she construed the relationship between her own parents. On the other hand, her relationship with her fiancé was seen as being quite different to these relationships but very similar to S's relationship with her father. Again the picture seems to provide some insight into S's current difficulties.

Ryle and Breen (1972) compared the results of applying such dyad grids to seven young patient couples who consulted a University Health Service for problems centring on personal relationships, with results from seven control couples. Not all

Figure 5 An Example of a Dyad Grid

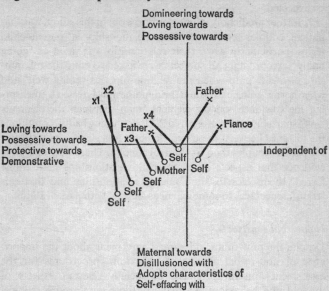

(Taken from Ryle and Lunghi, 1970, p. 324, Figure 1)

were married but all were in a long-term relationship with the prospect of eventual marriage. It was found that in several instances there was significantly more *variation* in the size of inter-construct correlations for the maladjusted couples. This was particularly true in the case of the relationship between the two constructs, 'sexually attracted to' and 'affectionate to'. This would seem to indicate a tendency for individuals in the maladjusted couples either to use these two constructs in an extremely similar fashion or to employ them in an extremely dissimilar fashion. Extremely similar use of these two constructs might suggest confusion between sexual attraction and affection, whilst extremely dissimilar use might be related to difficulty experienced in adjusting to a relationship in which both sexual attraction and affection would be expected.

A further prediction, which was borne out in this study, was that patient couples would see their relationship in parent–child terms, particularly when their relationship was rated as 'going badly'. Accordingly all subjects were asked to construe relationship elements both when the relationship was 'going well' and when it was 'going badly' and the hypothesis was tested by measuring the 'distance' on the element 'map' between the elements 'self→partner' and 'self→parent'. Under 'going badly' conditions the distance between these two elements was significantly shorter for patient couples than for control couples. There was thus some evidence that aspects of parent–child relationships had 'transferred' themselves to adult mating relationships and that this 'transference' was to some extent associated with patient status.

Non-verbal constructs

Despite the now quite widespread agreement about the importance of non-verbal aspects of behaviour, procedures for the assessment and measurement of socially relevant aspects of thought and behaviour, particularly those employed in clinical settings, continue to rest heavily on verbal aspects. This criticism applies in force to repertory grid procedures, despite the fact that Kelly himself, and others who have reviewed the theory and work derived from it (e.g. Bannister and Mair, 1968), have commented that 'personal constructs' need not be verbalized but may only be apparent in non-verbal, automatic, reflex-like, behaviour. Indeed the more verbal aspects of language, consisting of abstract symbols, which tend to have meanings *shared* throughout the social group or culture (we go so far as to circulate dictionaries in some cultures in order to try and ensure that meanings are shared), may be rather unlikely vehicles for expressing individual eccentricities in social meaning.

Cognitive structure

So far we have been discussing the *content* of S's implicit personality theory, whether it be the levels of certain attributes that he assigns to others or the implications that certain constructs have for others in his scheme of things. An alternative focus of concern is the structure of his implicit personality theory or construct system. How many constructs does he use? How many levels are available for use on each? And how independent are the constructs from one another? A popular notion here is that some systems are more complex than others and this has given rise to interest in the variable of 'cognitive complexity–simplicity'.

There is some evidence that at least some types of structural complexity may be related to important aspects of individual personality. For example, Sullivan *et al.*'s (1957) developmental theory of 'interpersonal maturity' makes clear reference to notions of structural complexity. The theory contains the idea that with increasing maturity perceptions of other people become progressively less simple and more differentiated.

In the field of mental disorder there is some suggestion that alcoholics resident in halfway houses are less likely to be helped if they display a relatively simple conceptual structure (Orford, 1974) and Hearn and Seeman (1971) have suggested that access to a large number of highly differentiated interpersonal dimensions for judging others is generally related to psychological integration.

Norris *et al.* (1970) have compared the conceptual structures of members of an obsessional neurotic group and a normal control group. A majority of the obsessional neurotic patients were found to have 'monolithic' structures, almost all constructs being related to each other at a fairly high level, so that any one construct implied the others. On the other hand the majority of normal control subjects had 'articulated' structures, groups of fairly highly related constructs being linked by significant, but lower level, correlations. Thus most constructs had implications for most of the others but there was a degree of 'freedom' about such a structure making it possible for many different combinations of attributes to be assigned to elements.

A further application is the development of a test for 'schizophrenic thought disorder' (Bannister and Fransella, 1966; Williams, 1971). Patients displaying 'thought disorder' produce a much less tight structure when applying a number of highly evaluative adjectives (such as 'kind', 'mean', 'selfish') to a standard set of elements (photographs of people) and this abnormal reaction is much more apparent when the elements consist of people than when they consist of physical objects. However, such patients also show a low level of consistency when the same exercise is repeated almost immediately, suggesting that their reactions may have more to do with confusion than with structural complexity. In a series of experiments Bannister (1965) has shown that this loose construing, characteristic of patients with 'thought disorder', can be produced, in the short term, in other people by a process of 'serial invalidation' whereby attempts to judge personality from photographs are repeatedly pronounced (not necessarily correctly) to have failed.

Implicit Personality Theories and the Dynamics of Social Behaviour
Prejudice and the IPT

There is plenty of evidence from general social psychology that interpersonal perceptual responses can be biased or 'structured' in accordance with previously held opinions or prejudices about O, or about a category of Os, or by information supplied about O from elsewhere; also that this influence combines with attitudes or beliefs about other people which we have subsumed under the term 'implicit personality theory' (e.g. Kelley, 1950; Thibaut and Riecken, 1955).

Assumptions contained in S's IPT operate therefore as types of prejudice, and presumably like social and political prejudices may or may not be resistant to change depending upon circumstance. An interesting example of the changeability of one, perhaps not very important, interpersonal prejudice, is provided by Argyle and McHenry (1971). Although their Ss attributed significantly more intelligence to Os wearing spectacles if they had no opportunity to talk to them, just five minutes interaction was sufficient to erase the effect. In their overall review of person perception studies, Warr and Knapper (1968) conclude that the effects of assumptions about construct implications are less as O is better known or as the amount of information about him/her is increased. Incorrect or maladaptive interpersonal beliefs held by people who are mentally ill may, therefore, as Kelly (1955) suggests, be most resistant to change when the person concerned is protected, or protects himself, from extra information which would invalidate his assumptions.

Self-fulfilling prophecies and the self-concept

The aspect of IPT relevant to illness or pre-illness behaviour about which most is known, concerns, yet again, the self-concept. Suggestions about the importance of self-attitudes in theories of mental illness and health need no repeating and not surprisingly constructs referring to self (e.g. 'myself as I really am', 'myself as I would like to be') occupy a central place in personal construct theory and practice.

A number of experiments show that levels of self-esteem or aspiration influence S's reaction to the opinion which Os express about him. In such experiments, self-attitudes are either *manipulated*, for example by arranging for S to experience, or to appear to experience, success (e.g. Deutsch and Solomon, 1959), or are *assessed* without any attempt at manipulation (e.g. Howard and Berkowitz, 1958). It is then arranged that another person evaluate S or S's performance on a task. Typically the findings are that Ss who are confident, or have been led to believe that they are successful, feel much more positively disposed towards an O who gives them a favourable evaluation than they are towards an O who is unfavourable. Ss who are low in confidence, or who have been led to believe that they are not successful, feel more equally disposed towards those who criticize and those who praise them.

Secord and Backman (1961) have proposed a 'two-factor theory' to explain such findings. One factor is the general preference, which it may be supposed people have, for hearing *favourable* things said about them. The second factor is preference for hearing evaluations *consistent* with one's own view of oneself. There is a great deal of support for consistency theories in social psychology and again the assumption that such a preference operates seems reasonable. For someone high in confidence these two factors would operate in unison in the direction of preference for favourable evaluations. For someone low in self-confidence, on the other hand, they would operate against one another, the first factor predicting preference for favourable evaluations, the second upholding preference for unfavourable evaluations consistent with the self-view. The latter type of person would therefore be expected to show a far less pronounced preference.

Secord and Backman (1961) have suggested a number of other mechanisms whereby the things other people say may be brought in line with S's own view of himself. For example S may simply disbelieve the things that he hears about himself if they are too discrepant with his own view, or he may make changes in the nature and composition of the group of other people with whom he compares himself, or to whose views he is exposed.

A number of experiments illustrate the influence of consistency upon actual behaviour. Amongst them is one by Aronson and Carlsmith (1962) in which subjects were led to believe that they were performing well, or badly, on a simple paired-comparison task (with a 50 per cent chance of being correct by guessing on each trial). After what appeared to Ss to be consistently good, or bad, performance on the first four 'rounds', half the subjects were led to believe that their performance on the fifth round was consistent with this previous performance, and the other half were led to believe that their performance was inconsistent (those who thought they had previously done well appeared to do badly, and vice versa). All subjects were then given a second chance to go through the fifth round again. Those subjects who had been led to believe that their fifth-round performance was *consistent* with their previous performance (whether good or bad) changed very few of their responses when given this chance to do so (adaptive for the 'good' performers but not for the 'bad'). On the other hand, most Ss who thought their fifth-round performance was *inconsistent* with previous performance (again whether good or bad) mostly changed 50 per cent or more of their responses. (Again adaptive behaviour for those Ss who thought they had done well on rounds one to four but not for the remainder. The latter would have maximized their scores by changing few, or none, of their last-round responses.)

Not all attempts to replicate this study have produced the same dramatic findings but at least this one experiment serves to illustrate that under some circumstances people are motivated by consistency, and that for people whose self-opinion is low this motivation may operate in a direction opposite to the motivation for self-enhancement.

In another experiment by Shaban and Jecker (1968) self-esteem was manipulated by false feedback of psychological test results (a strong indication, incidentally, of the potential for the misuse of such tests) and both 'high self-esteem' and 'low self-esteem' Ss were told that they would take part in a discussion with another subject and subsequently be evaluated by one of four judges whose judging styles varied from lenient to severe. Ss were asked to rate their preferences for being evaluated by each of these potential judges. Whereas 'high self-esteem' subjects displayed a preference for judges of moderate leniency, 'low self-esteem' subjects showed a preference for judges with extreme styles. The latter strategy may be thought of as a 'low risk' strategy as the probability of 'failure' is low if the judge is extremely lenient, and the 'cost' of failure is relatively low if the judge is extremely strict. On the other hand preference for a moderately lenient judge, or a moderately difficult task, represents a relatively 'high risk' strategy. Although it is somewhat inconsistent, the evidence that does exist suggests a link between psychological maladjustment and choice of tasks which are either extremely easy or extremely difficult, the setting of goals which are either extremely high or extremely low, and the holding of aspirations which are either very low or unrealistically high. (Kleiner and Parker, 1963; O'Connor and Franks, 1960.)

Although none of the experiments quoted above illustrate the total working of a feedback loop (it would be necessary to demonstrate that aspects of IPT were reinforced or modified as a direct result of the *consequences* of Ss behavioural or perceptual responses), nonetheless the direction of the results are all such that aspects of IPT to do with the self-concept would tend to be confirmed in the manner of a 'self-fulfilling prophecy'.

If it were true that mechanisms like this operate to perpetuate feelings of low self-esteem, it would undoubtedly have important implications for the study of mental disorder. However, the difficulty of studying such mechanisms objectively leaves us in the unfortunate position of knowing that whilst many people take the operation of these mechanisms for granted, largely on the basis of their observations in clinical practice, there is as yet no very telling evidence as to how important these mechanisms are in the etiology or maintenance of abnormal patterns of thinking, feeling and behaving.

Action, reaction and stability

A key link in the scheme presented in Figure 3 is represented by the arrow joining 'S's behaviour' to 'O's behaviour' which corresponds to the 'provoking' 'prompting' or 'eliciting' aspect of Leary's (1957) formulations. The idea that interpersonal attitudes or assumptions, the interpersonal behaviour which follows from them, and the behaviour which this provokes in other people, are all linked in a vicious circle which lends stability to each of the links in the chain and serves to maintain maladaptive behaviour patterns or beliefs, is an attractive idea, and one that is to be found in numerous non-scientific formulations of mental disorder (particularly neurosis) and its treatment. 'Paranoia' provides perhaps the most obvious example; it may be supposed that the hostile and suspicious behaviour which follows from the paranoid's social assumptions is particularly likely to provoke behaviour in other people which confirms his assumptions.

One of the few attempts which has been made to come to grips with such complicated matters at all objectively was that of Raush (1965) who, as already mentioned, studied sequences of friendly or hostile acts in the peer-group interactions of hyperaggressive and well-adjusted boys. For both types of boy it was found that the nature of an act (whether friendly or hostile) was determined in very large part by the nature of the immediately preceding act; if one boy acted in a hostile way the reaction was much more likely to be hostile than if the first act had been friendly. Sequences of interaction amongst hyperaggressive boys got off to a bad start (with an initially hostile action) more often than did sequences amongst socially adjusted boys, but even so the escalation of hostility proceeded at a relatively rapid rate amongst the hyperaggressive boys, a fact which, as already noted, can be attributed to the tendency of the hyperaggressive boy to interpret even friendly acts as hostile. Bandura and Walters (1959) have described a hostile mode of behaviour adopted by some adolescent boys. The style is characterized by active aggression, self-sufficiency, and mistrust of signs of affection. They believe that such boys are particularly likely to become unpopular with their peers as well as with people in authority. Watzlawick *et al.* (1968) proposed the existence of pathologies of 'symmetrical escalation' involving progressive changes in the course of interaction between individuals based upon equality or *similarity* (e.g. S boasting→O boasting→S boasting etc.) and of 'rigid complementarity' involving progressive changes based on *difference* (e.g. S assertive→O submissive→S assertive etc.).

A whole variety of other mechanisms for the generation of stable feedback systems are suggested by findings in general social psychology. A well substantiated finding, for example, is that interpersonal attraction is fostered by physical proximity between people, and by cooperation over shared activities. It may therefore be assumed that beliefs about other people, individuals or groups, which in any way involve *dislike* will tend to be associated with interactional events which serve to maintain these attitudes. This would be so if attitudes of dislike are associated with behaviour which puts physical distance or 'social distance' between S and the disliked Os and minimizes opportunities for cooperation and shared activity. A mechanism of a different sort is suggested by Bramel's (1969) finding that the *expression* of negative attitudes towards another person produced an enhancement of negative views about the other. This is important because it suggests that attitudes may be bolstered simply by their expression even without the intervention of a feedback loop through 'O's behaviour'. The operation of such a mechanism is in line with consistency theories, including the theory of 'cognitive dissonance' (Festinger, 1957).

It may be supposed that these vicious circles of action and reaction, attitude and behaviour, start to operate very early in life. There is probably a strong tendency for peer popularity and non-academic distinction to go together in school as well as out (Durojaiye, 1970) in a way that may confirm both a child's view of himself and the view that others hold of him. Even something as seemingly innocuous as a child's name may play a part in these processes. Bagley and Evan-Wong (1970) review a number of studies showing that child disturbance is associated with having odd first names and they themselves demonstrated that the same applied to surnames. On the basis of this and other evidence that unpopularity with peers is associated with oddity or unpopularity of the child's name, they suggest an explanation along 'symbolic interactionist' lines. Raised vulnerability to stress may be attributable to a low self-image consequent upon having an odd name and reinforced by rejection from other children.

The Simultaneous Study of Symptoms and Personality

Despite the traditional distinction between symptoms and personality, there have been some attempts to study the two simultaneously. Phillips and Rabinovitch (1958) have delineated what they believe to be three basic groups of symptoms: those reflecting 'avoidance of others' (e.g. withdrawal, suspiciousness, hallucinations); those reflecting 'self-indulgence and turning against others' (e.g. assaultive behaviour, drinking, destructive behaviour); and those reflecting 'self-deprivation and turning against the self' (e.g. bodily complaints, tension, suicidal ideas). Zigler and Phillips (1960) are of the opinion that these symptom clusters represent different levels of social maturity or competence and are of the view that the individual in becoming symptomatic does not change his habitual mode of response. Unfortunately in this research the measure of social maturity employed leaves much to be desired and there are some major sex differences in the incidence of symptoms in the different clusters which are difficult to reconcile with a simple one-dimensional social maturity approach. Men are much more likely than women to display symptoms in the 'self-indulgence and turning against others' cluster whilst women are much more likely to display symptoms in the 'self-deprivation and turning against the self' cluster.

A quite different, and perhaps more profitable, approach lies in the relatively intensive study of single cases. The approach is represented by the work of Gershon et al. (1968) who studied the

Figure 6 Two Illustrative Cases: Low Hostility–Out While Depressed and High Hostility–Out While Depressed.

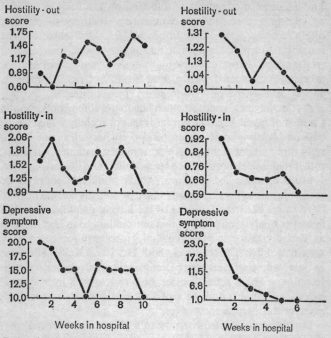

Patient 3. High hostility-in and low hostility-out while depressed

Patient 4. High hostility-out and high-hostility-in while depressed

(Adapted from Gershon *et al.*, 1968, pp. 230–31, Figures 1 and 2)

covariation of depressive symptoms and hostility in six individuals over a period of some weeks. When the results from all six cases were combined the correlation with 'hostility-out' (i.e. hostility directed towards other people) was found to be near zero but for individuals considered alone the correlation ranged from high negative values to high positive ones. There were some patients who became more hostile when they were more depressed and others who showed the reverse trend. The results for two extreme cases, representing each of these trends, are shown in Figure 6.

Conclusions

The importance of aspects of self-concepts has been recognized by writers and researchers representing a variety of different disciplines and persuasions. In general, a lack of self-confidence is associated with difficulties in, and anxiety about, interpersonal relationships. However, very high levels of self-esteem are not necessarily associated with mental health but may represent a variety of defensive or 'self-deceiving' mechanisms.

A relatively new concept which has found some application in the field of psychological disorder is that of socially skilled versus unskilled behaviour. However this concept, as well as the various self-attitude approaches, take a somewhat static, individual, rather than social, approach to 'personality' and mental disorder.

More dynamic formulations, which intuitively seem to do greater justice to the richness of human personality and interaction, have so far been the province of the largely non-scientific post-Freudian analysts and one or two outstanding contributors, such as Timothy Leary and George Kelly, who have presented more systematic ideas. Unfortunately both Leary and Kelly have come to be remembered more for the limited and relatively undeveloped techniques which their theories gave rise to (the interpersonal adjective check-list and the repertory grid methods respectively) than for the theories themselves.

For the present it is necessary to look towards 'normal' psychology for evidence of the association between skilled interpersonal performance, intimacy and interpersonal attraction, for evidence of the way in which particular styles of behaviour (particularly their non-verbal components) may elicit certain behaviours from other people, and for evidence of dynamic interpersonal processes whereby social attitudes, including self-attitudes, may be confirmed in a self-fulfilling fashion.

The implications for an understanding of mental disorder may be considerable but are as yet on the whole unrealized. For example there have been relatively few studies to date of the association between disorder on the one hand and prejudicial aspects of the Implicit Personality Theory, or non-intimacy or lack of skill in promoting rewarding relationships, on the other hand. Particularly noticeable is the relative dearth of investigations which focus simultaneously upon the traditional signs and symptoms of mental disorder, and the supposedly more enduring aspects of 'personality'.

Chapter 3

Husbands and Wives:
Marriage and Mental Disorder

Introduction

Heterosexual mate relationships, institutionalized in the form of
'marriage', are very likely the most important relationships
which most people have in their adult lives. A certain amount of
research on psychological disorder has been focused upon the
marital relationship and it is therefore appropriate that a chapter,
albeit a short one, should be devoted to this topic. It is important
to bear in mind, however, that this specialism reflects the pre-
dominating concerns of previous research and does not imply
that marriage is unique in having implications for mental health.
Many people do not experience conventional heterosexual marriage at all, and even for those that do the importance of pre-
marital and extra-marital, sexual and non-sexual, relationships
remains relatively unexplored.

There is a variety of interesting questions which can be asked
about marriage and mental disorder. Do people who have already
shown signs of mental disorder, or who are perhaps predisposed
towards it, make happy marriages? Do they choose their mates in
the same way as other people? Do they have as much choice as
others? What effect does mental illness have upon the 'well'
spouse and how does the latter cope? Does the 'well' partner
have a significant part to play in the process of recovery from
disorder? These and other questions which could be posed have
clear and undoubted implications both for an understanding of
mental disorder and for its prevention and treatment.

Much of the research in this area, as in other areas of potential
application for social psychology, has been bedevilled by one or
other of two one-sided approaches. Either the 'well' partner is
viewed as a 'victim' who has to 'cope' with 'stress' or 'deviance'
attributable to the other partner's illness, or alternatively he or she

is seen as more of a villain than a victim who provokes or encourages illness or who prevents recovery. At present there is a relative absence of more sophisticated social psychological study which takes the husband–wife relationship as the unit of study, rather than the contributions of the individual participants.

There are obviously a hundred-and-one ways in which this topic could be investigated. The relatively limited array of methods which have been used to date may appear to represent a somewhat arbitrary selection, but of course the selection is determined by existing systems of nomenclature in the mental disorder field and by existing methodologies in social psychology. As a consequence, studies are to be found in this chapter which concentrate on husband–wife similarities in terms of psychiatric diagnosis, questionnaire or interview studies of the way in which decision-making and task performance is shared or distributed within marriage, and studies of mutual interpersonal perceptions (John thinks Gill is bossy, Gill thinks she isn't, but Gill knows that John thinks she is, etc.). On the other hand, to take but one example, there is a relative dearth of investigations of the degree of husband–wife 'attachment' or 'affectional bonding' (the 'love' which the average lay person is likely to consider fairly basic).

Similarity and Complementarity
Deviant mate choice

Students of mental disorder and marriage often argue that there is some sort of satisfaction in being married to a spouse who, by general standards, is deviant or disordered in some way. For example, from a study of sixteen wives of drug addicts comes this comment: 'It appears to us that these women *seek out*, as husbands weak men whom they can control and dominate.' (Taylor *et al.*, 1966, p. 591, my emphasis.) Similar remarks have been passed about wives of male alcoholics and spouses of phobic patients. Those who stress deviant mate *choice* can point to the fact that many such wives know of their intended's abnormality at, or before, the time of marriage. Most of these ideas have stressed the *complementarity* of, or difference between, spouses. For example, they suggest that a controlling person may marry a younger, or particularly submissive, partner, to assist the expression of their controlling nature. These ideas particularly concern the dominance–submissiveness dimension of interpersonal behaviour.

In fact, the research that has been done on mate choice, friendship choice, and interpersonal attraction in general, suggests that the general picture is rather more mundane than these ideas would suggest. The major determinants of who forms attachments with whom turn out to be *propinquity* and *similarity*. People tend to pair up with others who are most readily available, because they are near, and with others who are similar to themselves in general social characteristics (such as race, social class, education, occupation), and values and interests. Even when it comes to more subtle 'personality' traits, the evidence is mainly in favour of similarity, rather than complementarity. However, it has to be said that theories of mate choice are becoming more sophisticated. For example, there are now a number of 'stage' theories, which suggest that the factors governing choice at a relatively early stage in bond formation, are not the same principles upon which progress may be based at a later, more intimate, stage (e.g. Winch, 1958; Kerckhoff and Davis, 1962; Murstein, 1970). Similarity might be the predominant factor at relatively early stages in the process, and more subtle factors, including complementarity, might operate at later stages.

Furthermore, although similarity, rather than its opposite, appears to be the general rule, relationships are uniformly weak and leave ample room for a wide degree of variation in the amount of similarity, or complementariness, to be found in individual couples. Winch (1958) noted that notions of complementariness in marriage had, for the most part, originated with authors who had treated neurotic patients and Cattell and Nesselroade (1967) found more evidence of similarity amongst 102 stably married couples than amongst thirty-seven couples who were separated or who voluntarily entered marital counselling. Differences were particularly apparent on scales contributing to the dimension of 'exvia versus invia' (which corresponds to the extraversion-introversion dimension of other personality systems). Stably married couples were likely to be similar in terms of this dimension whilst unstably married couples were likely to be dissimilar.

Another study which suggested that the degree of husband–wife similarity in personality might be related either to the degree of conflict in marriage, or to psychological disorder in one or other partner, is that of Kreitman *et al.* (1971). Joint interviews were carried out in the homes of each of sixty couples, within each of which the husband was a psychiatric patient with a diagnosis of neurosis or character disorder, and in the homes of each of sixty control couples. Each partner was assigned a score for assertiveness on the basis of interviewer ratings and counts made from the taped interviews. Although there were no between-group differences in average husband assertiveness, wife assertiveness, or husband–wife assertiveness discrepancy, the variation around each of the three averages was significantly higher for patient couples than for control couples. Amongst patient couples there were, therefore, more individual husbands and wives who were very assertive or very unassertive in the joint interview, and more couples who showed a relatively extreme degree of imbalance between husband assertiveness and wife assertiveness.

Similarity for disorder

Once again, however, this time in the psychiatric literature, it is *similarity* which is most apparent. Findings include a greater than chance probability of *both* spouses in a marriage being hospitalized for mental illness (Gregory, 1959); of husband–wife concordance for neurosis amongst general practitioner patients (Ryle and Hamilton, 1962), and amongst couples registered with a Canadian Health Insurance scheme (Buck and Ladd, 1965); a raised probability of both marital partners being referred to psychiatric facilities serving a single area (Nielsen, 1964); and husband–wife similarity in degree of mental ill-health revealed by a household survey (Hare and Shaw, 1965). There are also findings suggesting that, when both partners suffer from a mental disorder, there is a significant positive correlation between their ages at first symptom onset, and they are more likely to receive the same diagnosis than would be expected by chance alone (Kreitman, 1968).

There have also been a number of reports of significant and positive husband–wife correlations on tests or scales of psychological ill-health or neuroticism (e.g. Kreitman, 1964; Kreitman *et al.*, 1970), but correlations are usually very modest in absolute size (in the region of $+0.30$ to $+0.35$ at best).

Interaction and duration of marriage

Needless to say, assortative mating is not the only possible explanation for these modest, but fairly consistent, husband–wife similarities.

Nielsen (1964) suggests a number of alternatives. Firstly, some sort of interpersonal influence may take place whereby one partner 'infects' the other. Secondly, husbands and wives may be exposed to common sources of stress or deprivation. Thirdly, psychological ill-health in one partner may represent a reaction to breakdown in the other. Some of the sources of stress to which the 'well' partner is exposed as the result of the 'ill' partner's illness may, of course, be fairly incidental to the illness itself. For example, the loss of a family member, even temporarily, due to hospitalization, may in itself be a significant source of stress. Fourthly, there is the very real possibility that psychiatric treatment may be facilitated for the second spouse once the first spouse has been in contact with psychiatric services. This artefact may well operate in studies (e.g. Gregory, 1959; Nielsen, 1964) which rely on hospitalization or clinic attendance as an index of psychological ill-health.

Of these possible explanations, Kreitman (Kreitman, 1964; Kreitman *et al.* 1970) considers assortative mating and 'interaction' (the equivalent of Nielsen's, 1964, 'infection' and Ehrenwald's, 1963 'contagion') the two most serious contenders. Kreitman (1964) divided both patient and control couples into a number of groups on the basis of *duration of marriage*. He reported, firstly, a progressive increase in neuroticism score, and reported psychological and total symptoms of *patients*' spouses with increasing duration of marriage. Secondly, he reported a quite different pattern of variation of magnitudes of husband–wife correlations

Figure 7 Magnitudes of Husband–Wife Correlations for 'Neuroticism' for Patient and Control Couples Married for Different Lengths of Time

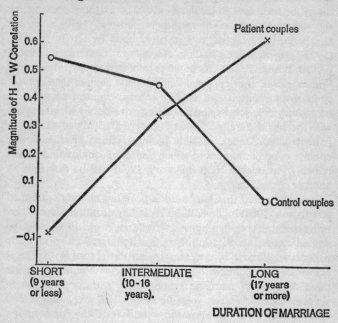

(Taken from Kreitman, 1964, p. 168, Figure 3)

with duration of marriage for the two groups. Fairly recently married *control* husbands and wives showed significant correlations on nearly all psychometric measures and correlations dropped in size in successively higher 'duration of marriage' groups. But the trend was reversed for *patient* couples. Zero or non-significant positive correlations were obtained for recently married patient couples and correlations *increased* in magnitude in successively longer duration of marriage groups. (See Figure 7.) It looked very much as if patient couples might be unusual in becoming more alike as marriage progressed. Perhaps one 'infected' the other, or perhaps they 'infected' each other, as time went on. Of course, though, no couples were actually followed over time in this study.

Kreitman (1964) speculated that the relatively restricted social life of the neurotic and his family might be partly responsible for the 'infective' effects of interaction. Nelson *et al.* (1970), analysing data from the same subjects reported upon by Kreitman *et al.* (1970), presented some findings consistent with this view. Firstly, *patient* husbands and their wives reported more intra-family (inter-spouse), and less extra-family, social contact than control couples. In addition, the trend revealed by control couples, for decreasing inter-spouse and increasing extra-family social contact with increasing duration of marriage, was markedly absent in the patient pairs. Similar, possibly harmful, effects of close family contact in some families to which young schizophrenic patients return from hospital (Brown *et al.*, 1962) will be discussed in another context below.

It must be said that later studies have not entirely confirmed Kreitman's (1964) initial findings regarding duration of marriage. For example, Kreitman himself (Kreitman *et al.*, 1970) reported limited success in replicating his original findings. Wives of neurotic patients appeared to be increasingly neurotic (according to clinical assessment) in comparison with wives of non-patients, across three duration of marriage groups (nine years or less; ten to sixteen years; seventeen years or more). However, neuroticism *scale* scores failed to show any similar trend. Furthermore, although husband–wife correlations were significantly higher for control pairs than for patient pairs when marriages were of short duration, the expected progressive rise in correlations for patient pairs, and the progressive decline for control pairs, with increase in duration of marriage, were not confirmed.

Interperson Perception and Marriage
Dyadic indices

Many social psychological hypotheses of potential relevance to the field of mental disorder are 'dyadic' in nature, concerning, as they do, relationships or discrepancies between scores obtained from one person (S) and those obtained from another (O). They are frequently couched in terms or phrases such as 'compatibility', 'similarity', 'complementariness', 'sensitivity', 'accuracy of person perception' and so on. Such 'dyadic indices' are prominent features of studies of interperson perception and marriage. Table 2 lists the various descriptions of themselves, and of their spouses, which subjects in these studies have been asked to provide. The reader may find it useful to refer to this table as these studies are described although, with the exception of Laing *et al.* (1966), investigators have never asked their subjects to provide each and every one of these descriptions.

Sensitivity and understanding

Researchers who are unaware of the many pitfalls in such work fairly consistently report a relationship between marital unhappiness and a lack of sensitivity, congruence or understanding (e.g. Luckey, 1960; Laing *et al.* 1966). For example, Luckey (1960) administered the Interpersonal Adjective Check List (LaForge and Suczek, 1955) to forty-one satisfied married couples and forty unsatisfied couples who were chosen from a much larger pool of couples on the basis of both husbands' and wives' responses to marital happiness scales. Each was asked to describe both him/herself and the spouse. There was significantly more congruence in the satisfied group, but only when the *husband* was the object of perception. In other words, amongst satisfied couples there was a higher level of H→H versus W→H agreement. Satisfied wives were better able than unsatisfied wives to describe their husbands as their husbands described themselves; satisfied wives thus appeared more sensitive than other wives. But there was no difference in 'sensitivity' between the groups of husbands. This finding, specific to wives, recurs in several studies.

Laing *et al.* (1966) have added a further dimension to the method in the form of perceptions at the 'meta-metaperception level' (e.g. how *she* thinks *he* thinks *she* describes *him*; alternatively written as W→H→W→H). At least two new dyadic indices can be calculated by taking advantage of data at the meta-metaperceptual

Table 2 Some Self- and Spouse-Descriptions, and Derived Dyadic Indices, Used in Studies of Interperson Perception and Marriage

Descriptions	Husband (H) as object of perception	Wife (W) as object of perception
Self-description	H→H (i.e. H describes himself)	W→W
Prediction of spouse's self-description	W→H→H (i.e. W describes how she thinks H describes himself)	H→W→W
Description of spouse	W→H (i.e. W describes H)	H→W
Meta-perception	H→W→H (i.e. H describes how he thinks W describes him)	W→H→W
Meta-metaperception	W→H→W→H (i.e. W describes how she thinks H thinks she describes him)	H→W→H→W

Derived dyadic indices

(a) Inter-perception indices (i.e. a comparison is made of a description provided by H with one provided by W, or vice versa).

Partner likeness	H→H	compared with W→W	
Agreement with spouse's self-description	{ H→W { W→H	compared with W→W compared with H→H	
Predictive accuracy	{ H→W→W { W→H→H	compared with W→W compared with H→H	
Understanding of spouse's perception of oneself	{ W→H→W { H→W→H	compared with H→W compared with W→H	
Realization of (mis) understanding	{ H→W→H→W { W→H→W→H	compared with W→H→W compared with H→W→H	

(b) Intra-perception indices (i.e. one description provided by one partner is compared with another description provided by the *same* partner).

Assumed similarity	{ H→H { W→W	compared with H→W compared with W→H	
Expectation of spouse's agreement	{ W→H→W { H→W→H	compared with W→W compared with H→H	
Feeling (mis)understood	{ H→W→H→W { W→H→W→H	compared with H→W compared with W→H	

level. These include the discrepancy between e.g. H→W and H→W→H→W (i.e. does he think that she knows what he thinks of her? Laing *et al.* call this index 'feeling (mis)understood'). A further new index is termed 'realization of (mis)understanding' by Laing *et al.* (e.g. W→H→W→H versus H→W→H; i.e. does she know how he thinks she describes him?).

Laing *et al.* (1966) compared twelve couples who had sought help with marital problems and ten control couples located in a general practice. They were compared in terms of congruence on a number of dyadic indices. As previous work would lead one to expect, less congruence of all types, at all levels, was found amongst the twelve couples who had sought help, and Laing *et al.* note the frequency of what they call 'straight flushes' in the data from the non-disturbed couples (i.e. almost identical responses were made by both husband and wife at all levels; e.g. I love her, I love him, she loves me, he loves me, she thinks I love her, etc.).

Dangers in interpreting dyadic indices

The dangers of misinterpreting such 'dyadic indices' have been pointed out forcibly on several occasions (e.g. Cronbach, 1955; Wright, 1968). Although accuracy may be a partial determinant of such scores, there are a number of other determinants which have relatively little to do with what most people would mean by accuracy or sensitivity. Amongst these extraneous determinants of distance scores are 'elevation' (e.g. if S rates himself consistently 'high', then Os, who also rate S consistently high, will appear to be accurate about S, although it may have more to do with the tendency of these particular Os to rate *everybody* high rather than their accuracy regarding this particular S) and 'stereotype accuracy' (i.e. the tendency to rate consistently high on some items and low on others in accordance with a stereotype of some kind, rather than on the basis of accurate knowledge or perception of a particular other person). There are many other biases, including those of social desirability, assumed similarity, assumed dissimilarity, acquiescence, and central tendency, which may give rise to apparent, or artefactual, accuracy.

As Wright puts it, the result of computing such an index is that, '. . . a given subject's score loses, for purposes of subsequent analysis, its independent identity' (Wright, 1968, p. 127–8). In other words, unparsimonious interpretations may be made of the relationship between individual scores, and the individual characteristics of subjects may be lost sight of. The danger lies in the likelihood that complex meanings may be forced on to essentially simple social psychological phenomena. This danger seems to be endemic to social theories of mental disorder and is present when two scores from the *same* individual are combined (intra-person comparison) as well as when two scores from different individuals are compared (inter-person comparison). For example, the importance of inconsistency in parental behaviour (and double-binding communications as special cases of inconsistency) may lie not in the relationship or discrepancy *between* two elements of behaviour but rather in the abnormality or extremity of one of those elements.

The individual contribution

When researchers have avoided complex dyadic indices, or have analysed more closely the contribution of individual scores to dyadic indices, the nature of sensitivity and understanding in marriage is seen more clearly. For example, in an early paper, Kelly (1941) found that marital happiness amongst seventy-six couples was associated with self-ratings which indicated relatively high self-esteem, and also with ratings by spouses which indicated even higher relative self-esteem. No attempt was made to calculate complex dyadic indices and the straightforwardness of the results is much in line with the expectations of writers such as Cronbach (1955) and Wright (1968).

Interestingly enough, Luckey herself, at a later date (1964), reported a purely monadic analysis of the same data which she had reported earlier in terms of dyadic indices (1960, see above p. 102). Adjective Check List (ACL) phrases in the categories 'sceptical-distrustful' and 'blunt-aggressive' were most often associated with lack of satisfaction in marriage, whether such phrases were being used to describe the self or the spouse. Items of self-or spouse-perception which were positively correlated with satisfaction were predominantly in the 'responsible-over-generous' category, the 'cooperative-over-conventional' category and in the 'docile-dependent' category. In addition, some of the milder items in the 'managerial-autocratic' category (e.g. 'makes a good impression; respected by others') and the 'competitive-exploitive' category, (e.g. 'self-respecting; self-confident') were positively associated with satisfaction whilst some of the more extreme items in these categories (e.g. 'dominating; dictatorial' and 'thinks only of self; selfish') were negatively correlated with satisfaction. One is forced to agree with Luckey's conclusion that the social desirability dimension is crucial. The items significantly associated with satisfaction are clearly evaluative in nature. The very general conclusion seems to be that people who report satisfaction in their marriages are much more likely than other people to describe themselves and their spouses in favourable terms.

Similar conclusions can be drawn from Murstein and Glaudin's (1966) monadic analysis. Twenty-six couples who were initiating marital counselling, and twenty-four control couples, were given the same ACL and asked to provide a number of descriptions, including self-description, description of ideal-self, description of spouse and description of ideal-spouse. Like Luckey (1960) these investigators found marital adjustment to be more strongly related to *wives'* perceptions. In particular marital adjustment loaded on two wife factors: 'spouse-dominant' and 'spouse-good'. Once again the results are straightforward. Maritally relatively well-adjusted wives are more likely to describe their husbands in favourable terms, and are more likely to describe them as assertive; their descriptions of their husbands appear to correspond with the approved male-role stereotype.

Stereotype accuracy and alcoholic marriages

A recent study of some sophistication is that of Drewery and Rae (1969). They asked each member of a group of twenty-two male alcoholics and their wives to describe themselves, their spouses, and how they thought their spouses saw them, and compared the results with those obtained from a control sample of twenty-six couples. A number of congruence indices were computed but the biggest difference between these groups lay in H→H versus W→H (wife's sensitivity to, or understanding of, her husband). Once again the largest group differences concerned perceptions with *husbands*, rather than wives, as objects.

Both the control husbands' descriptions of themselves, and control wives' description of their husbands, showed a number of marked 'peaks' and 'troughs', suggesting the possibility of a stereotype. Both these sets of *control* descriptions showed peaks on achievement, autonomy, dominance and endurance, and troughs for succorance and abasement. Drewery and Rae, who appear to have been aware of at least some of the possibilities of artefacts contributing to their results, were led to investigate the very real possibility that the highly significant group difference in terms of wife's sensitivity or understanding, 'might be unrelated to interpersonal insight and might be explained in terms of the presence or absence of a socio-sexual stereotype of masculinity' (Drewery and Rae, 1969, p. 294). They proceeded to demonstrate the soundness of this explanation by carrying out an intriguing piece of social psychological detective work. They first demonstrated the presence of a stereotype of masculinity shared by control men and their wives, but not shared by patients and their wives. This they did by demonstrating a higher degree of commonality amongst the self-descriptions of control men than existed amongst the self-descriptions of patients; by further showing that there was significantly more commonality between the control husbands' self-descriptions and descriptions of their husbands provided by all control wives than existed for patients and their wives; and finally by showing that the 'typicalness' of a husband's self-description and the 'typicalness' of a wife's description of her husband correlated highly for the control group (0·82) but scarcely at all for the patient group (0·07). Secondly, they demonstrated that this shared stereotype contributed to the apparent success of the control wives in describing their husbands. The correlation between the typicalness of a wife's description of her husband, and her sensitivity, was significantly higher for the control group than for the patient group (0·61 and 0·24 respectively).

In other words, Drewery and Rae (1969) had shown that the apparent greater sensitivity of non-alcoholics' wives did not necessarily have anything to do with sensitivity to the individual spouse. If data from the 'non-alcoholic' couples had been re-shuffled so that one husband's self-description was being compared with another wife's description of her husband, the non-alcoholic wives would still have appeared more sensitive. Because of the stereotyped manner in which 'normal' people describe married men, these wives were, on the whole, quite 'sensitive' to the non-alcoholic husbands of other women!

The overall conclusions which can be drawn from this section of the literature on marriage appear to be fairly clear-cut. Husbands and wives who take the view that their marriages are happy, adjusted, or compatible, describe themselves and their spouses in favourable terms. When further elements of an approved sex role are fairly widely shared, as is the case with assertiveness or dominance and the male role in industrial, English-speaking countries, then these same subjects will describe the husband in these stereotyped terms also. This 'set', to describe self and spouse, particularly the husband, in favourable and approved sex-role terms, does not apply, or at least not so uniformly, for spouses who consider their marriages to be relatively unhappy, maladjusted or incompatible. This is reflected in the dyadic indices. The happily married, as a consequence, *appear* to be more perceptive, understanding and sensitive. Because the stereotype is clearer for males, differences between the happily and unhappily married in terms of these dyadic indices are stronger when husbands are the objects of perception, than when wives are the objects of perception.

The Concept of Marital Aptitude

A monadic concept of extreme simplicity, and one that is much less fashionable amongst social psychologists now than it once was, is that of 'marital aptitude'. Despite an abundance of research over the years there is still little agreement on the factors making for marital stability or happiness (indeed there is little agreement on whether the concepts of marital happiness or success are useful at all). As recently as 1966 students of marriage were asking 'To what extent is success predicated on "readiness", "maturity", "mental health", and the like, compared to "compatibility", "right choice", or "good fit"?' (Murstein and Glaudin, 1966, p. 37). In fact many who have studied marriage, from a variety of perspectives, have been rather impressed with the probable importance of individual personality or temperament 'inputs' to marriage, although they have scarcely been able to *demonstrate* their importance.

Happily married man

On the basis of data from his large-scale study of American marriage, Terman (1938) had concluded that: 'What comes out of marriage depends on what goes into it . . . whether by nature or by nurture there are persons so lacking in the qualities which make for compatibility that they would be incapable of finding happiness in any marriage' (Terman, 1938). This is an extreme view and it has to be stated that there are some major logical problems in drawing this conclusion from his data. Terman went on to provide brief descriptions of the outstanding features of four types of married person: '*Happily married women* . . . are characterized by kindly attitudes towards others and by the expectation of kindly attitudes in return. They do not easily take offence'; '*Unhappily married women* . . . are characterized by emotional tenseness and by ups and downs of moods. They give evidence of deep seated inferiority feelings'; '*Happily married men* show evidence of an even and stable emotional tone. Their most characteristic reaction to others is that of cooperation'; '*Unhappy husbands* . . . are inclined to be moody and somewhat neurotic. They are prone to feelings of social inferiority'. (Terman, 1938, pp. 145–6, 155.)

Terman and Oden's (1947) study of gifted men and women and their spouses is also relevant. Their 'marital aptitude' score was based partly upon 'personality' and partly upon 'background'. Correlations with marital happiness were $+0.52$ for husbands and

+0·45 for wives when only 'personality' aspects were considered. In support of the contention that this aspect of marital aptitude reveals a tendency which existed *before* marriage, there is the finding that women rated twelve years earlier as having some, or marked, nervous symptoms had a significantly lower marital aptitude score, and that ratings of 'social adjustment' eighteen years earlier show significant relationships with 'marital aptitude'.

Using Thurstone personality inventory items, obtained *before* marriage and weighted for best discrimination, Burgess and Wallin (1953) report correlations with later marital success of only +0·25 for men and +0·18 for women. On the basis of these findings, and those of the other 'prediction' studies, Burgess and Wallin listed the following characteristics as the most decisive in differentiating happily married from unhappily married individuals: emotionally stable; considerate as opposed to critical of others; yielding as opposed to dominating; companionable as opposed to isolated; self-confident; emotionally dependent as opposed to emotionally self-sufficient.

One prominent reviewer of this type of research concluded, 'That individuals' neurotic traits are predictive of marital disharmony can be accepted as a demonstrated fact' (Tharp, 1963, p. 98).

Marriage-wrecking traits

Slater and Woodside (1951) came to similar conclusions on the basis of research of quite a different kind. The marriages of neurotic soldiers and their wives, and of control husbands and their wives, were categorized as satisfactory or unsatisfactory on the basis of direct statements made to an interviewer, and on the basis of the latter's impressions. It was stated that the neurotic husbands were 'conspicuously less successful in their marriages' (Slater and Woodside, 1951, p. 150), although numerically the difference does not seem to be a great one (35 per cent neurotic and 19 per cent control rated as unsatisfactory) and the rating method is obviously open to bias. Rather more important than group differences are the answers given by members of both groups to questions about sources and causes of happiness and unhappiness in marriage. Slater and Woodside record that qualities of personality appear to take the highest place and they describe a variety of 'marriage wrecking traits'. Depressive and hysterical characteristics are amongst those mentioned but moodiness and irritability are considered to be the commonest causes of overt unhappiness. The worst prognosis, they say, occurs when the husband is bad-tempered, irritable and aggressive, has a restless disposition and complains of difficulties in self-control. Anxiety may be considered to be relatively unimportant.

All in all, one has to agree with the conclusions of a review by Hicks and Platt (1970) that a balance of good or redeeming characteristics seems important for marital happiness. However, the same reviewers add the necessary caveat that the cause and effect relationships involved are quite unclear. Many of the earlier studies of marriage, including that of Terman (1938), were self-styled 'prediction studies' even though their design involved no prospective or longitudinal element. We have little knowledge of how the history of interaction in marriage, and the experience of marital happiness or unhappiness of varying degree, *affects* self and spouse-perception. In any case, there is little convincing evidence that the 'success' of a marriage can be predicted at all usefully at its outset on the basis of individual characteristics.

Marital Role Performance and Decision-Making

A procedure, which has often been applied in general studies of marriage, involves the categorization of couples on the basis of their answers (and sometimes on the basis of their children's answers) to questions concerning the relative involvement of husband and wife in a number of family tasks, or in the processes of decision-making. For example, Herbst (1954) attempted to categorize each of eighty-two urban Australian families. In the event, only thirty-two families could be pigeon-holed in this way: eight were described as 'husband dominant' (H makes decisions which W then carries out on her own or with H's help); seven 'wife dominant'; eleven 'autonomic' (in some areas of activity H decides and carries out the decision, whilst in other areas of activity

W both decides and acts); and six 'syncratic' (H and W make decisions jointly).

Similarly Blood and Wolfe (1965) categorized the decision-making patterns of each of several hundred American couples as 'egalitarian', 'male dominant' or 'female dominant'. They reported a high frequency of egalitarianism in family decision-making but a much greater degree of specialization in task performance. The theory of 'instrumental' and 'expressive' marital roles (the former, it is suggested, being played by the male in most societies, the latter by the female) (Parsons and Bales, 1955; Tharp, 1963) has been particularly influential in this area, although the 1960s have seen increasingly frequent attacks on this formulation both on empirical and logical, as well as philosophical and moral, grounds.

Neurosis and family decision-making

Collins *et al.*'s (1971) report of a study of 'executive decision-making' is one of a series of reports of the study of neurotic men and their wives carried out by Kreitman and his colleagues. The 'usual pattern' of family decision-making was explored in a semi-structured conjoint (husband and wife together) interview. Afterwards the interviewer rated the relative involvement of husband and wife in decision-making. Ratings were made separately for areas which included child rearing, choice of dwelling, financial arrangements, maintenance of social relationships, holidays, and entertainments.

Like Herbst (1954) and Blood and Wolfe (1965), Collins *et al.* categorized couples into types, although their categories were somewhat different ('husband-dominated', 'wife-dominated', 'cooperative' and 'segregated').

Although the focus of Collins *et al.*'s study was 'executive decision-making', also rated from the interview was 'husband's manifest behaviour' in two areas; housework and child care. In each of these areas the husband's involvement was rated as regular, occasional, or never.

Collins *et al.* (1971) found there to be more husband-dominated marriages in the neurotic group than in the control group (14/60 versus 6/60). Furthermore, of those families not clearly dominated by one partner, there were more segregated than cooperative patterns of decision-making amongst patient families, and fewer amongst control families. The average number of 'joint' decisions was significantly higher for control marriages. This was particularly so in the areas of child rearing and entertainment where the majority of decisions for control families appeared to be joint ones, but where only half the decisions, or fewer, were joint for patient families. However, the nature of the non-joint decisions in these two areas were, as one might expect, quite different. In the case of child rearing the majority of non-joint patient group decisions were wife dominated or divided, whereas the majority of such decisions concerning entertainment were husband dominated. Collins *et al.* remark that the results for these two areas, 'reflected the marked reluctance of the husband to engage in conjoint social activity and the effect of his veto on the couple's behaviour' (Collins *et al.*, 1971, p. 240).

Differences between patient and control families showed up in the two areas of 'manifest behaviour' as well as in the six areas of executive decision-making. Patient-husbands contributed significantly less in both housework and child care despite the fact that they as a group were found to spend more time around the house (Nelson *et al.*, 1970). Manifest behaviour and decision-making were related: combining patient and control groups, husbands in segregated and husband-dominated marriages contributed significantly less.

In summary, Collins *et al.* suggest that neurosis in husbands is associated with 'minimal cooperation' in marriage and that deviant role patterns produce conflict. Wives experience 'loss of support and lessened experience of sharing' (Collins *et al.*, 1971, p. 241). They speculate that wives in this situation may choose segregated roles as a defence against an irritable and self-absorbed husband.

Collins *et al.* suggest that *husband* domination may be a general feature of the marriages of neurotic patients (whether it is H or W who is 'ill') and indeed Bullock *et al.* (1972) record *less* relative decision-making control by depressed *women* than by matched control women.

Role transfer and disengagement

A transfer of role performance from a mentally disordered member of a household to other 'well' members (particularly the spouse) has been remarked upon by a number of writers. For example, there have been comments upon the adaptation of husbands of schizophrenic women to include a large part of their wives' roles; others have referred to the transfer of aspects of male role performance to wives whose husbands are suffering from alcoholism; and Clausen and Yarrow (1955) have referred to changes in family roles, particularly when patients are hospitalized, as being an important part of the impact of mental illness upon families.

A further development of the methodology employed by Herbst (1954) is relevant to this question of role rearrangements and transfer. The activities enquired about by Herbst were grouped into wives' household duties (HoW) (e.g. ironing, washing); common household duties (HoB) (e.g. setting the table, buying groceries); husbands' household duties (HoH) (e.g. doing repairs, chopping wood); child control and care (Ch); economic activities (E); and social activities (S). When Herbst looked at the number of these 'regions' in which husbands were active participants, he found that the pattern of participation across regions took a highly predictable order. The ordering was: E (all husbands participating), S, HoH, Ch, HoB, HoW (the smallest number of husbands, nineteen out of eighty-two, participating in this last region).

On the basis of this reproducible ordering, Herbst proposed a 'pathfield' along which the husband's activities progressed, one way or the other, depending upon whether his participation in family activities was on the increase or on the decrease. If on the decrease, HoW activities would be 'lost' first, HoB next, Ch next, and HoH next. He speculated that a husband's participation could not fall further so long as he was living with his wife. If participation was on the increase, the husband would engage in activities in the reverse order.

The same exercise was carried out for wives with very different results. No wives were found who did not participate in regions HoW, Ch, and S, and Herbst suggested that wives' participation could not normally fall below this level. Relatively few wives, at the other extreme, were engaged in HoH and E activities. The very different nature of the 'pathfields' of husbands and wives showed up the very different positions of these Australian husbands and wives in marriage. Whilst husbands had a relatively lengthy pathway, representing different degrees of possible engagement or disengagement in family activities, along which they could move whilst still remaining a member of the family, wives had relatively little room for manoeuvre. From a wife's perspective, there were many more activities in which her participation was mandatory, there were others traditionally belonging to the husband's role (HoH and E), leaving only one region (HoB) in which her participation varied very much.

The Influence of Family Factors Upon Treatment Outcome

There exist reports of a small handful of studies which have attempted to investigate the effects of family factors upon the course of a disorder during or following its treatment. Only one of this small number (Morrow and Robins, 1964) is exclusively concerned with *marital* relationships but the problems connected with these studies are so similar that they are most usefully considered together in this chapter.

Family emotional involvement

The first of these studies, reported by Brown *et al.* (1962), concerned 128 men, diagnosed schizophrenic and aged between twenty and forty-nine, who had been in hospital for at least one month and were being discharged from one or other of eight mental hospitals. Two hypotheses were tested, firstly:

'That a patient's behaviour would deteriorate if he returned to a home in which, at the time of discharge, strongly expressed emotion, hostility, or dominating behaviour was shown towards him by a member of the family'; and secondly 'That, even if a patient returned to such a home, relapse could be avoided if the degree of personal contact with the family was small.' (Brown *et al.*, 1962, pp. 55–6.)

Joint home interviews were held with the patient and a 'key' relative (usually a wife or mother) two weeks after the patient's discharge. Other adult members of the household were frequently present also. Questions were asked about problems connected with the patient's return home, future plans and relationships at home. Conversation was encouraged but the interviewer attempted to confine his own contribution to simple prompts and the introduction of new topics. Five four-point rating scales were completed by the interviewer. These concerned: emotion expressed by key relative towards patient; hostility expressed by key relative towards patient; dominant or directive behaviour by key relative towards patient; emotion expressed by *patient* towards key relative; and hostility expressed by *patient* towards key relative and other family members. Ratings were made on the basis of both verbal and non-verbal signs, and the reliability of ratings, which was adjudged to be acceptable, was determined in a series of preliminary interviews at which two interviewers were present.

A further interview was held with members of the household at the end of a year *or* (if he was readmitted during the year) at the time of the patient's readmission to hospital. Subsequently, for purposes of analysis, patients were divided into two groups: a 'deteriorated' group (55 per cent) including all those who had been readmitted as well as those who were 'definitely worse'; and the remainder termed 'not deteriorated' (45 per cent). At the same interview a time budget of the patient's social activities during a typical week (*before* any deterioration occurred) was constructed and the waking hours of the week were divided into various activity categories, including time spent in face-to-face contact with the key relative.

It was found that the percentage of patients subsequently categorized as deteriorated increased regularly with increasing scores on the three joint interview ratings relevant to behaviour of the *key relative*. For example, as ratings of the key relative's expressed emotion rose from absence, to normal or minimal, and to lesser or greater degrees of excessive expression, so the percentage of patients who subsequently deteriorated rose from 22 per cent to 42 per cent, 75 per cent and 89 per cent.

There was some support also for their second hypothesis concerning the relevance of amount of family contact. Amongst patients who were still 'ill' at discharge and who were returned to high-emotional-involvement families, those spending less than thirty-five hours a week with the key relative ('low contact') were less likely to show deterioration.

Brown *et al.* (1972) have recently reported a replication of this study which produced essentially similar results. In this latter study they conclude that 'number of critical remarks' about patients, made by relatives, is a crucial variable.

Tolerance of deviance

The second relevant study is reported by Freeman and Simmons (1963) in their book, *The Mental Patient Comes Home*. On the basis of prior findings Freeman and Simmons developed a 'tolerance of deviance' hypothesis which suggested that poor work and social performance of former hospital patients was associated with 'A continued acceptance of the former patient by his family members, even when he fails to perform in instrumental roles.' (Freeman and Simmons, 1963, p. 6.)

In the major study reported in their book, a first interview with a member of the patient's family was conducted as soon as possible after the patient left hospital, and a second interview with the relative was conducted either a year later, or on the patient's return to hospital if he was rehospitalized in the meantime. Patients were all diagnosed as suffering from a psychotic disorder. The 'most influential' relative was interviewed (30 per cent mothers, 18 per cent wives, 12 per cent sisters, 30 per cent husbands, 10 per cent others) and most interviews were conducted at home. 649 interviews were completed.

It is only possible to summarize briefly some of the major findings but in general the conclusion was that family factors predicted performance levels as expected. Performance level was related to type of family (living with *parents* was associated with low performance levels). Also performance levels were higher when the patient was regarded as the chief family bread winner (male patients only), and when there were relatively *few* other full-time workers in the home (both males and females). Low performance level was also associated with 'atypicality' of the relative's personality (e.g. authoritarian, rigid or withdrawn). High performance levels were related to greater willingness, on the part of relatives, to contact the hospital if the ex-patient behaved strangely. Subsequent high levels of performance were also predicted by indications, at the first interview, that relatives would expect, and/or insist upon, a relatively high level of performance from the ex-patient.

Subordination of the patient

The study by Morrow and Robins (1964) concerned twenty mothers admitted to one of two hospitals and diagnosed psychotic. Information about family relationships was obtained from husbands and wives during the latter's hospitalization. Information about the patient's post-hospital adjustment was obtained at a home visit made three months after the patient's return to her family, and a composite index of post-hospital adjustment was computed on the basis of information provided by both ex-patients and their husbands.

The family relationship variables significantly related to good post-hospital adjustment were: 'mutual love' (husband's report); 'husband's optimism re wife's post-hospital adjustment'; 'general concensus, pre-hospitalization' (reported by husbands); and 'non-subordination of wife pre-hospitalization' (reported by wives). The last mentioned of these variables was the one most strongly predictive of later adjustment. The scale measuring this variable consisted of four items concerning the extent to which the husband had more say than his wife in making important family decisions, made important family decisions without consulting his wife, pressured his wife into doing things she didn't want to do, and in general got his own way more often.

Individual patient variables

In each of these studies a family relationship variable (Y) has been assessed at one point in time and found to be predictive of an outcome variable (Z) measured at a later point in time. In all such predictive, correlational, studies in which the predictor variables are not under experimental control, there is the ever-present danger of neglecting the importance of a 'third factor' (X) with which Y is correlated and which is equally, if not more strongly, predictive of Z. This seems particularly likely to be the case when Z concerns the outcome (rehospitalization, performance level, adjustment, etc.) of A's condition (schizophrenia, neurosis, etc.) and when Y concerns the behaviour (hostility, tolerance, non-subordination etc.) of someone else, B, or aspects of the relationship between A and B (mutual love, etc.). Under these circumstances one would expect to find predictive variables of type X which concern the *earlier* behaviour of A.

The folly of ignoring X-type variables is obvious. Families are complex inter-reacting and 'open' systems (von Bertalanffy, 1966) with a lengthy prior history, so that any simple causal hypothesis of the type $X \rightarrow Z$ or $Y \rightarrow Z$ is obviously inadequate. Nonetheless an $X \rightarrow Z$ (both variables based upon A's behaviour) model has the decided merit of being the more straightforward. This is clearly the case when similar behaviours are assessed at both points in time, for then the hypothesis takes the even more straightforward form: $X_1 \rightarrow X_2$.

Some account was taken of X-type variables in each of the above studies. For example, the discharged patients of Brown *et al*'s. (1962) study were categorized, prior to their discharge, as symptom-free, nearly symptom-free, moderately ill, or severely ill, on the basis of a psychiatric interview. Subsequently 42 per cent of those categorized as symptom-free, or nearly so, were recorded as deteriorated in comparison with 64 per cent of those who were moderately or severely ill prior to discharge. There was also a significantly greater deterioration rate for those patients who had shown a decline in occupational level, or who had shown disturbed behaviour, prior to admission, and also for those who had been unemployed for twelve months or more in the two years prior to discharge.

It was also possible to show that predictive variables of type Y (family) and of type X (patient) were associated. A higher proportion of those rated as still ill prior to discharge returned to 'high emotional involvement' homes. In addition, patients with more than twelve months unemployment in the two years prior to discharge were more likely to return to such homes. As Brown *et al.*

comment, 'This does suggest that some of the high emotion shown by relatives was *elicited* by the patient's disturbed behaviour at discharge . . . [and] that his past history had influenced relatives.' (Brown *et al.*, 1962, p. 62, my emphasis.)

Freeman and Simmons (1963) have much to say about their 'third factor' problem. They summarize the position from which they embarked on their major study as follows:

In the development of our notions of differential tolerance of deviance and of post-hospital outcomes for the mental patient, we contended that the individual characteristics of the patient, both social and psychiatric, are of minor significance in determining his fate. Rather, we saw the patient as essentially a 'pawn' whose success or failure and post-hospital performance were a consequence of the interpersonal milieu of his post-hospital setting. (Freeman and Simmons, 1963, p. 12.)

There was evidence from their study that *patient* variables, measurable before or at discharge, were *predictive* of outcome criteria. For example the performance level of non-rehospitalized patients was inversely related to length of hospitalization. Furthermore, reported symptomatic behaviour at the time the patient left the hospital was moderately associated with both outcome criteria.

Morrow and Robins were also aware that: 'Personal characteristics of the patient herself, independently of her family situation, may play a major role in her post-hospital adjustment' (1964, p. 22). Six variables were assessed under the heading of 'severity of illness' and of these, one (sudden versus gradual onset of current illness) was highly predictive of post-hospital adjustment. However, whether patient characteristics were *independently* predictive is another matter. The two variables with greatest predictive value, one a patient variable (sudden versus gradual onset) the other a family variable (non-subordination of wife) were themselves associated.

Family and individual patient contributions

Brown *et al.* (1962) went some considerable way towards demonstrating that patient and family predictors make *independent* contributions. They were able to show, for example, that the relationship between the key relative's emotional involvement and subsequent deterioration remained significant, both for those patients who were completely or nearly symptom free prior to discharge, *and* for those who were moderately or severely ill at that time. They further showed that the *direction* of the relationship was preserved (although numbers were then too small for the relationships to be statistically significant in all cases) when the effects of both mental state at discharge, and months of employment in the two years before discharge, were partialled out (see Table 3).

Nonetheless, as Brown *et al.* remark, despite the strong evidence for the relationship between high emotional involvement and outcome, 'a causal relationship is not necessarily indicated . . . the findings could still be entirely due to clinical differences'. (1962, p. 64.) Even so it is their impression that this is not always the case. They note a wide variation in the response of relatives to the same kind of psychotic behaviour. Some wives, they say, remain tolerant and pleasant in the face of behaviour towards which others react with antagonism. Change over time is possible too. In their opinion some relatives markedly changed their behaviour and feelings towards the patient. In about one third of high emotional involvement cases Brown *et al.* formed the impression that the past or current behaviour of the patient could have been a sufficient cause of the high emotional involvement. In another third, the high emotional involvement seemed clearly to be due to unusual behaviour on the part of the relative who was in many cases mentally disordered her/himself. In the remaining cases it seemed a complex interactive matter. Of course, whilst it is of some interest that in the majority of high emotional involvement families one or other of the main participants (patient or key relative) gave the *impression* of being the 'cause' or the 'guilty party' (not Brown *et al.*'s expression) it is difficult to know what weight, if any, to place upon such one-sided constructions.

In many ways, then, the problems that go with trying to attribute cause (of recovery or relapse) to social factors are the same here as they were found to be in Chapter 1 when we were

Table 3 Employment in Two Years before discharge, Mental State at Discharge and 'Emotional Involvement' in the Home, Showing Percentages of Patients who Deteriorated

Months of Unemployment in the two years before Discharge	Level of 'Emotional Involvement'	Mental state at Discharge (degree of disturbance)											
		None and Minimal				Moderate and Severe				Total			
		Not Deteriorated	Deteriorated	Total	Percentage Deteriorated	Not Deteriorated	Deteriorated	Total	Percentage Deteriorated	Not Deteriorated	Deteriorated	Total	Percentage Deteriorated
More than 12	High	4	7	11	64	1	20	21	95	5	27	32	84
	Low	5	2	7	29	7	5	12	42	12	7	19	37
Less than 12	High	1	2	3	66	6	9	15	60	7	11	18	61
	Low	14	1	15	7	8	5	13	38	22	6	28	21

(Taken from Brown et al, 1962, p. 62, Table X)

considering the possibility that family factors might contribute to personality development or later mental disorder.

Conclusions

The gaps in our understanding of marriage and mental disorder are more impressive than the areas of established knowledge but a rough sketch of sorts is beginning to appear. It is reasonable to assume that there is a general trend towards husband–wife similarity in terms of a wide range of individual differences including those than can be construed as constituting mental health–ill health. The chances are that this is due partly to assortative mating and partly to the influence of one spouse upon the other during the years of their relationship. The pattern of role relationships in marriage is relatively likely to be unusual when mental disorder is apparent in one partner, at least when the 'ill' member is the husband: the degree of husband–wife contact may be relatively intensive, but the level of conflict may be relatively high. Studies of interperson perception suggest that mental disorder may be associated with incongruence between husband and wife perceptions at several different levels but this may be a general feature of unhappy marriages, whether or not complicated by mental illness.

There is evidence that when the 'well' spouse is relatively critical, unloving, or subordinating towards the 'ill' partner, then the prognosis for the latter's recovery is relatively poor. As a general hypothesis it might be suggested that the same aspects of interpersonal behaviour emerge as facilitative of mental health in this context as emerged in Chapter 1 in the context of caretaker-child relationships. Relatively high levels of affection or warmth, coupled with the granting of autonomy to the recovering spouse, may be most facilitative.

These very tentative conclusions rest upon a very small number of studies and it should go without saying that their generality can only be established by a great deal of further investigation using samples that differ in terms of factors such as age, socio-economic status and clinical diagnosis.

Once again efforts to establish truly *causal* relationships are foiled. The research designs employed by no means make it possible to conclude that disorder in one spouse *causes* disorder in the other, or that a lack of warmth or over-subordination *cause* relapse. Indeed there is every reason to suppose that husband–wife relationships should be viewed, like parent–child and psycho-therapist–patient (see Chapter 5) relationships, as two-way systems with system properties which are not simply predictable on the basis of individual properties alone.

Chapter 4
Mad or Bad ?
Alternative Constructions on
Mental Disorder

Introduction

Diagnoses of mental disorder are based upon evidence that
individuals are behaving, thinking, or feeling in ways which are
unusual or which give them or others cause for concern. The
relative prominence of these different ingredients varies widely
but in the case of the disorders which are usually felt to be the
most serious (the 'psychoses') and which are most likely to
result in hospitalization, overt behaviour is particularly likely to
be unusual and it is likely to be of concern to others whether or not
it is of concern to the individual. Close inspections, made by
sociologists or sociologically minded psychiatrists, of the events
surrounding the recognition of mental disorder, or hospitalization
for mental disorder, suggest that the matter is by no means cut and
dried.

The prevailing medical view of mental disorder is that it is a
property of the individual and that, given the right skills and
methods, it can be identified, and cases counted, as with certain
physical illnesses. Diagnoses are either 'correct' or 'incorrect',
disorder is either 'recognized' or not, and the incidence or pre-
valence of disorder can be established for any community given
reliable epidemiological methods. This is a relatively simple-
minded view of 'abnormal' human behaviour. However, this is
not to say that psychiatrists are simple-minded people; indeed they
are at the forefront of the movement to modify this view. Nonetheless most of us have to work within institutions which tend to
constrain us within a view of the world which is decidedly less
complex than our own private view. Mental health experts are no
exception.

The view has gained ground in recent years that the way people
react to rule-breaking or unusual behaviour is important in its

own right and may indeed help to create a form of 'secondary deviance' which may be more harmful than the 'primary deviance' to which it was a reaction. In particular the interpretation, or 'label', which is placed upon behaviour is thought to be crucial. All manner of crucial life events, including hospitalization and treatment, may follow from labelling behaviour as 'neurosis', 'mental disorder', 'schizophrenia', which might not have followed had behaviour been labelled differently.

Thus deviance may be 'amplified' by the labelling process. Relatively extreme upholders of this view maintain that deviance can be *created* by reacting to behaviour which is perfectly understandable, indeed 'normal', when viewed within the norms of the minority group to which the individual may belong, when viewed as unintentional behaviour, or when viewed as behaviour motivated by incentives for personal gain (Gove, 1970).

The overall questions to be considered in this chapter have thus been most clearly identified from a sociological perspective. Nonetheless an attempt will be made here to show that social psychology, with its greater emphasis upon the details of interpersonal behaviour and perception, has a distinctive contribution to make.

The Impact of Mental Disorder on the Family

An area of concern which has received very little attention from a social psychological perspective has to do with the interpersonal events surrounding illness behaviour itself. This is an area which has been studied far more by sociologists although it presents abundant scope for the social psychologist.

The impact of mental illness on the family has been considered at some lengths by Clausen and Yarrow (1955). They examined in detail the effects of the illness and hospitalization of thirty-three married men, particularly from their wives' perspective. Each wife was interviewed regularly from the time of her husband's hospitalization and in some cases interviews continued after the husband's return home. A number of points were noted. Several of these concern the wife's attempts, over a period of time, to understand and attach meaning to her husband's behaviour.

Table 4 Reported Problem Behaviour at Time of the Wife's Initial Concern and at Time of the Husband's Admission to Hospital

Problem Behaviour	Initially		At Hospital Admission	
	Psychotics N	Psycho neurotics N	Psychotics N	Psycho neurotics N
Physical problems, complaints, worries	12	5	7	5
Deviations from routines of behaviour	17	9	13	9
Expressions of inadequacy or hopelessness	4	1	5	2
Nervous, irritable, worried	19	10	18	9
Withdrawal (verbal, physical)	5	1	6	1
Changes or accentuations in personality traits (slovenly, deceptive, forgetful)	5	6	7	6
Aggressive or assaultive and suicidal behaviour	6	3	10	6
Strange or bizarre thoughts, delusions, hallucinations and strange behaviour	11	1	15	2
Excessive drinking	4	7	3	4
Violation of codes of 'decency'	3	1	3	2
Number of Respondents	23	10	23	10

(Taken from Clausen and Yarrow, 1955, p. 17, Table 1. Note that column totals exceed the number of respondents represented in each column as more than one type of problem behaviour was reported by many respondents.)

Wives were asked, 'Can you tell me when you first noted that your husband was different?' Clausen and Yarrow state that wives were usually unable to pinpoint the time at which problems clearly emerged, nor could they clearly separate problem behaviour from the context of his personality and family expectations. As they say: 'The subjective beginnings are seldom localized in a single strange or disturbing reaction on the husband's part but rather in the piling up of behaviour and feelings' (Clausen and Yarrow, 1955, p. 16).

Table 4 shows some of the types of problem behaviour of concern to these wives. When and how behaviour becomes defined as 'a problem' is apparently very individual: sometimes it is when a wife can no longer manage her husband; sometimes when his behaviour interferes with family routine; sometimes when she can no longer explain his behaviour. Clausen and Yarrow suggest that family members have a threshold for recognizing a problem and that the threshold depends upon an accumulation over a period of time of behaviours which are not readily understandable or acceptable.

Table 5 Initial Interpretations of the Husband's Behaviour

Interpretation	Psychotics N	Psychoneurotics N
Nothing really wrong	3	0
'Character' weakness and 'controllable' behaviour (lazy, mean, etc.)	6	3
Physical problem	6	0
Normal response to crisis	3	1
Mildly emotionally disturbed	1	2
'Something' seriously wrong	2	2
Serious emotional or mental problem	2	2
Number of respondents	23	10

(Taken from Clausen and Yarrow, 1955, p. 18, Table 2.)

Table 5 shows how wives initially interpreted their husbands' behaviour. It can be seen that early interpretations were not often organized around the idea of mental illness, or even emotional problems, and were frequently couched in terms of physical problems or character problems, the latter often growing out of a wife's long-standing appraisal of her husband as weak, ineffectual, spoiled, lacking in will-power or hypochondriacal. Others saw the problem as primarily environmental and expected changes in their husbands to be contingent upon changes in circumstances. Even when the problem was defined as emotional, wives were inconsistently 'judgemental' and 'understanding'. All in all, Clausen and Yarrow define the situation confronting the wife as one characterized by lack of clarity and an absence of clear directions as to how to cope. Jackson (1954) made exactly the same point with reference to the more specific circumstance of alcoholism in a husband. Whatever the initial interpretation a wife made, it was seldom held with confidence and many wives could recall early reactions of puzzled confusion and uncertainty, a feeling that something was wrong, but with no obvious explanation.

According to Clausen and Yarrow, wives' perceptions underwent a series of changes before hospitalization. There seemed to be three relatively distinct patterns. Rather less than half altered their interpretations towards seeing the problem as 'mental illness'. With this redefinition individual behaviours lost significance in their own right and came to be seen as signs of 'something deeper'. Even so some wives held negative conceptions of mental illness and used the term as an angry epithet or a threatening prediction for the husband, e.g. 'I told him he should have his head examined', 'I told him if he is not careful he will be a mental case'. Many of these wives saw the hospital as the end of the road. Others held a more positive conception but even so their feelings contained components equally as angry and rejecting.

Almost a third continued to deny that their husbands were mentally ill, whilst others never developed a consistent 'theory' to account for their husbands' behaviour. The use of the word 'theory' in this context is interesting and makes it clear that reactions to 'illness behaviour' could be examined from the perspective of implicit personality theory or personal constructs.

Clausen and Yarrow go on to argue that there are a number of factors which make it more difficult for a relative to recognize behaviour in a 'mental illness', 'emotional problem' or psychiatric framework. Firstly, there is the fact that abnormal behaviour very frequently follows a fluctuating course and a relative's reaction at any one time is likely to be over-determined by recent events. Secondly, there is the fact that behaviour may often appear to be simply an intensification of long-standing response patterns and it is therefore difficult to see it as 'symptomatic' of an 'illness'. Thirdly, poor communications between husband and wife often impeded recognition. Even after the husband's hospitalization about one fifth still did not interpret behaviour in the mental illness framework and a further fifth were ambivalent or inconsistent about it. Others had fully accepted a mental illness 'theory' and were likely to reflect upon their earlier tendencies to 'avoid' seeing things that way (e.g. 'I put it out of my mind – I didn't want to face it – anything but a mental illness'.)

Alternative constructions on behaviour

In general Clausen and Yarrow were impressed with the complexity and sophistication of wives' perceptions of these events. That 'mental illness' is just one of a number of possible constructions that may be placed upon abnormal or deviant ways of thinking, feeling or behaving has become a widespread notion. There are of course differences of emphasis amongst the experts. White (1964) contrasts the view that neurosis is a condition which an individual gets in the same way as one 'gets' tuberculosis, with what he calls the 'psychogenic hypothesis'. According to the first view, the possibility that some people with 'neurosis' may have had unhappy or eccentric personalities before their illness is largely irrelevant. From the second perspective on the other hand, neurotic symptoms or breakdown are the relatively unimportant end results of a long process of development.

What is rather more interesting, in the light of Clausen and Yarrow's observations, is the way in which this debate may take place within the perceptions and definitions of an individual relative or friend or within small groups of people concerned about the behaviour of an individual.

Schwartz (1957) also examined the various frameworks within which the wives of male mental patients defined their husbands' problems. Each of the patients was diagnosed psychiatrically as suffering from a psychotic illness. Defects were defined by wives as somatic, psychological or characterological and within each of these frameworks varying degrees of defect were defined. The way behaviour was construed therefore varied widely from 'physical sickness' and 'slight psychological upset' all the way to 'bad total character'. Schwartz raises the interesting question of how, or indeed whether, these perceptions are conveyed to 'the patient' and how this communication, whether accurate or inaccurate, affects the subsequent course of events.

Negotiated understanding

Scheff (1968) has argued cogently that the responsibility for events, such as those which a defending lawyer may discuss with his client, or those which a patient may discuss with his psychotherapist, is rarely if ever absolute, but depends upon the 'constructions of reality' which the partners in these discussions come to agree upon. The process of coming to an agreement is likened by Scheff to a 'negotiation' and as an example of the process Scheff draws upon a previously published example of an initial psychiatric interview. The patient, a married woman in her thirties, complains of being 'irritable, tense and depressed' (p. 7) but attributes this to the circumstances under which she is living, in particular to her husband's behaviour. In this particular interview, however, the psychiatrist's unwillingness to accept this definition is striking. He appears 'bored and disinterested' and whenever she says things like, 'I am a nurse, but my husband won't let me work' he changes the subject (p. 15). Scheff remarks that:

The psychiatrist appears to be trying to teach the patient to follow his lead. After some thirty or forty exchanges of this kind, the patient apparently learns her lesson; she cedes control of the transaction completely to the therapist answering briefly and directly to direct questions, and elaborating only on cue from therapist. The therapist thus implements his control of the interview not by direct coercion, but by subtle manipulation. (Scheff, 1968, p. 15.)

The session ends when the patient admits a guilty secret and cries, whereupon the therapist tells the patient that she needs and will get psychiatric help.

Although there is no way of knowing from Scheff's account how typical a case this is, it undoubtedly illustrates the fact that there are instances in which different observers of the same events surrounding mental disorder may hold quite different opinions as to how they are best construed.

If we take the view, discussed in Chapter 2, that sequences of interactional events can be viewed as feedback loops with no obvious origin or starting-point, then it follows that any attempt to see 'the problem' as being the exclusive property of one inter-actant is bound to be to some extent artificial. The fairly universal tendency to try and attribute cause at *one* particular point in a sequence of events has been referred to as an attempt to 'punctuate the sequence of events' (Watzlawick *et al.*, 1968). The latter authors give the vicious circle of a husband's passivity and his wife's nagging as an example. Whilst, in their view, a total view of the situation makes the impossibility of attributing cause quite clear, nonetheless the individual partners in the struggle are likely to attribute cause to the *other*, believing that their own behaviour is simply a *reaction* provoked by the spouse. Watzlawick *et al.* make the point that such artificial 'punctuating' of interpersonal disagreements is very likely to be associated with attributions of 'badness' or 'madness' at the point of the sequence where the cause is assumed to lie. It certainly seems that referral because of a 'personal problem' is more likely to be to a psychiatrist, rather than to a clergyman, physician or any other source of help, when the problem is defined by the individual concerned, or by others, as involving a defect that resides in him personally rather than in another person or in a relationship with another person (Gurin *et al.*, 1967).

Social crises surrounding breakdown and referral

An example of the way in which simple definitions may appear to do less than full justice to the complexity of events when those events are analysed in greater detail is provided by Lemert (1962), who challenged Cameron's (1943) idea of the paranoid's 'pseudo-community'. The latter idea suggests that the paranoid's view of his social world is a private and *false* one which provokes conflict with others. For example, 'the actions ascribed by him to its personnel are not actually performed or maintained by them; they are united in no common undertaking against him'. (Lemert, 1962, pp. 2–3.) Lemert suggests an alternative point of view, namely that although the 'paranoid' person reacts differently to his social environment, so too do others towards him. What is more, the behaviour of others commonly involves 'covertly organized action and conspiratorial behaviour ... [and] ... reactions are reciprocals of one another, being interwoven and concatenated at each and all phases of a process of exclusion' (Lemert, 1962, p. 3).

Accordingly he questioned whether a study of the individual is sufficient for a proper study of paranoia and he himself based his conclusions upon a particularly intensive study of the relatives, work associates, employers, police, doctors and others involved with each of a series of individuals.

Lemert found that the following train of events had usually occurred. The events began with persistent interpersonal difficulties within the family or at work, often surrounding a series of failures for the individual or a loss of status or threat of the same. At first the individual's arrogant and insulting behaviour fluctuated and was confined to certain situations; the reactions and tolerance of other people also varied. Benign interpretations of his behaviour were usually offered at this stage. However at some point a noticeable shift appeared to have taken place in others' perceptions and behaviour. In others' eyes the individual became either 'unreliable', 'untrustworthy', 'dangerous' or someone with whom they did not wish to be 'involved'. He was avoided, humoured or conversed with in a very guarded fashion. As a result the flow of information to the individual slowed down and discrepancies appeared between what people said to him and what they really thought and felt. Coalitions were formed against him and not infrequently an exclusionist group developed which demanded loyalty and solidarity of its members, held clandestine meetings, checked up on the individual and discussed his behaviour to the point of exaggeration and distortion. The individual's delusions grew as he recognized a conspiracy but lacked information about it and was progressively cut off from accurate feedback about other people's reactions to his own behaviour. In organizational settings, such as work, formal exclusion (discharge or transfer) was likely to occur and, in addition, the impact of the law and of the hospital services was often such as to 'nurture and sustain the massive sense of injustice and need for identity which underly the delusions and aggressive behaviour of the paranoid individual'. (Lemert, 1962, p. 15.)

In view of the alternative definitions of events which are possible it is not surprising that there are many occasions on which the process of referral to mental health services and personnel is not smooth and free of conflict. Clausen and Yarrow (1955) comment, for example, that there was often resentment, and even fury, on the part of the patient-husbands studied by them when referral was instigated, and they note that the suggestion that a person ought to 'see a psychiatrist' was in contemporary parlance (note that they were writing in the 1950s in the USA and therefore one has to consider whether the same is true of other places and times) a very common way of saying that one is irritated, exasperated or unsympathetic. In over half their cases hospitalization was associated with legal committment against the husband's wishes and in several such instances the husband reproached his wife for 'betraying' him. Some of these husbands later understood whilst others remained bitter, but wives were likely to retain feelings of guilt and shame in either case. In contemporary Britain, for example, the large majority of psychiatric admissions are now voluntary, but even about voluntary admissions Clausen and Yarrow remark that the process was one in which the husband acquiesced to strong pressure from his wife, from his parents, or from a doctor.

Polak (1967) reports on the setting up of 'admission assessment groups' which met at the time of admission of each of 104 consecutive patients. The patient, relatives, the referring agent such as the patient's general practitioner, hospital staff and representatives of other relevant community agencies (including the police in at least one instance) were involved. In the majority of cases a pattern of unresolved and recurrent problems (involving such things as separation, death in the family, physical illness and migration) appeared to have preceded the social crisis which precipitated admission. He concludes that the hospital, in addition to providing a medical service, provides a service of institutional supervision following failure to resolve life crises. This inevitably creates role confusion for hospital personnel, which must be heightened if they find themselves involved in advising on matters such as a patient's suitability for a particular sort of work, or on legal matters such as the custody of children.

The Attribution of Responsibility
Correspondent inferences

Attribution theory provides a powerful set of concepts for attempting to understand some of these important matters (Heider, 1944, 1958; Jones and Davis, 1965). This theory, which has to do with the way in which people perceive and react to other people's behaviour, assumes that the perceiver (whom I shall call 'S' to preserve the notation used in Chapter 2) looks for evidence of the actor's (O's) *intention* to act, for evidence that O had *knowledge* that his actions would produce the effects that they did, and had the *ability* to bring about the act and its effects. If there is satisfactory evidence of intention, knowledge and ability then S is likely to attribute to O a disposition towards making such actions. There are obvious parallels between this process and the legal process of assessing guilt.

On the basis of O's sullen and uncommunicative behaviour, for example, S may or may not make the 'correspondent inference' (Jones and Davis, 1965) that O is really a sullen and uncommunicative sort of person. 'Correspondence' would be low if S attributes O's behaviour to the special circumstances of the moment or to some special factor such as 'illness', which is beyond O's control. Any limits on O's freedom to choose how to behave, or any factors that suggest that O did not intend to behave in this way, did not know what effect his behaviour would have, or was not fully able to control his behaviour, would tend to decrease the degree of responsibility attributed to O and hence would reduce the chances of confident inferences being made about what O is 'really' like.

In their review of the evidence Jones and Davis (1965) conclude that S will be more likely to make confident inferences about O's dispositional state if the acts involved are fairly unique, non-conventional or generally unusual considering the role that O is playing (an example of 'out-of-role' behaviour is that of a job applicant who claimed not to have the appropriate abilities for the job for which he was applying, Jones *et al.*, 1961). They also conclude from a number of experiments that S's personal involvement is important. The more *relevant* O's actions are to S, the more S is personally helped or hindered, gratified or hurt, by O's acts, the more likely he is to infer things about O and the more likely he is to make extreme evaluations of O. Additionally the assignment of sanctions may be more likely to follow the attribution of responsibility when the outcomes from the actions are unfavourable and of high intensity (Shaw and Reitan, 1969).

Justification

As well as the intention to act, *justification* for actions is also likely to affect the attribution of responsibility (Heider, 1958). One of the ways in which abnormal behaviour may be seen as, in a sense, 'justified' is suggested by an experiment by Farina *et al.* (1966) on the question of stigma towards the mentally ill. The degree of 'stigma' was assessed by monitoring the intensity and duration of electric shock administered to O under the guise of a 'learning situation' (the 'learner' was 'taught' by being punished with shocks for errors). When O's (the 'learner's') current situation was described as 'stigmatized' (he was described as having no close friends and having been a patient in a mental hospital), the effect on the punishment given to him was reduced when his *childhood* was described as 'disturbing-pathogenic'.

Illness is also likely to provide a justification for help-seeking and dependency behaviours. Berkowitz (1969) summarized research which suggested that one person's willingness to help another depended upon whether the latter's need for help was perceived to be due to factors beyond their control ('external locus of dependency') or due to their own shortcomings ('internal locus'). Ss were more willing to offer help when dependency was 'externally' caused.

Variation with type of behaviour

Although attribution theory may provide a framework which might be applied to questions about definitions of abnormal patterns of thinking, feeling and behaving, the observations of Clausen and Yarrow (1955), Schwartz (1957) and others suggest that the answers will turn out to be rather complex. For one thing the nature of the attribution process is likely to vary considerably depending upon the exact nature of the abnormal behaviour concerned. This is suggested by some results outlined (but unfortunately not given in detail) by Fletcher (1969) who asked each of a hundred married couples in Connecticut, USA, how they would respond to a 'male aggressive case' and a 'male withdrawn case'. Both were described in the following way: 'He says that things are never right for him, and that people, even his own family, don't like him at all. He always gets very angry at people over little things.' (p. 154.) Both are said to have started behaving this way about six months ago and to have been behaving like it most of the time since then, but whilst the *aggressive* case is described as, 'So he is always shouting at them, even in his own family. No matter where he is, he always argues with people. He spends most of his spare time picking fights with them, even though they don't say much to him', the *withdrawn* case is described as, 'But he never tells them what he feels, even his own family. No matter where he is, he keeps it all to himself. He spends most of his spare time wishing that he could somehow get back at people, even though they don't say much to him' (p. 154). In each case respondents were asked to rate the degree to which the man was 'manifesting deviant behaviour' and the degree to which he was 'the cause of it himself'. They were also asked whether he should be referred to a psychiatrist, referred to some other source of help outside the family, or not referred.

Fletcher reports that, for the aggressive case, high estimates of self-cause were associated with a relatively strong relationship between estimates of deviance and desirability of psychiatric referral. In the withdrawn case, however, high estimates of self-cause were associated with reduced relationships between estimates of deviance and desirability of psychiatric referral. He suggests that whereas notions of 'sickness' appear to be governing ideas about referral to a psychiatrist in the withdrawn case, more traditional 'moral-normative' ideas appear to operate for the aggressive case. In the latter instance the psychiatrist is being seen, to some extent, as 'moral change agent'.

Evaluation and Mental Disorder

From all that has been said so far in this chapter, it should be clear that whoever is faced with the task of defining, construing, or making sense of deviant behaviour, whether that person be a relative, a friend, a member of the public, or the deviant himself, there exists a wide variety of constructions which can be placed upon the behaviour. It may be construed as 'bad behaviour', 'maladjustment', 'mental illness', or simply a nuisance; the individual concerned may or may not be held to have intended the behaviour and he may be perceived as the victim of circumstances, responsible for his plight, or just plain unlucky. In fact the very word 'deviant' implies that the behaviour is construed as deviant, abnormal or unusual, which it may or may not be. Not surprisingly under these circumstances, people often feel unclear and often highly ambivalent about what construction to place on other people's behaviour.

Of course different people at different times find themselves in different roles *vis-à-vis* other people and their behaviour, and the particular nature of the role relationship involved will partly determine the 'set' with which the problem of defining, construing, and making sense of behaviour is approached. The set which a member of a jury has for assessing the behaviour of a man on trial, the set which a husband has for assessing his wife's behaviour, the set a psychiatrist has for assessing the behaviour of a patient's wife, are all very different from one another. It seems reasonable to suppose that the psychotherapist would have a set to try and understand the genesis or cause of the behaviour concerned, whilst a close relative, on the other hand, would have a more complex, and possibly inconsistent, set.

Professional ambivalence

However, it should not be supposed that those who are charged with responsibility for the treatment of mental disorder are altogether free from ambivalence despite their specialized role. One of the circumstances under which this ambivalence is manifest arises when a professional therapist is caught out of his usual role when construing behaviour. Again Clausen and Yarrow's (1955) thought-provoking account provides an example. Wives of patients were asked about the nature of their contacts with their husbands' psychiatrists and a number of psychiatrists, in their turn, were asked about contacts with their patients' wives. Amongst other things psychiatrists were asked what personality characteristics made up the 'good wife' and the 'bad wife' of a patient. Although the question is a rather leading and direct one, the situation was in a way very similar to that involved in a repertory grid procedure, the answers to the question giving some indication of associational aspects of the psychiatrists' implicit personality theories.

In fact the majority of terms used in answering the question indicated that sound mental health was a main ingredient making up the 'good wife', and other terms used indicated that positive attitudes towards the hospital and the doctor were further ingredients. The 'good wife' was described as being aware of her own feelings, sincere, honest, straightforward, with insight. The 'bad wife' showed signs of 'emotional disturbance' or 'immaturity' and she lacked insight. The 'good wife' let the doctor alone, accepted the hospital's authority and cooperated with the hospital's plans. It seems that although psychiatrists accepted the likelihood of emotional disturbance in many wives, they nonetheless responded evaluatively on the basis of these individual differences. One can only assume that this was because they had no thereapeutic responsibility for their patients' wives, whilst at the same time individual differences in the wives' behaviour could have 'high consequences' for them in terms of interference with therapeutic plans for the patients. Wives' behaviour was therefore construed within a 'normative' framework rather than a 'pathology' framework and deviant behaviour on the part of the wife was defined as a 'nuisance' rather than as an indication of 'maladjustment' or 'mental illness'.

Use of evaluative constructs

Even when the professional therapist is acting within his normal role there may be considerable confusion about how behaviour is to be defined and this may be revealed by techniques akin to repertory grid procedures. Studies of the constructs used by individual social workers in construing their clients (Philip and McCulloch, 1968; Orford et al., 1975) reveal the use of many quite frankly evaluative constructs (e.g. 'someone I can't get on with', 'someone who expects you to accept all his failings') as well as a number of ambiguous constructs (e.g. 'someone who attempts to manipulate', 'genuine') which have a pseudo 'professional' or 'technical' meaning. In practice such constructs are correlated with the more frankly evaluative constructs and are therefore being used within a 'normative' or judgemental (as opposed to pathology or maladjustment) framework. Furthermore, it may sometimes be the case that constructs which one would confidently suppose to have a technical meaning, and to be used independently of evaluative constructs, turn out to be highly correlated with evaluative constructs or dimensions when used in practice to describe patients or clients. This has been shown to be the case for the construct 'depressed', for example, in at least two instances (Watson, 1970; Orford et al., 1975).

Watson's (1970) report is of particular interest because it illustrates the degree of concensus which can be reached amongst a group of people (in this case consisting of two therapists and a number of patients undergoing group psychotherapy) in the way in which they apply constructs to themselves and to other members of the group. Each member of the group was required to rate each fellow member in terms of a number of supplied constructs. The degree of concordance between the members of the group was very high for a number of the constructs (i.e. they tended to agree on who should be rated high and who low). The two therapists received fairly consistently high ratings on the construct 'like I'd like to be' and low ratings on 'like a child' and 'depressed'. Two particular patients in the group (one man and one woman) provided striking contrasts to the two therapists. They were seen by most of their fellows as 'like a child', 'depressed' and the opposite of 'like I'd like to be'. Watson remarks that the male patient concerned was both the most disturbed patient in the group and the group's 'scapegoat'.

Evaluation by fellow-patients

Watson's study concerned both therapists and patients together, but there are a number of other studies which throw light upon the place of illness or maladjustment constructs in the implicit personality theories of psychiatric in-patients. Pine and Levinson (1961) write of the categories to which patients assign fellow patients on the basis of a comparison between the latter's degree of illness and their own. In their experience the term 'mental illness' was often confined in its usage to fellow patients who were perceived to be worse than S, whilst those who were, like S, 'not so bad', were defined as merely 'nervous'. Tolerance of illness behaviour amongst patients varied from ward to ward. There was camaraderie and a relatively high degree of tolerance on the admission ward; on the convalescent ward there was less.

Kellam and Chassan (1962) studied the social life of a chronic female ward and revealed the existence of a 'status hierarchy'. 'Degree of sickness', as judged by the 'upper class' élite group of patients, was used as a major 'class' distinction. The ramifications of the hierarchy were considerable. For example, the élite group of patients sat at a certain 'reserved' dinner table and frequently the more isolated patients waited on them. They were more likely to have a private room and had fewer menial ward duties. It was Kellam and Chassan's impression that the staff used a different tone of voice, and even a different form of address, with these patients than with others. It was also their impression that different terms were used to describe the same behaviour in different patients. 'Lower status' patients might be said to be 'having a psychotic breakdown' whilst the élite group would refer to one of their own members as having a 'period of anxiety' or being 'slightly blue'.

Kellam and Chassan suggest that patients high in the hierarchy were more likely to get individual psychotherapy and Sinnett and Hanford (1962) are amongst others who have noted a similar association between treatment received and social factors which are not obviously associated with type or degree of illness (Freeman and Giovanni, 1969). Sinnett and Hanford found that male open-ward patients most often selected for psychotherapy were those who were most popular with their peers or who had the strongest, either positive or negative, emotional ties with fellow patients. Those patients who were not particularly popular or controversial were rarely chosen.

Brown (1965) tested the hypothesis that popularity amongst patients would be inversely related to degree of illness as judged by fellow patients. Patients, both male and female, on a single ward, were asked to sort the names of fellow patients into a category of those 'with whom he/she liked to associate in his/her leisure time', a category of those 'he/she least liked to associate with' and a third neutral category. Patients were also asked to nominate those 'whom he/she most wanted as members of his/her therapy group', those he/she least wanted and those who fell in a neutral category. Thirdly, patients were asked to sort the names of fellow patients into three categories according to whether the patients were regarded as 'sicker than', 'healthier than', or 'no different from' the sorter. It was thus possible to test whether, as hypothesized, popularity (either in terms of the leisure association criterion or the therapy group criterion) was inversely related to judged sickness. In fact, as expected, degree of sickness as judged by a consensus of patients (which, incidentally, agreed well with a consensus of ward nurses) was found to be significantly negatively correlated with sociometric rank determined by either criterion.

It should be noted that the patient-subjects of Brown's (1965) study were not asked *directly* about their assumptions concerning the relatedness of illness and personal choice, and the somewhat indirect procedure adopted could have elicited assumptions which operated only covertly. That this was indeed the case was suggested when patients were later asked the reason for their therapy-group choices. Brown states:

> ... they rarely mentioned either liking or illness as factors influencing their decisions. Rather they stated that some persons were more interesting than others, or that some persons could contribute more to the group, or that some persons had problems similar to their own. One subject claimed that he chose certain patients as co-members because he felt that he could help them to get well. Possibly the patients privately recognized the relevance of their liking to their choices but felt inhibited in expressing such sentiments owing to the prevalence of the therapeutic community philosophy. At any rate, it would appear that liking and degree of illness bore more relevance to their therapy-group choices than the subjects explicitly stated (Brown, 1965, pp. 244–5).

Concepts of Mental Health

Much of the foregoing seems to reflect the difficulty which people have, whether they are patients, therapists or others, in making a clear separation between moral judgement, preferences, liking versus disliking and so on, on the one hand, and statements about presence or absence, or relative degree of, psychological disorder or illness, on the other hand. This difficulty is reflected in prevailing conceptions of the nature of mental health itself (Jahoda, 1958 – see Chapter 2, p. 53, above; Offer and Sabshin, 1966; Smith, 1972).

A good illustration of the evaluative nature of concepts of mental health is provided by the operational definition used by Siegelman *et al.* (1970) in their study of the childhood antecedents of later psychological adjustment. They defined psychological adjustment in terms of the degree of match between ratings of each adult subject made by a number of psychologists and ratings of a hypothetical 'optimally adjusted personality' based on the consensus of 'nine experienced psychologists'. Ninety items were employed altogether in the rating procedure, but the flavour of the definition can be obtained by examining the items most, and least, defining of 'optimal adjustment', according to the 'experienced psychologists'. These are shown in Table 6.

Table 6 Items Most Positively, and Most Negatively, Defining of Optimal Adjustment

Most positively defining of optimal adjustment	*Most negatively defining of optimal adjustment*
Has warmth; has the capacity for close relationships; compassionate	Has a brittle ego-defence system; has a small reserve of integration; would be disorganized and maladaptive when under stress or trauma
Is a genuinely dependable and responsible person	Feels cheated and victimized by life; self-pitying
Has insight into own motives and behaviour	Handles anxiety and conflicts by, in effect, refusing to recognize their presence; repressive or dissociative tendencies
Is productive; gets things done	
Is socially perceptive of a wide range of interpersonal cues	Feels a lack of personal meaning in life
Behaves in an ethically consistent manner; is consistent with own personal standards	Is self-defeating
	Is vulnerable to real or fancied threat, generally fearful
Values own independence and autonomy	Keeps people at a distance; avoids close interpersonal relationships
Appears straightforward, forthright, candid in dealings with others	Is basically anxious
Able to see to the heart of important problems	Is guileful and deceitful, manipulative, opportunistic
Genuinely values intellectual and cognitive matters	Is subtly negativistic; tends to undermine and obstruct or sabotage
Is calm, relaxed in manner	Has hostility towards others
Behaves in a sympathetic or considerate manner	Tends to project his own feelings and motives onto others
Has a wide range of interests	Is emotionally bland; has flattened affect

(Taken from Siegelman *et al.*, 1970, p. 284, Tables 1 and 2.)

This operational definition was criticized by Miller (1970) for reflecting a relative rather than an absolute criterion of mental health. He considered that the items positively defining of mental health were biased towards qualities prized by members of the middle-class and which are of particular value to families 'whose breadwinners have managerial or professional jobs in bureaucratic organizations'. (Miller, 1970, p. 290.) He quotes with approval the conclusion reached by a meeting of the World Federation of Mental Health (Soddy and Ahrenfeldt, 1967) that a formal definition of mental health is difficult to arrive at, and should take into account the sex, generation, epoch and culture of persons being evaluated. It is noteworthy that Miller's criticisms are on the grounds of the generality of the definition used by Siegelman *et al.* (1970) and not on the grounds of evaluative tone.

In view of the 'goodie' characterization of mental health shown in Table 6, it is not surprising to find that questionnaire measures of psychopathology (such as the much-used Minnesota Multiphasic Personality Inventory or MMPI) correlate significantly with scales measuring 'social desirability' response bias. Furthermore, when psychologists are asked to sort a list of attributes into those that best, and least well, reflect the 'well-adjusted' person, and again sort the same attributes into those that represent socially desirable and socially undesirable attributes, the two sorts correlate almost perfectly (Block, 1962). Nonetheless, despite the high levels of these correlations there are some statistically significant, although slight, average differences in how psychologists place some of these attributes when sorting in terms of adjustment, and when sorting in terms of social desirability. The *adjusted* person is described as being somewhat more aggressive, egocentric, and comfortable with himself and other people, than is the *socially desirable* person. The latter, in turn, is described as more reliable, hard-working and self-disciplined.

There is much scope for social psychological study of the circumstances under which various diagnostic and characterological labels are applied. An illustration of the possibilities is provided by the study, referred to in Chapter 2, concerning the covariation of signs of depression and 'hostility-out' in each of a small number of depressed patients (Gershon *et al.*, 1968). Two of the patients displayed a pattern of positive covariation between these two signs i.e. they displayed more hostility towards other people at times when they were more depressed. The remainder showed the opposite pattern. Of present interest is the fact that the two former patients had the phrase 'hysterical personality features' attached to their diagnoses whilst the latter patients did not.

The Cost of Defining Mental Disorder

The possible advantages of defining certain behaviours as 'mental illness', in terms of a likely reduction in attribution of responsibility for the behaviour to the 'ill' person, have already been hinted at. But 'costs' may be incurred as well. Nunnally (1961) demonstrated that the very fact of attaching different labels to the same behaviour had a noticeable effect upon perceptions and judgements made by members of the lay public. They offered 'paranoid schizophrenic' and 'anxious-depressed' case descriptions to different subjects with different labels attached ('insane', 'mentally ill', 'emotionally disturbed') or with no label at all (the 'diagnoses' were not provided). On the whole, in both cases, negative evaluations of the behaviour depicted were *reduced* by offering a 'definition' especially when the definition was 'emotionally disturbed'. However, the effects of the labels upon ratings of 'immoral', for example, illustrated how different definitions could have quite different effects for different behaviours. Whereas labels lowered ratings of 'immorality' for the 'paranoid schizophrenic' case, they actually *increased* ratings of 'immorality' for the 'anxious-depressed' case. Hence, with labels attached, ratings of immorality were rather similar for the two cases, whereas without labels most subjects made a distinction between the two types of behaviour.

Diagnostic decision rules

Scheff (1964, 1966) has suggested that an important rule in general medicine governs the decision whether or not to diagnose illness in borderline instances. The general rule is that, when there is doubt, assume the presence rather than the absence of a condition. This follows from the assumption that type I errors (errors of failing to recognize a condition which is really there) are more serious in their consequences than type II errors (assuming an illness to be there when in fact it is not). This decisión rule, Scheff argues, has been carried over into psychological medicine where the assumption about the greater seriousness of one type of error may not be so true. Whereas in general medicine there may be important conditions that get worse if not diagnosed early, psychiatric illness often remains untreated in the community and gets better of its own accord. Furthermore, in the absence of reliable tests for psychopathology, similar to tests in physical medicine, there is little to hinder a pan-psychiatric bias (Szasz, 1961; Wootton, 1959) for reclassifying behaviour as mental disorder on a grand scale. In addition, type II errors may be *more* serious in psychological medicine where there may be formal costs (loss of voting and other rights etc.), informal costs (stigma etc.), and even the possibility of 'iatrogenesis' (the production or exacerbation of symptoms as a *result* of treatment or intervention) as a result of unnecessarily encouraging a person to occupy the 'sick role' (Mechanic, 1966). A tendency to see wide-ranging aspects of behaviour in terms of psychopathology is also likely to set up pressures for people to gain 'insight' and to 'recognize' illness in themselves and others. An instance of the negotiations that may take place to that end was given earlier in this chapter (Scheff, 1968). To put this same point a different way, Scheff argues that there are few rules in psychological medicine which enable one to define a 'non-case'.

Socialization and the mental health professional

The findings of Cumming and Cumming (1956) are relevant here. They were interested in the reputation that psychiatric nurses appeared to have for being better able than doctors to predict how patients would adjust in the community after hospitalization (incidentally they refer to some evidence that patients are even better). They thought it likely that this was because nurses retained, at least in part, normative as opposed to psychological standards of judgement. They compared doctors, supervising nurses, and trainee nurses at various stages in their training, in terms of 'recognition' of mental illness in short case descriptions which were also shown to members of the lay public. Firstly they found that the supervising nurses recognized considerably more mental illness in the descriptions than did members of the public, but nonetheless recognized less than the doctors.

Cumming and Cumming suggest that nurses go through a socialization process during their training which requires that they shift from a normative standard to a psychological one. In support of this hypothesis they were able to show a regular increase in the amount of mental illness recognized by nurses in the case descriptions with increasing numbers of years of training completed. When the various subject groups were ranked from those recognizing the least mental illness to those who recognized the most, members of the lay public came first ('failing' to recognize illness almost three times as often as they recognized it), first-year student nurses came next, followed in order by second-year nurses, third-year nurses, supervising nurses, and psychiatrists.

Subjects were also offered 'A description of what we considered a normal teenage girl'. (Cumming and Cumming, 1956, p. 83.) Only 12½ per cent of first-year student nurses thought there was 'something wrong' with this girl and none of them thought she was mentally ill. However, of third-year nurses 33 per cent thought there was 'something wrong' and 11 per cent thought that she was mentally ill.

The process of change, or socialization, which may affect nursing and other staff, is almost certain to affect patients as well. Manis et al. (1963) noted that psychiatric in-patients changed their opinions about the nature of psychiatric illness during their first thirty days in hospital, in a direction towards the views of the mental health staff who were treating them (e.g. they changed towards thinking that such factors as will-power and the avoidance of morbid thoughts were relatively unimportant). Furthermore, changes in this direction were associated with a more rapid discharge from hospital and greater gains in self-esteem.

The irrationality assumption

One of the areas of 'cost' in relation to mental illness diagnoses lies in the possible neglect of what psychologists generally suppose to be vital *situational* determinants of behaviour (e.g. Phares, 1972). The diagnostic approach is typological, i.e. it gives things a name, defines things as being of a certain type. It necessarily relegates questions of variation in behaviour, and the dependence of these variations upon changes in circumstance or situation, to a secondary position. If situation is ignored, unusual or deviant behaviour is likely to be construed as irrational or 'mad'. With specific reference to schizophrenia, Watzlawick *et al.* (1968) refer to two dramatically divergent frames of reference: the one assuming this behaviour to represent a progressive disorder of the mind; the second assuming it to be the only possible *reaction* to certain circumstances. Braginsky *et al.* (1969) also refer to the current conception of the mental patient as someone who is cognitively or otherwise impaired and incapable of rational action. They write of 'a kind of theoretical double standard . . . with one set of explanatory principles for human behaviour and another for schizophrenics' (Braginsky *et al.*, 1969).

The assumption of irrationality which may attach to a diagnosis of mental disorder can of course lead to varying degrees of rejection or invalidation of what the 'disordered' individual says about how he construes his circumstances. If O_1 is known to be 'mentally ill', S may be excused for assuming that O_2 (who is not 'mentally ill') is more to be believed in the event of a disagreement between O_1 and O_2. In some instances the events over which O_1 and O_2 disagree may even have important social or political implications. Szasz (1971) has likened the discrediting of the mentally ill to that which was once perpetrated upon the negro slave by the invoking of 'diseases' of running away and disinterest in work.

Role conflict

Siegler and Osmond (1966) have written of a number of possible 'models of madness' or ways of trying to understand schizophrenic behaviour. They refer to the medical model; the moral or behavioural model (behaviour is not called ill but rather inappropriate and rewards and punishments are applied in an attempt to modify behaviour); the social model (social circumstances are seen as responsible for producing illness) and so on. Although it is not at all clear that this is the best way of categorizing the different constructions that can be put upon schizophrenic behaviour, the important point is made that programmes of 'treatment', 'correction' or whatever, are very frequently based upon aspects of more than one model and that this is bound to lead to confusion. Szasz (1957) has made essentially the same point in drawing attention to what he believes to be abuses of the legal arrangements for the commitment of the mentally ill. He argues that the question of commitment is not a medical problem and concerns social restraint rather than treatment. The psychiatrist therefore finds himself playing the conflicting roles of therapist, on the one hand, and agent and protector of society on the other. He writes of the 'failure to explicitly differentiate between the manifold social roles and functions of the psychiatrist, some of which might – and usually do – conflict with some others' (Szasz, 1957, p. 305).

Erikson (1957) drew attention to role contradictions for the mentally ill patient. To fulfil this role, behaviour has to show signs of 'loss of reason', 'loss of control', 'inappropriateness', which are required, at least by the lay public (Star, 1955) for a definition of mental illness. But at the same time the ill person must be sufficiently in touch with reality to make a 'contractual agreement to cooperate in a therapeutic partnership, ... to want and appreciate treatment, to be realistic about the need for help, to volunteer relevant information, and to act ... upon recommendations of his therapist' (Erikson, 1957, p. 265).

Stigma and Public Attitudes

The stigma which can attach to mental illness has been recognized and discussed at length by Goffman (1964). Clausen and Yarrow (1955) have also referred to wives' expectations that mental illness will be regarded by others as a stigma. The majority of wives they interviewed thought that people would be suspicious, disrespectful or afraid of mental patients such as their husbands, or that some would assume their husbands to be crazy or uncontrollable. Even though people might not have expressed such feelings openly to them, wives were uncertain as to what people really thought. They feared discrimination over jobs, avoidance of the family by friends and the possibility of their children being taunted. These fears affected the patterns of communication which wives adopted with people outside the family. Roughly a third opted for a pattern of aggressive concealment, going out of their way to cut off former associations, minimizing threats stemming from other people's knowledge of their husband's illness, inventing stories about where the husband was, becoming over-sensitive to other people's remarks, whilst at the same time experiencing a strong need to find someone sympathetic to talk to. Others made a clear demarcation between people who were 'in', and could be 'told', and those who were 'out', from whom the truth had to be concealed. Others appeared to refer freely to their husband's illness, difficult though that might have been. Other investigators of American perceptions of a variety of illness conditions have noted the greater 'shame' attaching to conditions with a recognized psychological component.

The effects of stigma upon employment opportunities represents a whole subject in its own right but it certainly seems probable that many former psychiatric patients conceal their ex-patient status when seeking employment. In view of the fears which employers may have concerning the potential destructiveness of former patients, expectations of their occupational instability and doubts about the curability of 'mental illness', this concealment may be thought to be quite realistic (Rothaus *et al.*, 1963). Rothaus *et al.* suggest that the term 'mental illness', or other similar terms, may prevent other people 'getting to know' the person concerned and that the former patient, when applying for a job for example, would be better advised to explain a period of hospitalization in terms of 'interpersonal problems'.

One of the larger studies of public attitudes towards mental illness was carried out by Nunnally (1961), who investigated the opinions of high-school students, members of the general adult population, experts in mental health (psychologists and psychiatrists) and general practitioners. He also examined the contents of local and national (like most studies of attitudes towards mental illness, this one was carried out in the USA) mass media relevant to the topic of mental illness. Subjects were asked to rate on a number of scales the concepts 'neurotic man', 'insane man', 'neurotic woman' and 'insane woman' and the ratings were compared with those given to 'average man', 'old man', etc. It is difficult to tell how significant the findings of this study are as insufficient information is given on the degree of individual variation in ratings, but it certainly appears that ratings of the 'abnormal' concepts were very different from those given to the 'normal' concepts. Although there were some differences between average ratings given to 'neurotic man' and 'neurotic woman' on the one hand and 'insane man' and 'insane woman' on the other hand (the latter concepts particularly getting higher ratings for 'unpredictability', 'dangerousness' and 'dirtyness') *all* the abnormal concepts received higher average ratings for 'tense', 'sick', 'sad', 'passive', 'weak', 'delicate', 'cold', and also for 'foolish', 'ignorant' and 'insincere'. In general, ratings given to these concepts appeared to reflect an unfavourable overall evaluation and a low rating on 'understandability'.

Subjects were also asked to rate a number of mental health professional groups as well as a number of medical groups outside the mental health field. Table 7 shows these various groups ranked from those that were evaluated most highly, at the top, to those evaluated least highly, at the bottom. Scores ranged from 1.00 (negative evaluation) to 7.00 (favourable evaluation), 4.00 representing a middle or neutral point. It can be seen that moderately high positive attitudes were held towards mental health professionals although it was the medics from outside the mental health field who topped the pole. The 'mental patient' himself is the only one on the wrong side of the neutral point although it is a pity that no 'medical/surgical patient' was included amongst the groups to be rated. Mean scores for 'understandability' are also shown and the results are revealing. In comparison with 'nurses' and 'physicians' an aura of mystery seems to surround the 'psychologist' and 'psychiatrist'.

Table 7 Mean Evaluative and Understandability Scores Assigned by Members of the Public to Various Health and Mental Health Professional Groups

Evaluative		Understandability	
Concept	Mean Score	Concept	Mean Score
Physician	6·45	Nurse	5·32
Doctor	6·44	Me	5·22
Nurse	6·38	Physician	5·14
Research psychologist	5·96	Mental-hospital attendant	5·10
Social worker	5·95	Doctor	5·09
Clinical psychologist	5·91	Social worker	5·08
Mental-hospital attendant	5·91	Clinical psychologist	4·66
Psychologist	5·89	Psychologist	4·60
Psychiatrist	5·87	Research psychologist	4·52
Me	5·83	Psychiatrist	4·47
Psychoanalyst	5·76	Psychoanalyst	4·43
Mental patient	3·17	Mental patient	2·22

(Taken from Nunnally, 1961, p. 57, Table 5.4 and p. 58, Table 5.5)

Social distance

A number of investigators have made use of short hypothetical case descriptions originally used by Star (1955). Four of these are as follows:

Paranoid Schizophrenic Man ... is very suspicious, he doesn't trust anybody and he's sure that everybody is against him. Sometimes he thinks that people he sees on the street are talking about him or following him around. A couple of times now he has beaten up men who didn't even know him, because he thought they were plotting against him. The other night, he began to curse his wife terribly; then he hit her and threatened to kill her, because he said, she was working against him too, just like everyone else.

Simple Schizophrenic Woman ... she has never had a job, and she doesn't seem to want to go out and look for one. She is a very quiet girl; she doesn't talk much to anyone ... even in her own family, and she acts like she is afraid of people, especially young men her own age. She won't go out with anyone, and whenever someone comes to visit her family, she stays in her own room until they leave. She just stays by herself and daydreams all the time, and shows no interest in anything or anybody.

Anxious Depressed Man He has a good job and is doing pretty well at it. Most of the time he gets along all right with people, but he is always very touchy and he always loses his temper quickly if things aren't going his way, or if people find fault with him. He worries a lot about little things, and he seems to be moody and unhappy all the time. Everything is going along all right for him, but he can't sleep nights, brooding about the past and worrying about things that might go wrong.

Compulsive-Phobic Girl She seems happy and cheerful; she's pretty, has a good enough job, and is engaged to marry a nice young man. She has loads of friends, everybody likes her; and she's always busy and active. However, she just can't leave the house without going back to see whether she left the gas stove lit or not. And she always goes back again just to make sure she locked the door. And one more thing about her; she's afraid to ride up and down in elevators; she just won't go any place where she'd have to ride in an elevator to get there.

Phillips (1963) presented these four case descriptions and a description of a supposedly 'normal' person to each of 300 white married women in a single town in the USA. For each subject one of the descriptions had the following statement attached to it: 'He/she has been in a mental hospital because of the way he/she was getting along.' A second case had attached to it the statement: 'He/she has been going to see his/her psychiatrist regularly about the way he/she is getting along.' A third case had a similar statement attached but with the word 'psychiatrist' changed to the word 'physician'. A fourth case was similar but with the word 'clergyman' and the fifth description had no such statement attached at all.

Social distance was measured by answers to the following five questions:

'Would you discourage your children from marrying someone like this?' (*Yes* would obviously indicate greater social distance or rejection.)

'If you had a room to rent in your home would you be willing to rent it to someone like this?' (*No*)

'Would you be willing to work on a job with someone like this?' (*No*)

'Would you be willing to have someone like this join a favourite club or organization of yours?' (*No*)

'Would you object to having a person like this as a neighbour?' (*Yes*)

The 'paranoid schizophrenic' case elicited an average social distance, or rejection, of 3.84 (out of a possible 5) whereas at the other extreme the 'compulsive-phobic' case received an average score of 1.39 and the 'normal' case a score of 0.72. Almost as strong, however, was the influence on rejection scores of the attached statements concerning help source (this influence was independent of case description as different subjects had different statements attached to different cases, combinations of case descriptions and contact statements being systematically varied). At one extreme, when the person was described as having been in a mental hospital the *average* rejection score was 3.04, whilst at the other extreme, when no statement was attached concerning help received, average rejection was only 1.35. Seeing a psychiatrist was associated with less rejection than mental hospitalization, but with greater rejection than seeing a physician, and seeing a clergyman was associated with even less rejection.

In the light of these findings Phillips writes of rejection as one of the possible 'costs' of seeking help for mental illness and considers that the rewards and costs of seeking help have to be weighed in the balance.

Ideas about public views concerning mental illness have largely been based upon opinion surveys such as those of Nunnally (1961) and Phillips (1963). Hence these findings may possibly give a very misleading idea of how people actually act towards the mentally ill or the ex-mental patient, or even of the ideas about mental illness which really prevail and which might be conveyed, for example, to children. There is particularly likely to be a discrepancy between actions or privately expressed attitudes and *publicly* expressed opinions if certain attitudes have the stamp of 'approval' or are widely considered to represent a more enlightened or modern view. Nunnally (1961) obtained an even more extreme impression of public attitudes than was obtained by a survey approach, when he analysed the content of television, radio and newspaper references to the subject. This was especially true of a factor which Nunnally termed, 'look and act different'. Of eighty-nine references to mental illness which related to this factor, all but one affirmed it; that is they indicated or suggested that people with mental health problems looked different or acted differently from normal people. For example, 'In television dramas ... the afflicted person often enters the scene staring glassy-eyed with his mouth widely agape, mumbling incoherent phrases or laughing uncontrollably. Even in what would be considered the milder disorders, neurotic phobias and obsessions, the afflicted person is presented as having bizarre facial expressions and actions' (Nunnally, 1961, p. 74).

The recognition of mental disorder

Quite apart from the question of stigma and rejection, a number of investigators have been concerned with whether 'mental illness' is 'recognized'. Starting with Star (1955), the same case descriptions have been presented in a number of surveys and subjects have been asked whether the person described was 'mentally ill'. Although all the cases were designed so as to display some psychiatric symptoms, recognition of 'mental illness' has varied widely with the nature of the case description. Whilst the majority of subjects are willing to call the 'paranoid schizophrenic' man mentally ill, only a very small proportion (around 5–10 per cent in some surveys) have been willing to call the 'compulsive-phobic' girl mentally ill. Needless to say, results such as these can only be taken to apply to a relatively limited geographical area and to a relatively limited time period. Indeed there is some evidence that the 'recognition' of mental illness has grown in the USA over the last twenty years.

Fletcher (1969) asked his subjects whether they thought the aggressive and withdrawn cases, described earlier, required help with their problems. The results, which were fairly similar for the two cases, indicated that 60 to 80 per cent of subjects in different sex and socio-economic class groups thought that some referral for help was indicated, but only about 15 to 30 per cent thought that referral to a psychiatrist was indicated. The remainder suggested referral to a clergyman or a physician.

Differences between expert and lay opinion may lie not only in the 'recognition' of what constitutes 'mental illness' but may also concern beliefs about the origins and change of deviant behaviour. In particular, Nunnally (1961) found the lay public, and Manis *et al.* (1963) found psychiatric patients themselves, to be less likely than mental health professionals to disagree with statements suggesting that 'will-power' was the basis of personal adjustment or that the 'avoidance of morbid thoughts' formed the basis of mental health.

Experimental Studies of Prejudice

A series of experimental studies demonstrate that attitudes towards mental illness or maladjustment can act as true prejudices, that is, quite independently of how the person concerned really behaves.

Farina and Ring (1965) had subjects play a 'labyrinth' game in pairs (a board had to be correctly tilted so that a ball would reach its destination without falling through holes). Before the game each player received quite fictitious information about the other person. In some cases O was described as 'normal' and in the remaining cases as 'sick' ('certain problems . . . still bother me . . . somewhat different from most people . . . tend to keep to self . . . don't have any close friends . . . twice have been placed in . . . mental institution when I had a kind of nervous breakdown') (Farina and Ring, 1965, p. 48). A result of this experiment, which was contrary to expectations, was that when each of a pair received 'sick' information about O they performed significantly *better* during the game than when each of a pair received 'normal' information about the other. A variety of explanations for this finding suggest themselves but Farina and Ring speculate that one result of 'sick' information about another person may be the reduction of 'threat'.

More predictable results were obtained from answers to questions put to the players after the game. 'Sick' players were more likely to be seen by their partners as less able to get along with other people, less able to understand other people, less able to understand themselves and more unpredictable than 'normal' players. Whilst these perceptions might follow directly from the fictitious information provided before the game, the biasing influence of this pre-information was demonstrated by the finding that players paired with 'sick' partners were more likely to think that their partners had hindered during the game, and were more likely to say that they would prefer to work on their own in future. This was despite the fact that, on the whole, 'sick' players actually performed better during the game itself.

Similar results were obtained by Farina *et al.* (1966) in the teacher–learner experiment, already briefly described earlier in this chapter. Following the session in which subjects had acted as 'teachers', they were more likely to express liking for the person who had acted as 'learner' if they had previously been led to believe that the 'learner' had a 'normal' current level of adjustment, than if they were led to believe that the 'learner's' current adjustment was 'stigmatized' (previous mental hospital admission, few close friends). Ss were also more likely to express a preference for working with the same O in the future if O's adjustment had been described as 'normal', and the same Ss gave higher estimates of their team performance, although once again there was no objective basis for these higher estimates.

Jones *et al.* (1959) examined the reactions of subjects to favourable or unfavourable evaluations which they heard made, either about themselves or about another person. The normal pattern of reactions was to express greater liking for the person who made the more favourable evaluations; but in addition to this effect there was evidence of greater liking for an evaluator who was described as 'well adjusted' as opposed to an evaluator described as 'maladjusted' (unstable home life; inadequate emotional resources; underlying anxiety). This second effect was, under some circumstances, sufficient to upset the normally expressed greater liking for the more favourable evaluator.

The possibility of *ambivalence* in attitudes towards psychological disorder or abnormality has already been referred to. An experiment by Gergen and Jones (1963) begins to illustrate the circumstances under which it might be apparent. Subjects, who were non-psychiatric patients in a US Veterans Administration hospital, were required to predict the consumer choices of 'a patient' in an adjoining room. Some Ss were told that the person whose choices they were predicting was a psychiatric patient, whilst others were told that O was a patient suffering from a minor organic illness. Some Ss in both of these groups then found that the choices made were very *difficult to predict*, whilst others found the choices of the patient in the other room very *predictable*. A further variation in the experiment concerned the level of unpleasant consequences for S following an error in prediction. For some Ss consequences were high (an error produced a raucous buzzer noise of unpredictable duration) whilst consequences were low for other Ss (errors produced merely a signal light). In addition, S was told that the experimenter found the buzzer annoying and that it was up to S to try and avoid it by avoiding making errors.

The results, which are shown in Figure 8, are in terms of *evaluation change scores*, i.e. the degree of change in evaluation of the patient in the adjoining room from before to after the main part of the experiment. The results seem to illustrate a polarization of views about O when he is described as a psychiatric patient, and when the consequences of his behaviour are relatively high. Under those circumstances O's predictability is important. On the other hand, when consequences were low the predictability of the 'psychiatric patient' had no influence.

It was as if allowances were being made for unpredictability in the behaviour of the 'psychiatric patient' so long as the consequences of this unpredictability were not too great for S. Once the consequences were increased this tolerance could no longer be maintained and the degree of unpredictability of behaviour became a major source of devaluation.

These experiments all show that knowing another person to be maladjusted or mentally ill can bias perceptions of that person and can even alter behaviour towards him. But in this area, as in others, the nature of real life interaction is likely to be complicated and certainly not a one-way affair. Indeed Farina *et al.* (1971) have experimentally demonstrated another link in the probable chain of factors contributing to a stigma cycle. They were able to show that

Figure 8 Changes in Evaluation as a Function of Mental Status, Predictability, and Consequence

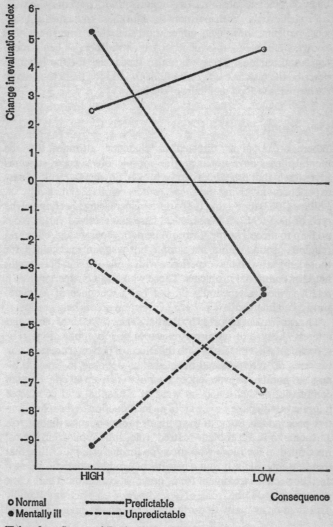

(Taken from Jones and Davis, 1965 p. 256, Figure 5)

Mad or Bad? Alternative Constructions on Mental Disorder **159** psychiatric patients performed less well in certain ways on a game task, when they were led to believe that their partner in the task knew of their patient status. In comparison with patients who were led to believe that their partners thought them to be medical/surgical patients, those who understood that their true status was known were rated subsequently by their partners as being more tense and anxious. There were also tendencies for the latter to describe the task as being more difficult, and for them to actually perform less well on their part of the task.

Changing attitudes

Whereas campaigns directed at changing attitudes towards mental illness have not met with conspicuous success, it seems more likely that prejudices can be broken down as a result of new experiences involving *personal contact* with the mentally ill. Phillips (1963) found that the pattern of increasing rejection (as the type of help which a hypothetical case had received varied from no help to mental hospitalization) held for separate age, class and religious groups within his sample but was *not* maintained for those subjects who had experience with a relative who had sought help for emotional problems. Those who had no experience of a relative who was mentally ill, but had experience of a friend, showed an intermediate pattern of rejection across help groups.

The experiment reported by Rothaus *et al.* (1963) is of particular interest because of its direct relevance to job applications. The experiment was concerned with the effects of personal presentation in terms of 'interpersonal problems' as opposed to 'mental illness'. A number of experienced interviewers from an employment commission visited an open ward of a hospital and conducted interviews with patients as part of an introduction to the rehabilitation programme. Some of the patients took a 'mental illness' role and some took a 'problem-centred' role. Job 'application forms' were filled in for those who took the former role indicating that they had entered the hospital because of trouble with their 'nerves' and the need for treatment for a 'nervous' condition. These same patients played the role of somebody who was emotionally disturbed or mentally ill during their interview, having practised this role previously with the help of fellow patients. They described their hospitalization in terms of therapy and treatment to help them relax, rest their nerves, to sleep better; they described treatment in terms of tranquillizers and other medications; they used terms such as 'doctor', 'ward', 'psychologist' and 'psychiatrist'. Other patients 'sent in' forms describing problems in their everyday interpersonal relationships. Hospitalization had occurred because of unsuccessful attempts to handle these problems on their own and the felt need for help in solving them. They continued to play this role in the actual interview, describing problems such as shyness, difficulty in accepting responsibility, tendencies to avoid other people, difficulty in getting along with authority figures, antagonism to other people, loneliness, stresses with wife or friends. They described hospitalization in terms of learning to solve these problems. In fact each patient who participated learnt to play both roles and played each role once with different interviewers.

After reading the application forms, and again after the interviews, the interviewers rated each patient in terms of expected ease of placing the patient in a suitable job. The main result was the more favourable average rating given *after* the interview itself rather than after seeing the application form alone. The role which the patient played only influenced those ratings made after the interviews. Interviewers expected to be able to place those patients who adopted the 'interpersonal problem' role more easily.

Conclusions

Once again it would be premature to claim that a satisfactory body of knowledge exists. On the other hand, the material presented in this chapter may have served to outline an area of study where some useful concepts are emerging with which to guide research and possibly action.

The idea that behaviour can be interpreted in various different ways, or that different constructions can be placed upon other people's behaviour, provides a major theme. 'Illness' or 'disorder' constitute one type of interpretation or construction which has to compete with others in individual cases. Relatives may only place this particular type of construction on a family member's behaviour after adhering to alternative interpretations, or vacillating for some long time, and indeed may never accept this interpretation fully even after a 'diagnosis' has been made.

An 'illness' interpretation implies at least a partial suspension of the 'normative' framework within which people usually judge others' behaviour. A process, aptly called 'negotiation', probably takes place during which a 'disorder' interpretation is recommended to patients and their relatives. In many cases this may provide a simplifying and acceptable solution to a confusing dilemma.

In practice, the normative framework for judging behaviour, whereby responsibility for action is attributed and evaluations are made on the basis of the outcomes of individual actions, is rarely fully suspended even by mental health professionals. A process of socialization undoubtedly takes place during training but indirect methods of attitude assessment reveal that evaluative constructs are used in association with illness constructs by professionals as well as by fellow patients. This is not surprising when the similarity between concepts of mental health and socially desirable behaviour is appreciated.

The availability of alternative ways of construing behaviour, and the mixture of types of interpretation employed in practice, is likely to be associated with 'role conflict' in those who interact with an individual whose behaviour is under discussion. Even the professional worker protected by the routines of an established institution is often likely to wonder whether his role should be to befriend, support, advise, train, or discipline his 'patient'. The dilemma is the more acute for those working in new settings, such as halfway houses, without such established procedures, and must be most acute for those, such as family members, unprotected by any professionalism.

The use of an 'illness' interpretation may not be without its costs in terms of stigmatization. Surveys and experimental studies show that prejudice persists and it seems likely that this may be particularly important when behaviour associated with mental illness has unpleasant consequences for other people.

Again it has to be stressed that generalization about these

processes, and about the degree of their importance, are certainly unwarranted at this stage. Deviant behaviour takes many forms and the matters discussed in this chapter may be of crucial importance for some and of relatively little importance for others.

Chapter 5

Therapists and Patients: Studies of the Psychotherapy Relationship

Introduction

Prominent amongst professional methods for attempting to restore to 'normal' ways of behaving, thinking and feeling which have been construed as 'mentally disordered' are a range of techniques which deliberately employ an interpersonal situation. They can be grouped under the general term 'psychotherapy' and the situation is very often a dyadic one, involving a 'therapist' and a 'patient'.

The most important question to ask here is relatively straight-forward: Can we specify the conditions under which such relationships will be effective in restoring mental health or 'normality'? By 'conditions' may be meant attributes of the therapist, aspects of the therapist's interpersonal behaviour, attributes or behaviours of the patient, or more complex 'conditions' to do with the fit of therapist and patient.

Apart from questions specific to psychotherapy, relationships deliberately engineered for the purposes of facilitating mental health provide settings in which more general questions can be asked about the importance of interpersonal behaviour for psychological normality and abnormality. Despite the impressive differences in terms of role relationships involved, it may be that the conditions under which psychotherapists are effective with their patients are similar to the conditions under which parents are effective in promoting mental health in their children, and to the conditions under which husbands or wives are effective in encouraging recovery in their spouses. General principles would be of much greater value in abnormal psychology than would a number of laws relating to their own specialities.

Commonalities in the psychotherapies

The word 'psychotherapy' is a very general one and covers a multitude of procedures. Frank has referred to 'The explosion of psychotherapeutic methods (which) has been accompanied by a proliferation of healers with all types of training, or even none at all' (Frank, 1971, p. 3). Frank suggests, and there are many who would agree with him, that this diversity of methods is more apparent than real. He argues that there is a great similarity between many psychotherapists, that many apparently revolutionary methods turn out to be rediscoveries of old methods, and that the choice of a particular method depends very largely on the personal predilection of the therapist.

Many other authorities on the subject have drawn attention to commonalities across psychotherapeutic methods (e.g. Strupp and Bergin, 1969; Goldstein, 1971). Strupp and Bergin (1969) have suggested that all the major forms of psychotherapy are utilizing a relatively small number of mechanisms: imitation, identification, persuasion, empathy, warmth, interpretation, counter-conditioning, extinction, discrimination learning, reward and punishment.

Almost without exception, however, the different schools and approaches to psychotherapy stress the essential importance of the nature of the relationship between 'the therapist' and 'the patient'. But as Goldstein points out the terms used to describe this relationship (reciprocity, transaction, empathy, trust, mutuality, etc.) and the techniques used to assess the nature of the relationship (projective tests, rating scales, sensitivity measures, etc.) are extremely diverse.

Optimal Therapy Relationships

Some time ago Fiedler (1950a, 1950b) asked the obvious question: 'Are these differences in theory semantic, or do they represent actual divergencies in the goals therapists set for themselves?' He attempted to answer the question by having a number of therapists, both experienced and inexperienced, sort a number of statements, descriptive of patient–therapist relationships, into those that were 'most characteristic of an ideal therapeutic relationship', those that were 'very characteristic', those that were 'somewhat characteristic', and so on (Q-sort method). Amongst the therapists who took part were some who espoused the psycho-analytic school of psychotherapy, others who followed the non-directive method (Rogers, 1959), one who followed the Adlerian tradition, and two who were eclectic. The way each therapist described the ideal relationship was compared with the way each of the others described it. Correlations between the rates were uniformly positive and significant (the median correlation was +0·67) and there was a tendency for the experts of different orientations to agree with one another at a slightly higher level than did the experts and non-experts of the same orientation. The judgements were pooled to obtain a picture of the concept of the ideal therapeutic relationship about which there seemed to be such a measure of agreement.

Table 8 shows the eight statements generally thought to be *most*, or at least *very*, characteristic of an ideal therapeutic relationship, as well as the eight statements generally thought to be *least* characteristic. Just a casual inspection of these statements reveals their very obvious evaluative content. Indeed it is hard to believe that a therapist, whatever his persuasion, could do other than sort such statements along an evaluative, or 'social desirability', dimension. For this reason it could be argued that Fiedler's (1950a) demonstration of inter-therapist agreement proved very little. Incidentally, Fiedler had one person sort the statements who had never done, nor been in, psychotherapy and the results showed, as one might expect, that it is not necessary to have experience of psychotherapy, either as a therapist or as a patient, to be able to achieve a high level of agreement with psychotherapists about the nature of an ideal psychotherapeutic relationship. Fiedler considers that this one demonstration provides some support for the very important hypothesis, 'that a good therapeutic relationship is very much like any good interpersonal relationship'. (Fiedler, 1950a, p. 244.)

On the other hand Fiedler may have demonstrated something of major theoretical and practical importance, if it could be shown that therapist–patient relationships do indeed vary along such a positive–negative, or *quality* of interaction, axis. In that case it could well be argued that it is the closeness of fit of a particular therapist–patient relationship to this ideal (which may well correspond with some more general notion of the 'ideal' as applied to relationships between people in general) which is the factor of greatest importance, besides which differences in 'style' due to the different orientations and training of therapists, are relatively trivial. Fiedler himself (1950b) went some way towards showing just this by having a small number of raters (themselves possessing different amounts and types of training in psychotherapy) listen to recorded psychotherapy sessions, and compare the relationships they witnessed on tape with the concept of the ideal. The therapists whose sessions were recorded also varied in

Table 8 Characteristics of an Ideal Psychotherapeutic Relationship

Most characteristic

The therapist is able to participate completely in the patient's communication.
The therapist's comments are always right in line with what the patient is trying to convey.
The therapist is well able to understand the patient's feelings.
The therapist always follows the patient's line of thought.
The therapist's tone of voice conveys the complete ability to share the patient's feelings.
The therapist sees the patient as a co-worker on a common problem.
The therapist treats the patient as an equal.
The therapist really tries to understand the patient's feelings.

Least characteristic

The therapist cannot maintain rapport with the patient.
The therapist's own needs completely interfere with his understanding of the patient
The therapist feels disgusted by the patient.
The therapist is hostile towards the patient.
The therapist is punitive.
The therapist is very unpleasant to the patient.
The therapist acts in a very superior manner towards the patient.
The therapist shows no comprehension of the feelings the patient is trying to communicate.

(Taken from Fiedler, 1950a, pp. 243–4)

experience and type of orientation. The relationships involving relatively experienced therapists were rated by all as approximating more closely to the ideal than did the relationships involving the relatively inexperienced therapists. There tended to be greater similarity between the relationships involving experienced therapists of different orientations than between experienced and inexperienced therapists of the same orientation. In several instances, when the therapist involved was inexperienced, the correlation between the rating of the relationship heard on tape and the ideal was *negative*. It seems possible, therefore, that there may be a general dimension for evaluating psychotherapeutic relationships and that 'experts', of whatever orientation, may have a higher standing on it than 'non-experts'.

Three conditions

Fiedler suggested that the most important ingredients of this 'expertness' were, 'the therapist's ability to understand, to communicate with, and to maintain rapport with the patient' (Fiedler, 1950b, p. 444).

Truax and Carkhuff have reviewed a programme of research concerned with three therapist 'conditions' thought to be necessary for a favourable outcome of psychotherapy. The first of these conditions, 'accurate empathy',

... involves both the therapist's sensitivity to current feelings and his verbal facility to communicate this understanding in a language attuned to the client's current feelings (Truax and Carkhuff, 1967, p. 46).

The second condition, 'non-possessive warmth', or 'unconditional positive regard',

... ranges from a high level where the therapist warmly accepts the patient's experience as part of that person, without imposing conditions; to a low level where the therapist evaluates a patient or his feelings, expresses dislike or disapproval, or expresses warmth in a selective and evaluative way. It involves valuing the patient as a person, separate from any evaluation of his behaviour or thoughts ... a prizing of the patient for himself regardless of his behaviour. (Truax and Carkhuff, 1967, p. 58–60.)

The third, 'genuineness' or 'self-congruence' is,

... at a very low level where the therapist presents a façade or defends and denies feelings; and [is at] a high level where the therapist is freely and deeply himself ... he is being himself in the moment rather than presenting a professional façade. But the therapist's response must be sincere rather than phoney; it must express his real feelings or being rather than defensiveness. (Truax and Carkhuff, 1967, p. 68-9.)

As well as claiming that high levels of these therapist conditions are related to favourable therapeutic outcome, Truax and Carkhuff also claim that the effectiveness of psychotherapy may be increased by *training* therapists to offer high levels of these conditions. In particular they present some important evidence that lay people can be trained to offer levels similar to those offered by a group of experienced counsellors, after something like a hundred hours of training over a period of a few months. In view of the importance, in hospitals and other settings, of contacts between patients or clients and social workers, nurses and untrained personnel, and the shortage of people trained in clinical psychology or psychological medicine, such a claim is obviously of the utmost importance.

Frank (1961, 1971) has argued that there are striking similarities between some of the things that go on in psychotherapy and components of other change processes as diverse as healing in primitive societies, religious revivalism, miracle cures, thought reform and placebo effects in medicine. Goldstein (1971) has noted that the literature contains reports of successful 'treatment' carried out by nurses, psychiatric aides, patients' parents, students, technicians, convicts, housewives, auxiliary counsellors, and foster grandparents. Frank (1971) also argues that many psychotherapy clients could be supported by non-professionals, in some cases with professional supervision.

In most of the research reported by Truax and Carkhuff, or carried out since then, the levels of therapeutic conditions offered by therapists are rated by trained raters from segments of tape recordings of therapeutic interviews. It seems there is considerable support for the claim that therapeutic change is related to higher levels of these conditions but the evidence is strongest from studies where the 'patients' were delinquents, and there are some contradictory findings (Truax and Carkhuff, 1967; D. Shapiro, 1969). It seems also that whilst it is true that training can produce higher levels of the therapeutic conditions, there is little evidence that this necessarily increases the effectiveness of psychotherapy (D. Shapiro, 1969).

If there are therapist conditions which can be reliably assessed and which are related to therapeutic outcome, this immediately raises interesting questions concerning the *processes* whereby these conditions produce their effects. One of the hypotheses which receives some support (Truax and Carkhuff, 1967; D. Shapiro, 1969) and which is of particular interest because of its connections with matters discussed in a different context in Chapter 2, concerns the patient variable of self-exploration or 'interpersonal openness'. There is some evidence that a patient's 'readiness to convey personal information about one's life, one's feelings, one's impressions of other individuals' (Whalen, 1969) is related to therapy outcome (Truax and Carkhuff, 1967) and that the application of the therapeutic conditions of empathy, warmth and genuineness may result in selective reinforcement, and hence an increase in frequency, of patients' self-exploratory behaviour (D. Shapiro, 1969).

Non-verbal therapist behaviour

The scales for rating the Truax and Carkhuff conditions make reference almost exclusively to therapist *verbal* behaviour, thus ignoring non-verbal aspects which others have supposed to be of crucial importance in understanding both patient and therapist behaviour (e.g. Ekman and Friesen, 1968; Lewin, 1965). Lewin, for example, suggests a whole range of non-verbal aspects of therapist behaviour which may influence the nature of the therapist–patient relationship. They include such obvious things as the therapist's appearance, manner of walking and sitting, and his personal attractiveness as well as other factors to do with his 'performance' (Goffman, 1959) such as furniture arrangement (the presence and positioning of chairs, couch, desk etc.), whether, when, and how the therapist laughs, whether he takes notes, where he looks and so on. He even suggests that the size and positioning of an ashtray (indicating tolerance or encouragement of smoking) and whether the therapist's own lighter works easily (on the basis of which assumptions may be made about his dependability or his humanness) are amongst the sort of non-linguistic aspects of the therapist's behaviour to which a patient may be most responsive.

In fact there is some evidence that there may be aspects of the therapist's behaviour, both verbal and non-verbal, which are associated with high levels of the Truax and Carkhuff therapeutic conditions, but which do not require a knowledge of how they 'fit in with' what the patient says, in order to be reliably rated. For example, Truax (1966) found that therapists' accurate empathy and non-possessive warmth could be rated just as well from tape recordings from which the patients' statements had been excluded. Furthermore, J. G. Shapiro *et al.* (1968) showed that judges, trained to use the linguistically-oriented scales of therapist behaviour, could agree fairly well amongst themselves about the levels of therapist conditions being offered by a number of counsellors, when they were presented merely with *still photographs* of the counsellor alone. A comparison of judgements based on photographs confined to the counsellor's face and those based on photographs of the rest of the body, suggested that raters were largely responsive to facial rather than bodily cues. In a further study J. G. Shapiro (1968) reported significant positive correlations between ratings, made by trained raters, of audio-only recordings, and ratings, made by the same raters, of video-only recordings of the same therapy segments.

Patient–therapist similarity

Attempts have been made to link a wide range of therapist and therapist–patient variables both with 'remaining' in, as opposed to 'terminating', psychotherapy, and to psychotherapy outcome (Luborsky *et al.*, 1971). Amongst those which have been consistently positively related to outcome on a number of occasions are some reflecting therapist–patient *similarity* in terms of interests, needs or values. It has to be noted however that measures of similarity are likely to involve dyadic indices with all the difficulties (discussed in Chapter 3) they entail (Wright, 1968; Cronbach,

1955). Sapolsky (1965), for example, used the Fundamental Inter-personal Relations Orientation–Behaviour scales (FIRO–B, Schutz, 1958) with a number of hospitalized, largely psychotic, women (of whom there were twenty-five) and their doctors (of whom there were three). Patients were randomly assigned to a doctor at admission. The scale identifies three areas of interpersonal need – inclusion (the need to interact, or associate with people), control and affection – and for each need one score indicates how S states she treats others, and a further score indicates how she wishes to be treated by others. A comparison of the scores obtained by an individual patient and the scores obtained by her doctor can be analysed to yield a total *compatibility* score. These compatibility scores correlated positively and significantly with post-discharge ratings of patient improvement made by a senior psychiatrist. (A random reshuffling control analysis – see Chapter 3, p. 107 – suggested that compatibility scores did reflect 'true' compatibility and not simply an artefact.)

Goldstein (1971) has reported a study in which twenty-four mental hospital patients were selected from a much larger group of patients on the grounds of being the most totally compatible (FIRO–B again) with one of twenty-four ministers who were taking part in a training programme. An additional twenty-four patients were chosen on the grounds of being least compatible. Thus each trainee therapist had one highly compatible and one highly incompatible patient assigned to him. Psychotherapy took place twice a week for twelve weeks and the personal reactions of both participants were tested after the third and again after the eleventh weeks. On both occasions of testing high compatibility patients were more attracted to their therapists than were low compatibility patients. There was also a tendency, though not statistically significant, for therapists to be more attracted to their high compatibility patients than to their low compatibility patients.

In fact the FIRO–B compatibility variable is not completely correspondent either with 'similarity' or 'complementarity' and a similar debate about the relative importance of compatibility, similarity and complementarity has been entered into with regard to the outcome of therapy dyads as there has been in the area of mate and friendship-choice (Goldstein, 1971).

The A–B therapist variable

Further empirical support for the notion that certain types of therapist do better with certain types of patient comes from research on the 'A–B therapist variable'. The variable contrasts those therapists (type A) who produced the highest rates of improvement amongst hospitalized schizophrenic patients, and those therapists (type B) who produced the lowest rates (Betz, 1967).

Therapists of type A produced no more improvement for *neurotic* patients than did therapists of type B and a subsequent study (McNair *et al.*, 1962) actually found that therapists of type B were significantly *more* successful with patients in a non-schizophrenic male out-patient sample. Although the basic studies in this field are very few in number and not totally free of contradictory results, it is this possibility of a significant interaction effect between type of therapist and type of patient that has led to much recent investigation of the A–B variable.

There have been many speculations as to why As should be better with schizophrenic patients. For example it has been suggested that such patients show a marked deficit in sex-role identification and that the less 'masculine' A-type therapists find it easier to be empathic and respectful of such patients (Berzins *et al.*, 1971). Alternatively it has been suggested that As are more able to persuade schizophrenic patients to trust them on account of their readier awareness of idiosyncratic perceptions (Razin, 1971).

The situation may in fact be even more complex than the therapist–patient interaction picture which work on the A–B therapist variable suggests. Razin (1971) quotes one study in which a therapist–patient-outcome criterion interaction effect was noted: As were more effective than Bs, especially with schizophrenics, if outcome was measured in terms of the relief of subjective distress; but Bs were more successful, especially with schizophrenics, when outcome was assessed in terms of 'impulse control'. Such findings should be sufficient warning against expecting simple answers in the field of psychotherapy research.

There is in fact fairly general agreement now that the single question 'Does psychotherapy work?' should be replaced by a number of questions of the form: 'Does X achieve Y for type of person or problem Z?' Nonetheless it is true that evidence on the overall effectiveness of psychotherapeutic procedures has been difficult to obtain (Rachman, 1971; Eysenck, 1960). The possibility has to be faced that whilst psychotherapy may have the potential for being facilitative or restorative of mental health or adjustment, it probably fails to realize that potential in many instances and in some cases may be actually harmful. This should scarcely surprise us if the therapist–patient dyad is considered, as it should be, as a special case of dyadic relationships in general, albeit one that is deliberately manufactured for therapeutic purposes.

Studying Therapy Processes

Most of the research on psychotherapy discussed so far in this chapter is in the tradition of *outcome* research, being concerned with the connections between therapeutic conditions and psychotherapeutic change, success, failure, favourable outcome and so on. A somewhat different research tradition concerns itself with *processes* with little or no concern, directly at least, for outcome. An important paper by Scheflen provides an example of this tradition and at the same time offers some intriguing hypotheses having to do with the regulatory function of non-verbal aspects of patient and therapist behaviour. Scheflen (1963) described the research method known as 'context analysis' or 'communicational analysis' in which the concern is with speech, body motion, touch, bodily noise, decor, dress and other behaviours of 'communicational import'. A film is made of each psychotherapy session, and each observable behaviour of each participant (linguistic, non-linguistic verbal or paralinguistic – gestures, postures etc.) is recorded on a time graph. The graphs are examined for 'patterns of repetitive behaviour' and each is examined in the context of preceding, simultaneous and following behaviours. Scheflen's general conclusion from analyses of this sort is that, 'the same linguistic, gestural and postural configurations appear over and over again [and] . . . recur again and again in the same configurational context' (Scheflen, 1963, p. 129). Furthermore, deviations from normal patterns appear to be accompanied by new behaviours which appear to have a regulatory function and which continue until the old pattern recurs or until a new pattern is established.

A number of examples of this regulatory function are given by Scheflen. In one example a male therapist and a young female patient appeared to mutually regulate the degree of intimacy or closeness between them, by means of a repetitive cycle of events, in which attempts at greater intimacy by the patient were followed by periods of lessened attentiveness by the therapist. To this the patient responded by becoming overtly remote, to which the therapist in turn responded with physical contact and increased activity, which served to start the cycle off again.

Other examples provided instances of the, apparently unconscious, use of non-verbal signals for regulation purposes. These include the widely understood raised eyebrow and 'umm-hmm' as well as less generally acknowledged signals such as 'sweeping the side of an index finger across the nostrils'. Scheflen suggests that this gesture is regularly associated with negation or disapproval and is used fairly generally as such in American groups.

Different styles of therapy

Much of the psychotherapy research in the *process* tradition concerns different therapist *styles*. Even if we ignore for the moment the many physical and behavioural treatments, and confine attention to treatments which rely exclusively upon talking and listening as the media through which change is to be brought about, there are quite dramatic differences in the treatment philosophies espoused by different therapists. Just one instance need be quoted: Steiner (1969) describes the philosophy of 'transactional analysis' applied to alcoholic patients. The assumption behind this philosophy seems to be that the therapist can too easily be caught playing a sympathetic role towards his patient and that in terms of patient change this is unlikely to be productive. As he says, the transactional analyst 'will tend to avoid expressions of pity, empathy, or even compassion, and insists that the alcoholic take responsibility for his behaviour' (Steiner, 1969, p. 933). He has to admit, perhaps not surprisingly, that his patients know him as a 'tough cookie'. The point here is not whether this approach is any more successful than any other, but simply that it represents the stated philosophy behind the treatment approach of at least one therapist, and that this philosophy appears to be diametrically opposed to another philosophy, that of non-directive, client-centred, therapy (Rogers, |1959) which stresses the importance of the therapist conditions of empathy, genuineness and warmth.

Although Fiedler (p. 166, above) found the similarities between the views of therapists of different schools more striking than their contrasts, nonetheless differences between schools were apparent in his study particularly in terms of the status which therapists assumed towards their patients: 'the Adlerian and some of the psychoanalytically oriented therapists tend to place themselves in a more tutorial role, whereas non-directive therapists tend toward the opposite direction' (Fiedler, 1950b, p. 444). In certain treatment settings the availability of different personnel with different roles and status positions may allow the nurturant-supportive therapist role, and the critical-directive therapist role, to be played by different people; for example it may be the expectation that doctors (who are more likely to be male) will play the latter role, and nurses or social workers (who are more likely to be female) the former. It is certainly not unusual for psychiatric patients to rate their contacts with nursing staff as having been of greater therapeutic benefit to them than contacts they may have had with other staff (e.g. Ferguson and Carney, 1970).

In practice, of course, the behaviour which psychotherapists display in actual psychotherapy sessions may be quite different from the therapeutic attitudes which they express. In practice inter-therapist differences may not be so extreme. It has already been pointed out that therapists of different 'schools' may define the 'ideal therapeutic relationship' rather similarly. Nonetheless there are likely to be some differences and a study by Auerbach (1963) illustrates this. He reported a content analysis of three individual sessions taken from the 'multiple therapy' of a single eighteen-year-old girl by two therapists (both present in the same sessions) and compared this with a previously reported content analysis of the therapy of a single middle-aged woman carried out by a single

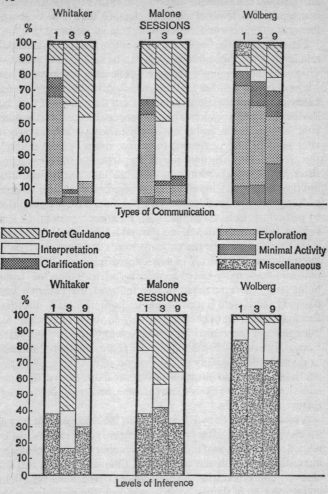

Figure 9 A Comparison of Three Psychotherapists in Terms of Types of Communication and Levels of Inference

Types of Communication

- Direct Guidance
- Interpretation
- Clarification
- Exploration
- Minimal Activity
- Miscellaneous

Levels of Inference

- Level 1, Least Inference
- Level 2, Moderate Inference
- Level 3, Most Inference

(Taken from Auerbach, 1963, p. 140, Figures 1 and 2)

Studies of the Psychotherapy Relationship 177

therapist. In each case the first, third and ninth sessions were analysed and comparisons were made in terms of types of therapist communication, levels of therapist inference, the dynamic focus of therapist utterances and the levels of therapist initiative.

Figure 9 shows the results for types of therapist communication and levels of therapist inference. It can be seen that, as might be expected, the 'multiple therapy' colleagues (Whitaker and Malone) behaved rather similarly, although in some respects their behaviour in later sessions departed from the pattern of their behaviour in the first session. The comparison therapist, on the other hand, showed considerably less change in behaviour from early to later sessions and continued to behave more like the multiple therapists did in their first session. In particular, the comparison therapist (Wolberg) continued to 'explore' and 'clarify' whilst the multiple therapists showed a great predominance in later sessions of 'interpretation' and 'guidance'. The differences are paralleled by differences in levels of therapist 'inference': even in the first session Whitaker and Malone showed a lesser tendency to stay close to the content of the patient's words and were much more interpretative. Whereas Wolberg showed relatively little 'initiative' and made much use of comments such as 'go on' or 'Umm hmm' the others relatively rarely followed the patient's lead passively and were much more authoritative and directive. Examples are given of challenges ('why do you act so crazy?' for example) and contradictions of the patient ('I don't think that's true . . .') made by these therapists. There are admittedly problems to do with the reliability of the method of analysis used in this study, but it serves to illustrate the types of dimensions of therapist behaviour which are likely to reveal some, perhaps quite startling, therapist differences.

A piece of research by Klerman *et al.* (1960) suggests the way in which the personal values and temperaments of therapists can be related to their choice of therapeutic techniques. It also provides an interesting link with the concerns of Chapter 2, which was exclusively concerned with the patterns of interpersonal behaviour and perception of those who are *patients* or who may become so. In this study a significant correlation was found between the amount of drug treatment which individual psychiatric interns used, and their scores on scales of authoritarianism and other values. Those who made greater use of drugs in treatment tended to value assertiveness, self-control and forceful leadership and were themselves willing to assume authority. Those who prescribed fewer drugs were, on the other hand, more likely to be opposed to status hierarchies and to assertive behaviour. They tended to prefer psychological treatments which maximized the patient's role. They were likely to see some conflict existing between the traditional medical role and the role of psychotherapist.

Klerman *et al.* ask, 'to what extent are irrational feelings and motives involved' (p. 115). They suggest that there may be a degree of prejudice and inflexibility in either orientation. They suggest that relatively high levels of drug prescribing may reflect defensive needs to control impulsive and disturbed behaviour, whilst relatively low levels may reflect an inhibition of, and aversion to, acting in a directive or assertive manner. The latter may, under certain circumstances, be just as dysfunctional from the patient's point of view if it results in delaying the administration of necessary treatments.

Such suggestions are of course purely speculative but they serve to make the important point that concepts (such as behavioural rigidity, prejudice, implicit personality theory, etc.) introduced in one context, and thought to have particular application to certain interpersonal situations or to people occupying a certain role (patients, relatives, therapists, etc.), are *generally* applicable to human behaviour whatever the role-position concerned.

Dimensions of psychotherapy

Mintz *et al.* (1971) have recently reported an attempt to define the major 'dimensions of psychotherapy' by factor analysing the intercorrelations of a number of therapist and patient variables based on ratings of whole tape recorded psychotherapy sessions. Fifteen experienced psychotherapists each contributed recordings of two early sessions for each of two patients. The therapists were predominantly of psychoanalytic and eclectic orientation and the total length of treatment varied from as little as one month to as much as four and a half years. Patient diagnoses were 'neurosis' or 'personality or character disorder'. Each session was rated independently by three raters whose ratings were then pooled. The factor analysis produced four factors, which were interpretable, and accounted for about 60 per cent of the total variance. The first of these ('optimal empathic relationship') was defined by *therapist* variables: secure, reassuring and warm, skilful, accepts patient, likable, perceptive, empathic, and fast speech tempo. As Mintz *et al.* say: 'This factor describes a therapist who is easy-going and relaxed, natural, spontaneous, warm and highly involved. The therapist is seen as highly perceptive and empathic.' (Mintz *et al.*, 1971, p. 109.) In many ways it seems to embody Fiedler's (1950a, 1950b) ideal relationship and Truax and Carkhuff's (1967) therapist conditions.

The second factor ('directive mode') consisted of therapist directiveness, activity, creativity, experiential approach, hostile-defensiveness, intrusiveness, and therapist interpretations and impact. Mintz *et al.* comment that 'therapists scoring high on factor II seem to feel that the provision of a nurturing atmosphere is not enough. They attempt to provide something more striking: direction, advice, emotion, or even criticism' (Mintz *et al.*, 1971, p. 110).

The third factor was a *patient* factor ('patient health versus distress') with contributions from patient health-sickness, anxiety, guilt and shame, depression, and dependency.

The fourth ('interpretative mode with receptive patient') was marked by patient receptiveness, therapist interpretations and impact, and therapist 'transference focus'. Mintz *et al.* interpret this dimension as representing the depth of therapy, reflecting the focus and involvement of both participants in intensive therapy.

They find these factors to be consistent with factors that have emerged from other studies based on analyses of patient or therapist reports about therapy. Other than the factor structure itself, which suggested that variation was apparent both in the degree to which an optimal relationship was established and, independently, in the degree to which therapists were directive and interpretative, there are two other facets of this study which are of rather general interest.

Firstly, there is the question of whether differences in ratings are to be attributed to variations in therapists or in patients. Although no one patient was seen by more than one therapist, so it is impossible to detect contributions from patients which are independent of therapists, it was possible to apportion variations in factor scores to therapists, to patients (within therapists) and to sessions (within therapist–patient pairs). Scores on the first factor were found to be relatively stable from patient to patient, and from session to session for any given therapist, suggesting that therapists have certain styles, with respect to 'optimal empathic relationship', which were largely independent of patient behaviour. The reverse was true for the third factor: as might be expected variations in patient health versus distress were largely attributable to differences between patients and not to differences between therapists or sessions.

The picture for the second and fourth factors, however, was much more mixed. Approximately equal percentages of variance were accounted for by therapist and patient differences and almost as much was accounted for by differences between sessions. It seemed that different therapists were characterized by different levels of directiveness but that, in addition, some patients characteristically received from the same therapist a more directive approach than others. The same could be said of factor four.

Auerbach (1963) makes a similar, but not uncontentious, point concerning the role of the *patient* in producing the therapist differences noted in his study. He suggests that the younger patient (treated jointly by two therapists) may have been treated more like a child just because she *was* a child both chronologically and emotionally. He says: 'Clinically speaking, it would have been inappropriate to relate to this immature, hysterical, psychotic girl as to an adult' (Auerbach, 1963, pp. 142–3). The point is the same very general one, concerning the location of sources or causes of events in social systems, which we have considered in earlier chapters and to which we shall return again.

Heller *et al.* (1963) have also demonstrated the likely 'reciprocally contingent' (Jones and Thibaut, 1958) nature of psychotherapy interaction by showing that interviewer behaviour is affected by client behaviour very much in the manner suggested by Leary (1957). (See Chapter 2, p. 71, above.) Heller *et al.* trained each of four student actors to play a 'standard client role'. The roles were: dominant–friendly client, dominant–hostile client, dependent–friendly client, and dependent–hostile client. Each of thirty-four trainee psychotherapy interviewers interviewed each actor for thirty minutes within a period of twenty-four hours. The four interviews were held in counter-balanced order and were observed through a one-way mirror by a rater who rated the interviewer's behaviour on a form of the adjective check list (see Chapter 2, p. 67, above) modified so as to refer specifically to interviewer→actor–client behaviour.

The results were as predicted, and in fact they provide some of the strongest objective support for the hypotheses about the 'evoking' or 'prompting' of social behaviour put forward by Leary (1957) and discussed in Chapter 2 of this book. Actor–client dominance produced significantly *less* interviewer dominance than did actor–client dependence, and actor–client friendliness produced significantly *more* interviewer friendliness than did actor–client hostility.

The second matter of general interest arising from Mintz *et al.*'s (1971) analysis concerns the relationship between the dimensions and outcome. Outcome was rated by the therapists in a number of different ways but there were few straightforward relationships. However, a significant interaction was noted between the first two factors. Relatively high levels of treatment success and patient satisfaction were found under conditions which combined *either* high levels of 'optimal empathic relationship' and low levels of 'directive mode', *or* the reverse, namely high levels of directive mode and low levels of optimal empathic relationship. When both factors were high, or both low, the success plus satisfaction outcome criterion tended to be low also. This would seem to suggest that empathy, etc., may correlate positively with certain aspects of therapy outcome when the therapy is relatively 'non-directive', but that this relationship may not hold when therapy is relatively directive. Again the warning against simple generalizations in this field is clear.

Psychophysiological response in psychotherapy

Along a different line of research, attempts have been made to correlate aspects of the interpersonal situation between therapist and patient and aspects of the patient's bodily functioning. A study by McCarron and Appel (1971) is illustrative. They synchronized a continuous recording of patient galvanic skin response (GSR, a measure of sweating often used to give a psychophysiological indication of anxiety or arousal) and verbatim transcripts of twelve psychotherapy sessions from a *single* patient–therapist pair, as well as single sessions contributed by twelve *separate* patient–therapist pairs. They found it possible to code nearly all therapist verbalizations into one of four categories: 'confrontation', 'interpretation', 'interrogation' and 'reflection'. These categories were designed to reflect decreasing amounts of *information specificity*. Confrontation was considered highly 'specific'. It was of high information-value and was most limiting of the patient's options of what to say next. Reflections, at the other extreme, convey little information, are highly 'ambiguous', and scarcely limit the patient's response at all.

McCarron and Appel give a number of examples of what they mean by these categories. An example of confrontation would be a therapist statement such as, 'Whatever happened to make you think of yourself as so fragile as this?' As an example of interpretation, 'You wanted to be a child rather than take care of one' (in response to the patient's statement that she had never liked looking after children after helping to look after her little sister). Examples of interrogation would include, 'How do you feel about that?', 'When was the first time?', 'Do you have difficulty sleeping?'; and examples of reflection would include 'Mm-mm', 'I see', 'You feel nervous and panicky' (in response to the patient's statement, 'I have anxieties and fears').

Patient GSRs emitted during the five seconds following the completion of each therapist verbalization were compared between therapist verbalization categories. Both for the individual patient, in each of twelve sessions, and for each of the twelve separate patients, the type of therapist utterance was a major source of variation in patient GSRs (although there was, in addition,

Studies of the Psychotherapy Relationship   183

considerable variation between patients and also, for the single patient studied intensively, considerable variation from session to session). The order of the verbalization categories was as expected. Highest patient G S Rs occurred in response to confrontation by the therapist, and the lowest in response to reflection. Interestingly enough the therapists themselves were not immune to the physiological effects of their own verbalizations; when therapist G SRs were monitored in a similar way (except that therapist G SRs were measured for the five seconds *prior* to the completion of an utterance by the therapist) they were found to vary with the type of verbalization the therapist was making, in a very similar fashion.

The system of categories used by McCarron and Appel is of considerable interest and has been used in the same or similar form by other researchers. The different categories have obvious parallels in Auerbach's (1963) content categories, and Mintz *et al.*'s (1971) dimensions, as well as in the philosophies of a number of different psychotherapy schools. Furthermore the scheme would appear to have application beyond the psychotherapist–patient dyad and could conceivably have application in the analysis of family interaction sessions and indeed for an analysis of interpersonal behaviour in general. For example, the categories seem likely to have their counterparts in the circumplex schemes of interpersonal behaviour discussed in earlier chapters. Some further data on the categories from McCarron and Appel's (1971) study are of interest: In terms of frequencies of occurrence, confrontation was rare (only 4 per cent), the other three categories occurring much more frequently, interrogation being the most frequent (42 per cent). Nor were utterances in the different categories of equal duration; confrontations averaged sixteen words, interpretations thirteen, interrogations seven-and-a-half and reflection merely three.

Increasing psychotherapeutic attraction experimentally

Goldstein (1971) has pointed out that most of the evidence for the importance of the nature of the patient–therapist relationship in psychotherapy (there is even evidence of its importance with therapies which make use of specific techniques such as the behaviour therapies (Goldstein, 1971, pp. 36–7)) at best demonstrates merely an association between aspects of the relationship and treatment outcome, and hence provides little convincing proof that relationship factors are *causal*. In his book on *Psychotherapeutic Attraction* he summarizes a series of experiments which, as well as employing a strict experimental design and therefore offering the hope of establishing truly causal relationships, take the bold step of attempting to demonstrate the applicability to psychotherapy of a number of findings from general social psychology. A number of experiments are reported. Some involved psychiatric patients at hospital or clinic. Others involved students under counselling at a student counselling centre for problems of a mainly neurotic nature. Others employed students in analogue, simulated-therapy. Experiments with students are seen as 'bridging the gap' between findings from the social psychology laboratory and the applied field of psychotherapy.

One of the more convincing experiments in this series concerned 'therapist structuring' whereby subjects (graduate students in clinical psychology with an average age of twenty-five to twenty-six years) received prior information about a 'patient' via an 'intake staff report'. The first two paragraphs of this report were the same for all subjects and contained factual information about the 'patient', his reason for coming to the clinic and so on. Thereafter the report varied and different subjects received different information about diagnosis and about the 'patient's' motivation. There were three different diagnostic conditions ('neurotic', 'psychopathic', and no diagnosis given) and three motivational conditions (motivation for therapy said to be 'high', motivation said to be 'low', no comment made about motivation). All subjects then viewed the same film of the 'patient' (actually an actor playing the part of a middle-aged man seeking help with a drinking problem) being interviewed. The film was stopped on several occasions, each time for thirty seconds, and the viewer asked what he would say to the patient at that point. The responses were content analysed for 'empathy' and 'warmth' and in addition subjects filled out a number of questions and scales after seeing the film.

The results indicated that structuring for diagnosis affected empathy, warmth and subsequent attraction towards the 'patient' (highest levels of these variables being associated with the diagnosis 'neurotic' and lowest levels with the diagnosis 'psychopathic'). Structuring for motivation affected prognosis, willingness to treat the patient, and perceived similarity to the patient. The 'high motivation' label resulted in significantly more favourable prognostic estimates, greater willingness to treat the 'patient', and greater perceived similarity between the patient's age and the subject's age. This experiment seems to constitute a rather neat demonstration of the possibility of the biasing effect of interprofessional communication in the mental health field, and has obvious implications for the matters discussed in the previous chapter.

In other experiments attempts were made to modify the attractiveness of the therapist for the patient by such means as 'direct structuring' (involving messages suggesting that the therapist possessed particular characteristics such as 'warmth' or experience), or manipulations of the therapist's apparent status.

Summarizing the results of the whole series of experiments, Goldstein (1971, p. 164) concludes that the experimental manipulations derived from findings in general social psychology were mostly effective with YAVIS subjects (young, attractive, verbal, intelligent, successful; Schofield, 1964), but were mostly ineffective with non-YAVIS subjects (generally speaking the students were YAVIS subjects and hospital or clinic patients non-YAVIS). He suggests that this is hardly surprising when one realizes that many of the basic findings in general social psychology are derived from studies which almost exclusively use YAVIS students as subjects.

Some Special Techniques

So far in this chapter a rather general approach to the nature of the psychotherapeutic relationship has been adopted with little regard for the means whereby the therapist exerts his influence. The influence process in psychotherapy could be studied from a number of perspectives corresponding to the mechanisms which Strupp and Bergin (1969) have suggested underlie all the major forms of psychotherapy.

Imitation and modelling

One of these suggested mechanisms was 'imitation' which is worthy of special mention here in view of the link which the concept provides with general social psychology and with other areas of application of social psychology to mental disorder (see Chapter 1, pp. 23–5). One of a number of concepts (others are 'copying', 'observational learning', 'vicarious learning') used to describe the process of imitation is 'modelling'. The concept has been applied to traditional forms of psychotherapy on the assumption that the therapist serves as a model demonstrating desirable behaviours for the patient to imitate (Whalen, 1969). In addition a variety of attempts have been made to use the process explicitly in therapy. Most of these direct applications have so far used children or psychotic patients and have attempted to directly modify fearful behaviour, aggressive behaviour, mutism, etc. by having models demonstrate appropriate behaviour (Heller, 1969; Goldstein, 1971). There have been other studies on the effects of modelling on increasing 'appropriate' in-therapy behaviour. For example Schwartz and Hawkins (1965) constituted psychotherapy groups of schizophrenic in-patients in such a way that a high level of patient emotional expression would be modelled in one group, by two patients chosen for that purpose, a low level would be modelled by two chosen patients in a second group, and no models would be assigned in the third group. Over sixteen group sessions the group leader attempted to reinforce all emotional statements, but nonetheless significant between-group differences emerged as predicted. Patient emotional statements increased in rate over sessions in the first and third group but decreased significantly for the second group.

Goldstein (1971) reports an exploratory study of the clinical applications of 'planting' stooge patients whose task is to model appropriate social behaviour in psychotherapy groups. The study involved two groups; one consisting of six university students meeting at the university counselling centre, the second of six psychiatric out-patients. Each group had two therapists and in addition a graduate student planted as a 'patient'. The 'plants' modelled a variety of behaviours, as appropriate. Therapy supervisors, therapists and plants held regular planning and role-playing sessions in order to define and redefine the manner in which the plants could best serve the interests of their groups. For example, at an early stage the plants modelled a relatively high level of self-disclosure. At a later stage they modelled a wider variety of behaviours and played a variety of different roles. In some cases the intention was not to model behaviour which would be imitated by the group members but rather to enact a role which provoked other members into appropriate behaviour. For example, by enacting the role of 'opinion deviate' the plant attempted to provoke other group members into a greater cohesiveness. Although the study was exploratory and no controls were employed, both groups showed an increase in inter-member attraction over time and sociometric questions showed that the plants were consistently seen as the most pro-therapeutic members in their respective groups, although they were not the most popular.

In that study, of course, there was an element of deception involved. The 'plants' were not real patients, and it was necessary to maximize their credibility as models by providing each with a 'cover story'. In practice however, there seems no reason why 'plants' should not be ex-patients, or even patients who were 'senior' or advanced in their therapy. The similarity of plants and other group members, which this would ensure, would be likely to enhance modelling effects, and indeed most group psychotherapists probably unsystematically practice a degree of 'planting' of this sort.

Operant training in elementary social skills

Reward and punishment training was also amongst the common mechanisms listed by Strupp and Bergin (1969). Over recent years there has in fact been an ever increasing number of applications of operant conditioning procedures in the modification of disordered behaviour in children, institutionalized adults, and non-institutionalized adults (Bandura, 1970). In some cases the modification procedures have been in the hands of professional therapists whilst in many other instances nurses, parents, husbands and wives and other non-professional personnel have acted as the 'behavioural engineers'.

One example of this approach will suffice. It is of particular relevance here both because the reinforcements involved were partly social in nature, and because the 'target behaviours' included elements of skilled social performance. The subjects of the study by King *et al.* (1960) were described as 'schizophrenics with extreme symptoms' (p. 276) and were patients in a large locked ward of a mental hospital. A small number of these subjects were given 'operant-interpersonal' therapy three times a week for fifteen weeks. During this time they were trained to make increasingly more complex motor responses at a 'multiple operant problem-solving apparatus'. At the beginning patients were required simply to depress a lever for a reward of sweets, cigarettes or the presentation of a picture on a screen, along with definite social acknowledgement ('good', 'very good', 'good work', etc.). At a later stage more complex motor responses were required in response to visual stimuli (a certain type of movement was required following a green light, a further but different movement following an amber light and so on). Later still, verbal responses (for example to questions such as, 'Now where do you go next') were required for reinforcement (several of the patients had been mute at the beginning of therapy) and finally patients were required to cooperate in a team in order to obtain rewards. At first the therapist joined the patient in a two-man team, later patients were paired in patient–patient teams and finally teams were required to operate with other patients observing them. In this way behaviour was 'shaped', from the simple and solitary at the beginning, to the more complex and cooperative at the end.

Change was assessed in a number of ways including the use of an 'extreme mental illness schedule' involving ratings on a number of simple interpersonal tasks (e.g. responding to a hand shake, responding to the offer of a chair or a cigarette) and ratings of a variety of behaviours of social relevance, with the emphasis on non-verbal behaviours such as postures, gestures, etc. The operant-interpersonal method produced greater changes in scores on this schedule than were produced by verbal therapy, recreational therapy, or than occurred in patients who received no special treatment. It is interesting and instructive to consider the similarity of the effects, in terms of social behaviour, produced by this operant method and the 'social psychological' methods used by Fairweather (1964), whose work will be discussed in the following chapter (pp. 220–25), despite the radically different nature of the methods used.

Assertive training

Possible methods for training, or retraining, in social skills at a different level are illustrated by the work of McFall on the use of 'behavioural rehearsal' in assertive training. 'Non-assertive' subjects were obtained by advertising in student classes, '. . . for persons who feel they would like to be more assertive in various social situations. For example, such a person might find it difficult to deal with one of those salesmen who call you on the phone.' (McFall and Marston, 1970, p. 297.) The expectation was that these subjects would be 'similar to a clinical population of self-referred non-assertive subjects' (p. 297), although this seems somewhat unlikely to be the case. Before and after 'treatment' subjects took a test in which they were instructed to respond to a number of tape recorded stimulus situations requiring assertive responses. Examples of situations included in the test were: friends were interrupting the subject's studying; the laundry had lost his cleaning; the waiter brought him a steak that was too rare; his boss asked him to work overtime when he already had plans; someone pushed in in front of him in a theatre queue.

Those subjects who received the behaviour rehearsal treatment practised responding assertively to a number of similar situations (again tape recorded) and it was suggested that they should evaluate their performance by considering whether responses were direct and to the point, whether they really communicated the subject's feelings, etc. In some later sessions the subject heard on the tape a more extended encounter in which a moderately assertive response to the 'antagonist' was heard on the tape and the antagonist (e.g. the mechanic who had supposedly overcharged for servicing the subject's car) was heard to respond again. The subject was required to make an assertive 'counter-response'. Some of the behaviour rehearsal subjects received feedback on their performance by being able to listen to the play-back of their own attempts at making assertive statements. Others had no opportunities to get this feedback. In terms of post-treatment tests, behaviour rehearsal subjects, either with or without feedback, made greater improvements in assertive behaviour than did other students who received no treatment, or students who simply spent the time discussing their non-assertive behaviour with the therapist. There was a tendency for feedback to be an additional help (McFall and Marston, 1970).

To quote McFall and Lillesand (1971), this 'role-playing ... permits the patient to simulate problem situations and practice new modes of responding without concern for the immediate, real-life consequences of his experimental behaviour' (p. 314). In a later study by McFall and Lillesand, 'modelling' and 'therapist coaching' were added to the role-playing rehearsal used by McFall and Marston. Subjects were again a selected group of university students who identified themselves as people who found it difficult to assert themselves and who were willing to participate in a programme of 'treatment' designed to improve their assertiveness. Subjects were trained in the ability to 'refuse unreasonable requests' (e.g. being asked to lend a book to someone who had previously borrowed a book and failed to return it on time) and in addition to role-playing practice, subjects heard both a male and a female model respond to the taped situations in an assertive way, and received coaching regarding what constituted a good assertive response.

Similar procedures are now being used in a more general way, for example to 'improve the interpersonal functioning' of hospitalized mental patients (Vitalo, 1971), or to 'increase the social interaction of asocial psychiatric patients' (Gutride et al., 1973). Vitalo's account is of special interest because the declared aim of the training method adopted was to increase *patients'* levels of empathy, positive regard and genuineness, the very same 'skills' thought by some to be the makings of the good *therapist*.

The sorts of treatment régime outlined in this section follow from conceiving of some social problems in terms of lack of 'skill'. A common-sense approach to training a skill (e.g. driving a car) probably consists of some combination of demonstrating skilled performance (modelling), instruction (coaching) and providing opportunities for practice (role-playing). Whether or not such a common-sense approach has more than limited application in helping with the problems of people who are sufficiently upset to seek help of mental health experts remains to be seen.

Role-playing and attitude change

The term 'role-playing' has been used in at least two relevant contexts other than that of behaviour rehearsal. One of these concerns *attitude* rather than *behaviour* change. Amongst the variety of consistency theories in social psychology, dissonance theory (Festinger, 1957) is particularly concerned with the general motivation towards consistency between what a person thinks and feels and how he actually behaves. Contradictions between behaviour and attitudes are said to give rise to an unpleasant state of 'dissonance' which motivates the person concerned to reduce the discrepancy by changing either his behaviour or his attitude. The theory has received some application in the use of role-playing procedures for changing attitudes. The argument is that if a person can be given the opportunity to behave in a model fashion (and the more freedom of choice he feels he has in doing so, the better) then the contradiction between this and old attitudes will create the necessary motivation for attitude change. For example, in some of the original experiments on the phenomenon (e.g. Festinger and Carlsmith, 1959) students were induced to behave in a way inconsistent with their attitudes by being asked to describe, as interesting and exciting, a task which they had just performed and which they knew to be dull and boring. In other experiments attitude change has been brought about by having subjects make public speeches advocating certain positions on social issues (Janis and King, 1954).

Role-playing has been used in a similar way in an attempt to change racially prejudiced attitudes (Culbertson, 1957) and to change attitudes towards smoking (Janis and Mann, 1965). In the latter study each smoker acted the role of a patient who was informed that she had lung cancer, and who then discussed with her doctor preparations for hospitalization and surgery. This role-playing experience, which was described as being highly upsetting for the subjects, was followed by a greater subsequent reduction in cigarette smoking than was reported by subjects who witnessed such role-playing sessions but did not themselves take part.

Frank (1961) is well known for his view that the reorganization of beliefs and attitudes underlies a wide variety of change processes. He also believes that this reorganization is encouraged by high expectancy, by faith in the agents of change and their procedures, and by behaviour consistent with change (e.g. behaviour reflecting commitment to change and to procedures which are likely to bring change about, such as travelling to 'treatment', taking part in public 'confessions' concerning previous behaviours, etc.). There has been a number of recent suggestions that forms of behavioural treatment, such as aversion therapy, originally assumed to work through conditioning and learning, may at least partly have their effects through attitudinal change for which dissonance theory could account (Carlin and Armstrong, 1968; Feldman and MacCulloch, 1971; Rachman, 1972). In addition, many of the procedures such as public confession and commitment to change, used by self-help organizations such as Alcoholics Anonymous, Gamblers Anonymous and Weight Watchers, can be easily subsumed under the same principle.

Role-playing and psychodrama

Psychodrama (Moreno, 1946; Corsini, 1966) represents yet another relevant use of role-playing procedures which should not be confused with their use in behaviour rehearsal and attitude change. In these procedures patients act out interpersonal situations relevant to their problems, usually in front of fellow patients. Ingenuity alone sets the limit on the variations of this procedure which are possible. Corsini has outlined a number of basic role-playing formats which may be employed and some of these are illustrated in Table 9. It might be expected that A would gain a greater understanding of interpersonal events involving A and B, and perhaps a more accurate perception of B's position, on account of the variety of new perspectives with which A's parts in the role-

Table 9 Some basic psychodrama role-playing formats

A is the major participant and the psychodrama involves his/her relationship with B. The actors (A, B, C, D) are indicated by letters outside brackets and the parts they play by letters within brackets. A′ and B′ are A's and B's 'alter egos'.

Straight role-playing ⎱⎰	$A(A) \times B(B)$	i.e. A and B play themselves
	$A(A) \times C(B)$	i.e. A plays self but C takes B's part.
Role reversal	$A(B) \times C(A)$	i.e. A plays B and C takes A's part.
Alter ego	$A(A) \times C(B) \times D(B')$	i.e. A plays self, C plays B and D speaks what he imagines to be B's inner thoughts.
Mirror technique	$D(A) \times C(B)$	(A is a spectator) i.e. A watches while C plays B and D plays A.
Doubling	$A(A) \times B(A')$	i.e. A plays self and B speaks A's inner thoughts (A and B may stand back to back in this format).

(Based upon Corsini, 1966, Chapter 4)

played scenes provide him. The connection with concepts of interpersonal perception at various levels (see Chapter 3, pp. 100–103) is clear, and it is in the area of interpersonal perception that one might expect this type of role-playing to have its effects. Unfortunately there appear to have been few attempts to study the results of such procedures objectively.

Conclusions

The amount of research which has been done on the subject of psychotherapy is colossal and the illustrations given in this chapter can scarcely begin to do it justice. At best it has been possible to provide a glimpse of some of the lines of investigation which have been pursued. This area of study has become a specialized one and general references to other types of dyadic relationships with implications for mental disorder are rarely found. This is despite the fact that many of the concepts being used to describe elements of the psychotherapist–patient relationship are remarkably similar to those used in other contexts and referred to in earlier chapters of this book.

For example, there is considerable evidence for a major dimension of therapist behaviour which is associated with therapeutic effectiveness. This dimension may have much to do with the general 'non-criticalness' or 'warmth and affection' which are so prominent in discussions of family life and mental illness and, furthermore, there is evidence that this dimension is manifest as much on a non-verbal as on a verbal level, as the material reviewed in Chapter 2 would lead us to expect.

It is clear, however, that different psychotherapists have different styles of behaviour quite apart from their standing on the major dimension referred to above. In particular some therapists are more directive, more intrusive, more inferential, and more confronting. The relationship of these therapist behaviours to therapeutic outcome is likely to be a highly complex one, depending upon other aspects of the therapist's behaviour, aspects of the patient's behaviour and the particular outcome criteria involved. Research on psychotherapy dyads provides some of the best demonstrations of the 'reciprocally contingent' nature of social interaction: to a degree both therapist and patient 'train' the other to behaviour in a complementary fashion.

Attempts to experimentally manipulate therapist or patient attitudes, such as attraction, have not met with a great deal of success but, on the other hand, a number of specific therapeutic techniques have been successfully designed which take advantage of interpersonal processes and which aim to modify aspects of social performance. Amongst these are 'social conditioning' and 'modelling' in various guises and the use of role-playing and feedback directed at increasing socially skilled behaviour.

The individual psychotherapy setting is likely to be one that will continue to excite research interest, although it is to be hoped that it will be seen in a wider context.

Chapter 6

Sociotherapy:
The Use of the Treatment Context

Introduction

It can fairly be argued that the amount of research effort devoted
to the topic of psychotherapy has been out of all proportion to its
real importance. The overall usefulness of psychotherapy in the
treatment of mental disorder remains a very open question and
many people are unclear as to how the psychotherapist expects to
effect change when the techniques he uses concern, '. . . only a
small fraction of the total environmental stimulation to which the
patient is exposed' (Scheff, 1966, p. 17). There has in the past been
an over-emphasis on the events of the 'treatment hour' and insufficient attention has been paid to the events of 'the other
twenty-three hours' (Stanton and Schwartz, 1954, p. 9).

The most salient aspects of the patient's environment may consist of his family, his work, his leisure pursuits and so on. The importance of the first of these has been elaborated in Chapter 3.
There is however a growing awareness that contact with helping
agencies results in exposure to a wide range of experiences not all
of which occur in the specific context of 'treatment' or 'therapy'.
Of course this is particularly the case when the receiving of help involves temporary removal to a new residential setting.

The aspect of treatment milieux which has perhaps received
most attention is the social structure of the large traditional mental
hospital. Sociologists and psychiatrists have characterized many
such hospitals as highly authoritarian in the means whereby staff
maintain control over patients. Goffman's (1968) characterization
of the 'total institution' of the mental hospital in his book *Asylums*
is particularly well known. As Freeman and Giovanni have put it,
'The mental hospital has come under severe criticism for violating
the medical dictum "do no harm" . . .' (1969; p. 694). The terms
'institutionalization', 'institutionalism' and 'disculturation' have

been used to describe the supposed process whereby the demands of the social system of the mental hospital produce in its patients

Table 10 **The Psychotherapy–Sociotherapy Ideology (PSI) Scale**

(P items express the Psychotherapeutic position. S items express the Sociotherapeutic position.)

(1) A personal psychoanalysis is by far the most valuable part of a psychiatrist's training. (P)

(2) The use of the social milieu without specific treatments may help to get the patient over an acute episode, but it rarely effects any lasting improvement in the patient. (P)

(3) Staff meetings devoted to clinical case presentations should be open to all non-medical as well as medical personnel. (S)

(4) Psychodynamic interpretations to hospital patients by non-psychiatric personnel are likely to do more harm than good. (P)

(5) Those who take a mainly social milieu approach to hospital treatment of patients are for the most part unable to recognize and deal effectively with the deeper levels of personality. (P)

(6) The mental hospital psychiatrist should try to avoid informal social relations with his patients. (P)

(7) The psychiatrist's treatment of hospital patients would be greatly improved if he spent more time than he now does learning to utilize the hospital as a therapeutic influence and less time on individual psychotherapy. (S)

(8) If a hospital like this one had to choose between somatic and psychotherapeutic treatments, it would do well to choose psychotherapy. (P)

(9) The most important consideration in administering a hospital like this one is to make sure that patients get enough psychotherapy. (P)

(10) A good deal needs to be done to decrease the status differences that exist in this hospital. (S)

(11) A psychoanalyst who devotes himself primarily to intensive, long-term analysis of a few is failing to meet his social responsibilities. (S)

(12) A medical degree should not be a necessary prerequisite for practicing intensive psychotherapy. (S)

(Taken from Gallagher *et al.*, 1965, p. 304, Table 2)

states of apathy, depersonalization, resignation, dependence, loss of self-esteem, and reliance on fantasy (Caudill *et al.*, 1952; Wing, 1967).

A somewhat different way of looking at the mental hospital (different perhaps because they studied a different hospital) has been put forward by Braginsky *et al.* (1969). They think that the mental hospital serves as a sort of resort or 'cooperative retreat' and they liken the activities of patients there to week-end or holiday activities. They consider that the psychiatric examination, the diagnosis, the formulation of a treatment plan, and so on, are unnecessary ceremonies through which the poor, oppressed, tired and marginal in society have to go in order to get a rest. The mental hospital, they propose, would be better staffed by a hotel manager, with the help of such as teachers and artists to help inmates pursue a chosen activity.

Despite the interest which hospital milieux have provoked, not all helpers or practitioners are equally motivated to investigate or deliberately make use of the milieu in the treatment of mental disorder. Different treatment interests and ideologies operate here as they do in relation to the use of physical and drug treatments (see p. 179 above) and behavioural treatments. This was illustrated, for example, by Gallagher *et al.* (1965). Whether acutely ill mental hospital patients received psychotherapy or not depended upon characteristics of the patients (younger patients, less authoritarian patients, and higher social class patients were more likely to receive psychotherapy) but also depended on characteristics of the doctor's treatment ideology as assessed by a 'psychotherapy–sociotherapy ideology scale'.

Some of the items from the scale are shown in Table 10. If a patient had a doctor with a higher than average score he had a 60 per cent chance of receiving intensive psychotherapy, but if his doctor scored lower than average his chances were reduced to 35 per cent.

Attitudes of Hospital Staff
Custodialism v. humanism

There have been a number of studies of the attitudes of hospital staff. Gilbert and Levinson (1956), for example, studied at three

Massachusetts mental hospitals the variable of 'custodialism' (agreement with such items as 'As soon as a person shows signs of a mental disturbance he should be hospitalized' and 'Abnormal people are ruled by their emotions; normal people by their reason') versus 'humanism' (e.g. 'Mental illness is an illness like any other' and 'Patients are often kept in the hospital long after they are well enough to get along in the community') amongst staff (doctors, nurses, student nurses and attendants). There were fairly consistent differences between the three hospitals in terms of the custodialism of their staff, and consistent differences between status groups within each hospital (doctors being the least custodial and attendants the most). But *within* each status group *within* a hospital there were high positive correlations with broader aspects of personality; preference for a custodial orientation appeared to be part of a broader pattern of personal authoritarianism. Those in favour of custodialism towards mental patients tended, for example, to be in favour of a relatively autocratic approach to family life.

The results of this study provided a fascinating example of congruence between ideology at an individual personal level, and ideology at a collective policy level. Where the prevailing policy was relatively custodial, staff tended to subscribe to a custodial ideology and tended to be generally authoritarian in personality although the correspondence was of course far from complete. These results raise a number of questions relevant to organizations in general and not just to mental hospitals. For example,

To what extent do relatively homogenous systems maintain themselves by recruitment and selective maintenance of individuals whose personalities are receptive to the structurally required ideology? To what extent do systems change the personalities which initially are unreceptive to the prevailing policy? (Gilbert and Levinson, 1956, p. 271).

Pearlin and Rosenberg distinguished two separate elements in the 'humanistic' or 'democratic' approach of staff at a mental hospital. Two varieties of social distance might, in their view, separate staff from patients. One of these, 'status distance', concerned the 'extent to which nursing personnel are guided by a consciousness of their own status superiority in defining their relations with patients'. (Pearlin and Rosenberg, 1962, p. 56.) When status distance is high the nurse 'sees his relations with the patients in terms of a superordinate–subordinate arrangement' (p. 57). 'Personal distance', on the other hand, is high when there is, 'a lack of positive affect for patients ... lack of emotional attachment to patients ... no investment in relations with patients beyond that formally prescribed by the institution' (p. 57).

More than 1,000 nurses at a single US Federal mental hospital answered questions about the degree of their social distance from patients and a number of questions about their jobs. Questions about social distance included: 'You have to keep your distance from mental patients, otherwise they are liable to forget you are a nurse or a nursing assistant' (high status distance), 'One patient is more or less the same as any other' (high personal distance), and 'I often become quite personally attached to patients on my ward, and in a way I am sorry to see them leave the ward' (low personal distance) (Pearlin and Rosenberg, 1962, p. 58).

The important finding here was that whilst these two measures were correlated, the relationship between them was slight and the two scales correlated with different aspects of the job. *Status distance* tended to be high when nurses were themselves of relatively low status (e.g. not fully trained and therefore not able to obtain the rank of 'registered nurse'), when nurses were on wards with relatively 'low status' patients, and particularly when the nurse was, in addition, dissatisfied and felt that there were few career prospects. On the other hand *personal distance* tended to be low when nurses were assigned to patients of opposite sex (i.e. female nurses on male wards) and when nurses and patients were of similar ages. Pearlin and Rosenberg conclude that, whilst status-relevant aspects of the hospital regulate status distance from patients, status distance and personal distance are not the same and an authoritarian and hierarchical organization need not necessarily lead to high levels of personal distance.

Restrictive control and protective benevolence

Ellsworth (1965) assessed the degree of 'non-traditionalism' amongst sixty-five psychiatric hospital nurses and aides. Non-traditional staff were those who tended to reject statements such as: 'One of the main causes of mental illness is a lack of moral strength or will-power', 'When a person has a problem or worry it's best not to think about it, but keep busy with more pleasant things', and 'People who are successful in their work seldom become mentally ill.' In this sample traditionalism correlated positively with two other types of attitude, 'restrictive control' and 'protective benevolence'. Those who were restrictively controlling in attitude tended to agree with statements such as: 'Although patients discharged from mental hospitals may seem all right, they should not be allowed to marry', and 'People with mental illness should never be treated in the same hospital as people with physical illness.' Those whose attitudes were protectively benevolent tended to agree with items such as, 'Patients should never be locked up alone in an isolation room', 'Patients should be paid for any work they do in the hospital' and 'Mental patients who cause the least trouble in the hospital are likely to get along well after discharge.'

Unlike the study by Pearlin and Rosenberg (1962), an attempt was made in this study to find out what implications these attitudes had for staff *behaviour* as witnessed by patients. Patients were asked to describe each of the staff members with whom they came into contact in terms of a number of adjectives or phrases descriptive of interpersonal behaviour. The implications of non-traditional attitudes appeared to be considerable: there were high positive correlations with patient descriptions of staff as, 'sensitive and understanding', 'dependable and reliable', 'open and honest with me', and high negative correlations with items such as, 'hard-boiled and critical' and 'bossy and domineering'. Of particular interest was the nature of the descriptions assigned to staff relatively high on one or other of the two traditional attitudes. Those high on restrictive control tended to be described as 'impatient with others' mistakes' and 'hard-boiled and critical' and *not* 'sensitive and understanding' and 'open and honest with me'. Those high on protective benevolence tended to be described as 'stays by himself' and 'reserved and cool' and *not* 'lets patients get to know him' and 'talks about a variety of things'.

In some respects therefore the findings of this study show that attitudes such as restrictive control and non-traditionalism have rather predictable consequences. In other respects, relating to *protective benevolence* in particular, attitudes have consequences that might not have been so easily predicted. Staff members high on this attitude scale expressed attitudes that appeared to suggest 'kindliness towards patients' and yet they appear to have been seen by patients as basically aloof, distant and non-interacting. Ellsworth speculates that this type of staff member may find it preferable to indulge and placate patients and may therefore adopt a philosophy of 'it's better to leave the patient alone because if you confront him he just gets upset'. Such a philosophy may lead to telling the patient what he wants to hear rather than being 'honest and straightforward'. Maybe such staff are motivated to maintain 'a superficially comfortable relationship with the patient' (Ellsworth, 1965, p. 197).

Furthermore staff attitudes may have some of the practical consequences outlined by those who have written on institutionalism or disculturation. This is suggested by a study, by Cohen and Struening (1964), of the association between staff attitudes and discharge policies in twelve mental hospitals. Over 7,000 employees of these hospitals, in sixteen separate occupational groups, were given an 'opinions about mental illness questionnaire' which yielded scores, among other things, for authoritarianism and social restrictiveness. The seven hospitals whose staff in general had high scores on these two scales were compared with the remaining five in terms of the number of days which their patients spent outside hospital in the twelve months following admission. Even when 'days in the community' was adjusted for individual patient characteristics known to be associated with time spent out of hospital, patients from hospitals in the former group spent significantly fewer days in the community in the follow-up period. Cohen and Struening conclude that, 'The professional leadership which fosters authoritarian-restrictive attitudes amongst its employees also sets policies which delay the release of their patients' (1964, p. 297).

The effects of hospital policies and staff attitudes may be pervasive. Morgan and Cushing (1966) have considered the mental hospital patient's personal possessions, for example. They note large differences in the number of personal possessions of chronic patients in different hospitals and they attribute these differences very largely to hospital attitudes. For male patients, having a greater number of personal possessions was predictive of being out of the hospital three years later.

Individual Patterns of Adjustment to the Hospital

Needless to say, individual patients do not come empty-handed to treatment. They necessarily bring with them their personal modes of behaviour (some aspects of which will be construed as illness and others as personality or temperament) and these will interact with the social context to which they are exposed. For example, Morgan and Cushing (1966) noted that the number of personal possessions of long-stay mental hospital patients varied not only with the hospital, but with clinical condition also. The number of possessions was associated at a highly significant level with the severity of social withdrawal. Indeed, whilst some have emphasized the importance of the milieu in shaping treatment processes and outcome, others have stressed the individual contribution. We could at this point refer back to much of the discussion of Chapter 2 which suggested that recognized mental illness might be associated with or even preceded by, characteristic types of, or biases in, interpersonal behaviour and perception. In particular there was the suggestion that much of this could be subsumed under the very general phrase 'lack of social skills'.

The schizophrenic 'no-society'

Sommer and Osmond (1962) can be cited as an example of those who have emphasized individual factors contributing to the social organization and climate of chronic mental hospital wards. They argue that, typically, groups of patients on such wards do *not* constitute societies, communities, or cultures. They point to the absence of spontaneous cooperative activity amongst such patients, the absence of signs and symbols of a patient organization which does not derive directly from the staff, the absence of leaders, an absence of 'trading' or dealing between patients, an absence of organized protest or any sign of patient government, a noticeable absence of reciprocated friendships, and even very little conversation. They conclude that long-stay mental patients simply form 'aggregates' of discrete individuals and that 'the mental hospital is unique in the persistence of a no-society among people living together over long periods of time' (Sommer and Osmond, 1962, p. 252).

Although it is by no means clear how thorough were the observations upon which these conclusions were based, the picture presented by Sommer and Osmond probably conforms in general outline to the impression which the 'back wards' of a large mental hospital may convey. What many would dispute however is Sommer and Osmond's apparent assumption that this state of affairs is largely attributable to 'illness'. They write:

Schizophrenia has accomplished what no tyranny, no inhumanity of man to man, has ever been able to do – it has kept people from communicating with one another . . . it is surely more probable . . . that the lack of social organization . . . is an attribute of the most common illness found there than a consequence of hospital conditions (Sommer and Osmond, 1962, pp. 252–3).

Sociometry and sickness

Sommer and Osmond are careful to point out that their conclusions apply to long-stay mental-hospital patients and Caudill *et al.* had earlier emphasized the point that:

. . . psychoneurotic patients on a less disturbed ward of a mental hospital should not be thought of as an aggregate of individuals, but as a group which tries to meet many of its problems by developing a shared set of values and beliefs translated into action through a system of social roles and cliques (Caudill *et al.*, 1952, pp. 329–30).

Brown (1965) has discussed the evidence for and against the existence of an inverse relationship between having reciprocated friendships and degree of 'sickness'. In her own study of sociometric patterns amongst patients on an intensive treatment ward, she found a significant negative correlation between sickness ratings and the proportion of an individual's positive sociometric choices which were *reciprocated* by other people.

Murray and Cohen (1959) studied the sociometric choices of a total of more than a hundred patients in three wards of a large Army hospital. The three wards were ranked in terms of the degree of mental illness displayed by their patients. One was a control medical ward, the majority of patients having limb fractures or amputations. The second, an open psychiatric ward, contained patients with a variety of diagnoses but they were considered by the staff to be almost well enough to be returned to duty or otherwise discharged. The third, a locked psychiatric ward, contained patients whom staff felt to be considerably more disturbed; they were escorted to all activities and were not allowed passes. The wards were of roughly equal size but a number of major differences emerged. For a start there were differences in the average number of names of other patients which patients could state. The average medical patient knew around fourteen names compared to an average of nine and seven on the open and locked psychiatric wards respectively. There was variation between wards in the average number of *positive* sociometric choices made (4·1, 2·8, 2·3 respectively) and in the percentage of patients with one or more *positive reciprocated* choices (74 per cent, 50 per cent, 25 per cent). Interestingly enough the same trend was apparent with negative choices. Numbers of *negative* sociometric choices averaged 2·5, 1·5 and 1·0 and the percentages of patients on the three wards with one or more reciprocated negative choices were 26 per cent, 6 per cent and 0 per cent. Murray and Cohen take this to suggest that mental illness is associated with general withdrawal rather than with a differential effect on positive and negative aspects of interpersonal relationships. Whilst none of the medical control patients were 'total isolates' (i.e. receiving no choices at all from other patients) 18 per cent and 21 per cent were total isolates on the open and locked psychiatric wards.

McMillan and Silverberg (1955) had earlier attempted a similar study comparing five hospital wards, three psychiatric and two non-psychiatric. However, their methods of analysis were somewhat more complicated than those used by Murray and Cohen (1959) and the results less clear-cut. Although there was a tendency towards fewer reciprocated choices amongst patients on the psychiatric wards, the rank ordering of the psychiatric wards was not as predicted. In particular, the level of reciprocations was lowest amongst patients on a ward of anxiety neurotics and not, as had been expected, amongst patients on a closed ward composed chiefly of actively psychotic patients.

Patient roles and staff contacts

A study by Perrucci (1963) is of interest because it builds upon the traditional sociometric method of investigating patient–patient relationships. The study concerned an open ward of fifty-four female patients most of whom were diagnosed as having some type of schizophrenic reaction. The study concerned both the patient group structure and patient–staff social distance.

Patients were asked to nominate two fellow patients whom they would most like to room with, two whom they would least like to room with, and the one whom they would choose to be chairman of a committee of patients on the ward. In comparison with positive room-mate choices, negative room-mate choices and leader-choices were relatively highly concentrated on a few individuals. 50 per cent of the negative room-mate choices fell upon four particular patients and 50 per cent of the leadership choices were concentrated on only two patients. McMillan and Silverberg (1955) also found negative sociometric choices to be more concentrated than positive choices. The nature of staff–patient contacts in Perrucci's study was assessed by counting the number of individual contacts which each patient had with staff in the nurses' office over a period of fifty-six hours. The content of each contact was also categorized as either 'attention and information', 'service request', 'staff favour', 'criticism' or 'formal business'.

Patients who received most *positive* room-mate choices from fellow patients had relatively few contacts with staff and these were concentrated in the areas of 'attention and information' and 'service requests'. These contacts were seen as being within formal organizational bounds. On the other hand, those few patients who either received many negative room-mate choices from their fellow patients, or received many leadership choices, tended to have many more contacts with staff over the period of observation and a much higher proportion were in content areas involving departures from formal staff–patient roles. Those receiving many *negative* room-mate choices had many contacts in the area of 'staff favours' (e.g. patient to staff member: 'Can I get your lunch today?' or 'I'll go over and pick up the medicine basket'). These patients tended to identify closely with staff members, they did a great many favours for the staff, who become quite dependent upon their help and information. They were accorded certain privileges although from time to time staff took steps to restore a more formal relationship.

Those receiving many *leadership* choices showed more contacts in the areas of 'criticism' and 'formal business'. However, one of the two 'leaders' was relatively high on one of these contact patterns, the other being relatively high on the other. The 'formal leader' (high on formal business contacts) was in fact the elected ward president. The 'informal leader' (high on criticism) was reported by many of the staff to be the most troublesome patient on the ward. This patient was observed to come to the defence of almost any patient, against the ward staff, and appeared to be a means by which much of the unexpressed aggression and hostility of other patients could find some expression. Perrucci suggests that it is just because of this openly critical attitude, combined with the rather conservative leadership style of the 'formal leader', that the informal leader gained her popularity.

Although the numbers are very small it is interesting to note that staff were particularly likely to say of those few patients with many *negative* room-mate choices: 'As she is now you have to treat her firmly and let her know who is boss' and also 'If you don't watch her closely she'll try to run things her own way.' Such remarks are strikingly similar to remarks which some parents express about their children and which have been construed as displaying an 'autocratic' attitude.

Patient reputations

From a somewhat different perspective Fontana (1971) has considered the *reputations* which patients may acquire amongst staff during their stay in hospital. He had previously found there to be three factors amongst items of staff comment drawn from patient–staff meetings and ward rounds. Day nurses, evening nurses and doctors appeared to use the same factors in construing their patients' behaviour. The factors appeared to define the roles of 'critical manipulator', 'involved helper' and 'model patient'. The first was someone who tended to contest staff judgements and policies, to question staff decisions, to successfully persuade other people to grant their requests, to express anger to other patients and to disobey hospital rules. The 'involved helper' on the other hand was someone who tended to calm other patients, provide staff with information, be receptive to offers of help from other people, to speak up in meetings, to aid fellow patients in discussions with staff and to exercise leadership. 'Model patients' tended neither to contest, nor to work, with the staff. They gave a psychiatrically healthier appearance than others, showed steady progress in treatment, they obeyed rules, were liked by staff and were popular with fellow patients. Although Fontana assumed that reputations in this setting would develop in accordance with the principles of reputation formation applicable in any social system (i.e. as a product of continuing transactions and negotiations between the different role-occupants), he expected that reputations would also be partly a consequence of a general adaptational style adopted by the individual patient which would be independent of the specific context. In one respect, at least, the results bore out this expectation. In two separate studies, with different groups of patients, significant positive correlations existed between 'critical manipulator' reputation and scores on a scale of Machiavellianism (Christie and Geis, 1968) which is designed to measure the degree to which the individual adopts a 'cynical, exploitative, manipulative orientation towards interpersonal relations'. (Fontana, 1971, p. 253.) There was some suggestion that this correspondence was more likely to emerge in certain milieux. Where patients tended to be treated alike, in accordance with specified rules and procedures, the correspondence tended to be strongest. It was least strong where patients were treated individually and where important decisions were made on a one-to-one basis.

Patient hospital knowledge and activity

Individual styles of adaptation to the mental hospital have also been examined in a programme of research reviewed by Braginsky *et al.* (1969). For example, the selective acquisition of information about the hospital has been studied and reliable individual differences emerge. Some patients get to know more about the names of staff and locations of staff offices, whilst others get to know more about places for recreation, leisure and socializing and become more knowledgeable about such matters as visiting times. Cross-sectionally these interests were related to length of hospitalization: long-stay patients were less likely to know staff names and the locations of staff offices but were more likely to possess knowledge of other matters. At least for female patients, an early relative interest in, and knowledge of, non-staff areas was *predictive* of remaining for a relatively long time in the hospital. Braginsky *et al.* (1969) therefore argue that the relationship between length of stay and type of knowledge cannot solely be attributed to staff ignoring longer-stay patients. On the contrary they assume that patient 'invisibility' is largely due to individual differences in the rates with which patients attempt to *initiate* contacts with staff.

The types of activity which patients engage in are not accidental either. For each of a hundred patients the activities of a 'typical twenty-four-hour day' were categorized into three groups: 'on-ward activities', 'work', and 'off-ward socializing'. Activity styles were related to different types of information acquired about the hospital, and to attitudes towards mental illness, and were predictive of length of stay in the hospital. For example 'workers' were relatively unlikely to leave the hospital within the few months following the assessment whilst 'socializers' were relatively likely to.

Other important material on patient attitudes, or styles of adjustment, to hospitalization is to be found in Caine and Smail (1969) and Moos and Houts (1968).

Conflict in the Hospital
A case study of misunderstanding

Whilst the above investigations have concentrated on such matters as the reputations or staff contacts of individual patients, others have dwelt upon more general sources of staff–patient strain or discrepancy in values, ideologies, or ways of construing events. For example, Caudill has particularly noted the effects in the hospital setting of the psychiatric bias for interpreting patient behaviour 'almost solely in individual dynamic-historical terms', with little recognition of possible causes of behaviour lying in the immediate situation (Caudill *et al.*, 1952, p. 330). He further remarked that, in many instances, friction between patients and the hospital routine appeared to give rise to frustration which led to behaviour, on the part of patients, which closely resembled 'neurotic' behaviour which could have been attributable to personal emotional conflicts. In other words, neither an interpretation in situational terms, nor one in terms of individual psychopathology, had obvious superiority over the other, although staff observed by Caudill tended to favour explanations of the latter type.

In his book on *The Psychiatric Hospital as a Small Society*, Caudill (1958) provides a lengthy case history of the progress of one patient, Mr Esposito (a fictional name of course), during his eight-week stay. In this account he attempted to trace the origins and effects of a series of staff–patient interpretative discrepancies. The case history drew on material from a variety of sources including actual observations of the patient's behaviour, extracts from nursing notes and transcriptions of interchanges at staff meetings. The doctor's notes from the early period of the patient's stay make many references to the possibility of an organic diagnosis, and to the results of various tests relevant to such a diagnosis. The patient's account of the situational determinants of his behaviour, including conflicts with nursing staff, remained relatively unexplored. The patient was subsequently transferred to a locked part of the ward and negotiations between Mr Esposito, nurses and doctors clearly illustrates discrepant perceptual biases. One of the senior doctors displayed his preference for interpreting events in terms of individual psychopathology and is quoted as saying: 'The patient will have to show us that he can be calm and demonstrate his rationality before we let him out of seclusion.' (Caudill, 1958, p. 44.) Mr Esposito's view was quite different. He stated that he had been observing people for thirty years and in most of his dealings, 'It turned out that people had been bad to him' (p. 47). Events in the hospital had tended to confirm this.

Over the weeks he acquired a reputation amongst the nurses for being something of a clown, and joking remarks began to be passed about him at staff conferences. A content analysis of nursing notes about Mr Esposito showed that whilst the incidence of specific remarks about behaviour (e.g. 'He tore up bits of paper and gave them to X') exceeded the incidence of general remarks (e.g. 'Usual playful silly self') during the early weeks of Mr Esposito's stay, the reverse was the case towards the end. This seems to illustrate the hardening of his reputation. His behaviour had come to be seen, in some senses, as more predictable, and it was less likely to be examined in detail. Caudill comments upon the final note written by Mr Esposito's doctor about him at the time of his discharge. It dwelt almost entirely on the patient himself, his diagnosis, the insight he had gained, and his hostility towards the hospital and its staff. 'It failed to indicate the significance of the context of hospital life for this schizophrenic patient. As such, this final note read like hundreds of others to be found in the case records of almost any psychiatric hospital' (Caudill, 1958, p. 57).

Ideological conflict in a therapeutic community

Disparities between staff and patient views and values may of course take many different forms. Rapoport (1960), for example, records the disparity between treatment ideologies of staff and new patients at the social rehabilitation unit (now the Henderson Hospital) at Belmont Hospital in England. Staff tended to subscribe to the concept of the 'therapeutic community' (Maxwell Jones, 1953), and therefore tended to agree with propositions such as: 'Patients should help decide how their fellow patients should be treated', 'If a patient is very abusive or destructive in hospital, it is better to discuss it with him than to discipline him', 'If it were possible, staff and patients should share all facilities and activities in common – cafeterias, work shops, socials, meetings, etc.' and 'Everything the patients say and do while in hospital should be used for treatment.' They tended to disagree with propositions such as: 'Many things a patient thinks whilst in hospital are nobody's business but his own and he shouldn't have to talk about them', 'Psychiatric hospitals should provide a change from ordinary life with emphasis placed on rest, comfort, and escape from stress and strain' and 'Psychiatry is for the treatment of sick people and belongs in hospitals and doctors' offices, and not in homes, schools and outside communities.'

Whilst the majority of staff members held to most of these views, the majority of *new* patients did not. During the course of their stay most of the patients appeared to shift their values but most of these shifts were moderate in degree and as many patients shifted away from the general staff attitude as shifted towards it. However, patients who stayed for more than a hundred days in the unit were significantly more likely to shift *towards* the staff ideology, and those who did shift in that direction were more likely to be judged 'improved'.

Raphael *et al*. (1967) studied the attitudes towards mental illness of patients at a hospital dealing primarily with acute psychiatric problems and having a relatively high staff–patient ratio. The attitudes of patients being readmitted were more congruent with the views of a sample of psychiatrists and psychologists, than were the attitudes of a number of patients who were being admitted for the first time. A number of possible explanations could account for this difference, but as a follow-up study showed that attitudes congruent with the experts were predictive of *later* readmission, there is some support for an explanation in terms of a process of *selection* of patients for readmission (both patients and staff presumably being active in the process of selection) on the basis of expert or 'correct' views.

Inter-level staff conflict

Disparities may of course exist amongst staff themselves. Rapoport's data (1960, p. 65) show considerable variation in the treatment values of individual members of staff and Caudill (1958) has elaborated on this matter at some length.

In the small hospital which he observed in such detail there was much evidence of differences of opinion between nurses on the one hand, and doctors on the other. The former were, on the whole, charged with administrative responsibility, and the latter were largely engaged in psychotherapy. Furthermore, the hospital was at the time going through a transition period, changing slowly from a traditional approach to a more psychodynamic one. There appeared to be a broad, and not openly stated, disagreement between nurses and junior doctors, the former tending to think that the latter were too permissive with patients. In the case of Mr Esposito, for example, it was the nurses who were in favour of the patient's seclusion in a locked ward and the doctors who were in favour of his being allowed to stay on the open ward. The miscommunication, which appeared to be a result of these strains, had consequences in terms of misunderstandings over administrative decisions. Caudill described one such misunderstanding in detail. It concerned an unnecessarily time-consuming and fractious chain of events following the request of a group of patients to watch TV 'after hours'. The confusion which followed the presentation of the patients' petition on the matter appeared to indicate 'serious defects in making and channelling of observations about behaviour in the hospital system' (Caudill, 1958, p. 82). Nurses were in possession of information which would have placed the matter in its appropriate context for the benefit of all staff concerned. It was particularly important that the more senior doctors should know the background to the petition as the resolution of the matter was their decision. However, apparently because of the strain between staff levels and the differences in background and training of staff at different levels, the necessary information was not efficiently transmitted. In particular, information which gave evidence of, or was phrased in psychodynamic terms, was given greater weight at the staff conference and less weight was given to observations couched in administrative terms, which were the terms favoured by the nursing staff.

It may be noted here that Caudill's analysis of staff participation at daily administrative conferences illustrated dramatically the very general phenomenon of the interaction of individual personality and social role in interpersonal behaviour. It was found that senior staff consistently talked most, resident (junior) doctors next, and other personnel and nurses least. Consistent individual differences within these status-role groups were noted but they were less important as determinants of amount of talk. Even the most retiring resident doctor spoke more than the most assertive of nurses (Caudill, 1958, p. 337).

Symptom infection and interpersonal relationships

The question remains whether various aspects of interaction in a treatment setting (patient–patient, staff–staff, staff–patient), intriguing though their study may be, have any consequences, in the short- or long-term, for reducing the symptoms and increasing the health and happiness of the mentally ill. The study by Kellam and Chassan (1962), already referred to in Chapter 4, illustrates one of the ways in which this matter might be investigated. Essentially what they did was to examine the fluctuations in symptoms of a number of individual patients, and to look for parallels in the fluctuations of pairs of patients who might have influenced one another. Nurses and doctors rated the level of illness of each patient each evening for a total of eight months. The ratings were 'personal', i.e. each separate patient had his own rating scale couched in terms of his own particular symptomatology. Each patient's sequence of ratings was correlated with that of every other patient. The 300 correlation coefficients (from twenty-five patients) ranged from high negative values to high positive values (approximately half were positive and half negative), but the distribution of correlations showed many more to be significant than would have been expected by chance alone.

The effects of race and education upon the ebb and flow of symptoms in different patients were detected by this method. All six inter-correlations from the four black patients on the ward were positive, and when the four most racially prejudiced white patients were selected, on the basis of staff knowledge about them, fourteen of sixteen correlations within black–white patient pairs were *negative* (nine were significantly negative and none significantly positive). It seemed that the black patients tended to be well together and sick together, and the most racially prejudiced white patients on the ward tended to be well when the black patients were sick, and vice versa. When white patients were divided into groups, in accordance with the level of education they had received, a regular increase in average correlation with black patient sequences was apparent; better educated white patients had on average the most positive correlations with black patients and the least well educated had the most negative correlations.

The method did not detect any systematic effect of friendship or antipathy other than that between patients of different races. Kellam and Chassan suggest that race and education, being static attributes, may have had effects lasting over a period long enough to be detected by this method whereas other aspects may have been insufficiently long-lasting to be detected. Nonetheless they speculate that negative, hostile, competitive relationships between patients may be responsible for negative correlations. Subsequent interviews with patients suggested that certain individuals and certain relationships held key positions in the social organization of the ward. For example, one relatively stable and tranquil middle-aged woman was mentioned by a number of fellow patients as being a source of their own symptom fluctuations. They hypothesize a 'growing ground swell' (Kellam and Chassan, 1962, p. 379) with symptom increase in one patient, particularly if that patient is a key patient, being followed by increasing symptomatic behaviour on the part of other patients who are positively associated with this source person.

Oscillations in ward atmosphere

Rapoport (1960, Chapter 6) introduced the concept of 'oscillation' in the 'emotional climate' and social organization of the therapeutic community. In periods of greatest equilibrium, tension was relatively low and patients' behaviour largely conformed to expectations. At other times incidents of deviant behaviour became more frequent, interpersonal tensions were generated, defensiveness, aggression and withdrawal occurred, and attendance at groups and other indices of participation showed a decline. Disintegration might reach crisis proportions, and at such times disturbances on the ward at day and night, as well as outside complaints from local citizens, the police or the larger hospital, placed severe strains on staff. Coincidentally with these changes in 'atmosphere' Rapoport reported changes in patient treatment values and patient–staff disparities. It was his impression that periods of equilibrium were characterized by consensus about values but that, at other times, 'anti-unit' values were more openly expressed. At such times prestige among patients was to be gained by demonstrating such *deviant* values, whilst patients who were staunch supporters of the unit ideology became targets for the hostility of other patients. Attitudes towards important aspects of the treatment process appeared to be much affected; communication with staff, which in better days was seen as commendable, was increasingly seen as 'squealing', helping an uncommunicative patient to discuss his problems in groups was called 'needling' and staff were increasingly called 'snoopers' (Rapoport, 1960, pp. 135–42, 155–8).

Collective disturbances

Caudill too was convinced that aspects of the wider social organization of the hospital had implications for patient care. As he put it, 'the patients became heir to many of the tensions which more properly belonged to the staff' (Caudill, 1958, p. 322). Material from another part of his book adds further weight to this conclusion. He hypothesized a 'covert emotional structure' to the hospital which affects all, staff and patients alike, but operates largely out of awareness and is maintained even during periods when overt communication at a cognitive or informational level has partly or completely broken down. 'Mood sweeps' may occur (see Kellam and Chassan, 1962, above) which may develop into 'collective disturbances' if they are severe enough.

Caudill made a number of attempts to quantify aspects of the hospital's social organization and at least one of these produced some revealing results. Different types of remarks made in daily administrative conferences over a period of several weeks were counted. An 'index of withdrawal' was calculated by expressing the number of topics brought up in any one week which were restricted to the bare reporting of descriptive material, as a proportion of the total topics brought up in that week. Total topics included 'questions' and 'requests'. It follows that when the index of withdrawal was high, relatively few questions were being asked and/or relatively few requests being made. It was felt that more 'push' was required to make a request or raise a question, and that when staff confined themselves largely to reporting descriptive material they were tending to withdraw from active participation.

An 'index of administrative difficulty' was calculated by expressing the number of administrative topics as a proportion of total topics (which included matters relating to therapy and 'human relations'). Thus when the index is low, administrative matters are receiving relatively less attention than at other times.

In fact the major administrative misunderstandings (the TV petition and the moving of the locked ward patients), as well as the major collective disturbance, all occurred towards the end of a period of apparent withdrawal and avoidance of discussion of administrative matters at the daily conferences.

Schottstraedt *et al.* (1963) have attempted to illustrate how physiological processes, and the emergence of signs and symptoms of psychosomatic illness, are associated in time with interpersonal stresses and strains on a metabolic ward, and Stanton and Schwartz (1954) have provided detailed accounts, in their much quoted book, *The Mental Hospital*, of the coincidence of tensions, at staff level, and patient symptoms and behaviours such as agitation and incontinence.

Alternatives to Custodialism

One way of offsetting some of the difficulties in the social organization of the hospital would be to have a 'clinical social scientist' appointed to watch over such matters and to feed back his observations constantly (Caudill, 1958, Chapter 14). Another would be to experiment with alternative residential settings (Caudill *et al.*, 1952) such as half-way houses (Raush and Raush, 1968; Keller and Alper, 1970), community lodges, farms, etc. (e.g. Fairweather *et al.*, 1969). Doubtless, though, alternative settings give rise to problems in social organization, some new and some familiar. For example, collective disturbances similar to that described by Caudill (1958), and apparently having multiple causes at all levels of organization, have been noted in alcoholism rehabilitation half-way houses (Otto and Orford, 1976).

The alternative that has perhaps received most attention is the idea of harnessing the tensions that arise amongst and between patients and staff for therapeutic benefit. The idea is of course one of the core ideas of the 'therapeutic community' (Maxwell Jones, 1953; Rapoport, 1960). Rapoport discerned four themes which he felt covered what was particularly distinctive about the ideology of the therapeutic community which he studied. These were: 'democratization', 'permissiveness', 'communalism' and 'reality confrontation'. It was the unit's view that decision-making about the community's affairs should be shared equally amongst members of the community; that all members should tolerate from one another a wide degree of behaviour that would normally be thought distressing or deviant; that the atmosphere should be informal, everything should be shared and relationships should be close but never exclusive; and finally that patients should be continuously given interpretations of their behaviour as other members of the community saw it. Status-role divisions, observed by Caudill (1958) for example, would be minimized thereby, a high premium would be placed upon good communication, and tensions, misunderstandings and disturbances would be used to throw light on patients' 'personality disorders' in an attempt to aid in their correction (Rapoport, 1960, pp. 54-64).

Despite the widespread enthusiasm which there continues to be for the idea of the therapeutic community it has been pointed out that the concept is vague and that the effectiveness of a therapeutic community is extremely difficult to evaluate (e.g. Freeman and Giovanni, 1969). The term 'therapeutic community' certainly overlaps in meaning with a number of other terms such as 'milieu therapy', 'relationship therapy', 'administrative therapy', 'sociotherapy' and 'collective therapy'. Some of the dangers, for example the danger of indoctrination into the ways of a particular community and dependence upon the authority of the leader of the community, have been pointed out by others (e.g. Zeitlyn, 1967). Rapoport too has discussed at length some of the inherent contradictions of the concept. He noted, for example, that the ease with which the themes or principles of the community's ideology could be applied varied with the state of the unit's social organization. High levels of permissiveness, democracy, and so on, could be maintained without much difficulty at periods of equilibrium and low tension, but tension was not usually allowed to rise above a certain level without staff intervention. At some point limits were set upon permissiveness and the 'latent authority' of the staff was exercised (Rapoport, 1960, p. 141).

The individual in context

Once again it is necessary to remind ourselves of the probable importance of individual 'disorder'-related differences. Rapoport, for example, stressed the importance of patient group composition in the therapeutic community. He referred to the disturbing and destructive influence of new patients 'of exceptionally disruptive or psychotic personality' (Rapoport, 1960, p. 144). He declared that the unit could accommodate only a certain proportion of such individuals and the aim had to be a balance analogous to that of a 'balanced aquarium'. Removal of the more disruptive individuals by discharge, or transfer to more traditional wards of the mental hospital, figures large in Rapoport's account of the actions which were taken at periods of extreme social disorganization in order to restore equilibrium (pp. 135–45).

Individuals *do* have different temperaments, and varying degrees of disorder or illness, and these are bound to interact with aspects of the social setting. Both sets of variables, the individual and the contextual, need to be taken into account if anything like an adequate understanding of what is going on in a treatment setting is to be achieved.

The matter is highly complex and the methodological problems in the way of objective study of such 'treatment' systems are formidable. The problems are the same as those outlined in earlier chapters of this book when considering the relative contributions of family environment and individual characteristics for the development of (Chapter 1, pp. 46–9), and recovery from, (Chapter 3, pp. 117–22), mental disorder.

Murray and Cohen's (1959) study of the sociometric organization of different wards also suggested the importance of both individual and contextual factors. Although their major finding concerns the different nature of organizations on wards containing patients with different degrees of mental disorder, a subsidiary study pointed to the importance of the milieu. The organizations on two psychiatric wards with roughly similar types of patient (one using milieu therapy, the other using somatic therapy on a closed ward) were compared with that on a non-psychiatric control ward. The degree of social organization on the milieu therapy psychiatric ward was very similar to that on the control ward, but that on the somatic therapy psychiatric ward was significantly different. Only a minority of patients on the latter ward were involved in reciprocal relationships.

An experiment in non-traditionalism

The considerable difficulties in the way of evaluating the effectiveness of attempts to harness aspects of the social context of treatment for therapeutic benefit have already been referred to, as have the difficulties of studying the contributions of individual and contextual factors simultaneously. One investigation which goes a long way towards accomplishing both is that of Fairweather (1964). In his book entitled *Social Psychology in Treating Mental Illness*, he and his colleagues present in detail the results of randomly assigning mental hospital patients to one or other of two wards; a 'small-group ward' and a 'traditional ward'.

The programmes on the two wards were designed to be identical in all but a few important respects. Table 11 shows the daily schedules for the patients on the two wards. The differences concern two of the morning hours during which patients on the small-group ward engaged in a group ward housekeeping task and later met together as a group to discuss decisions and recommendations about group members. Traditional ward patients had individual jobs assigned to them instead. The differences between the wards were in fact much more fundamental than the daily schedules alone would suggest. In the traditional programme all patient problems were discussed individually with staff members and staff made final decisions about all matters. A psychologist was responsible for scheduling patient activities, discussing problems with patients and leading meetings. Other members of staff (nurse, psychiatrist, social worker) occupied their traditional roles. On the small-group

Table 11 **Daily Ward Schedules**

		Small-Group Ward	Traditional Ward
A.M.	6.00– 6.30	Lights on in dormitory	Lights on in dormitory
	6.30– 7.30	Bedmaking, shaving, bathing	Bedmaking, shaving, bathing
	7.30– 7.55	Breakfast	Breakfast
	7.55– 8.00	Medication	Medication
	8.00– 9.00	Task group ward housekeeping	Individual work assignments
	9.00–10.00	Ward meeting hour	Individual work assignments
	10.00–11.00	Recreation hour	Ward meeting hour
	11.00–12.00	Autonomous meetings of task groups	Recreation hour
P.M.	12.00–12.05	Medication	Medication
	12.05–12.30	Free time	Free time
	12.30– 1.00	Lunch	Lunch
	1.00– 4.00	Individual work assignments	Individual work assignments
	4.00– 5.30	Ward activity – patients' choice (recreation, shower, socialize, etc.)	Ward activity – patients' choice (recreation, shower, socialize, etc.)
	5.30– 6.10	Dinner	Dinner
	6.10– 9.00	Off-ward recreation i.e. library, dance, etc.	Off-ward recreation, i.e. library, dance, etc.
	9.00– 9.05	Medication	Medication
	9.05–10.00	Free time	Free time
	10.00	Bedtime	Bedtime

(Taken from Fairweather, 1964, p. 28, Table 3.1)

ward, on the other hand, the patient was immediately, on admission, introduced to his own task group who were made responsible for orienting him to the ward. The task group was responsible for the successful completion of ward assignments and for the individual progress of its members through a number of graded steps. Pocket money, week-end passes and other privileges were assigned in accordance with this step-wise progress and it was the function of the task group, who met on their own without staff members on four days out of every week, to make recommendations about the upgrading of individual members of their group or about any other matter relating to patient problems. Staff roles were also quite different as a consequence. The total experiment was conducted for twenty-seven weeks and staff switched wards half-way through the experiment so that half were on the traditional ward first and the other half were on the small-group ward first.

The immediate effects of the different structures were seen in a number of different ways. Dramatic differences were apparent, for example, in terms of a 'location activity inventory'. The locations, and activities, of all patients were noted, on a time-sampling basis, during the recreation hour following the large ward meeting. Very basic aspects of social behaviour were affected. The number of patients observed to be talking to other patients was significantly greater on the small-group ward (see Figure 10). The more demanding or complex the category of social behaviour counted, the more the incidence of behaviour on the small-group ward exceeded that to be found on the traditional ward. For example, the number of times three or more patients were seen to be interacting together was exceedingly small on the traditional ward but considerably greater on the small-group ward. Patients were more likely to be observed asleep or inactive on the traditional ward and more incidents of 'pathological behaviour' were observed there (but only for the second period of the experiment after the 'staff switch'). The differential responses of patients to pathological behaviour in fellow-patients was noted. Whilst hallucinating patients on the traditional ward typically drew no interest or attention from others, bizarre behaviour on the small-group ward met with concern, particularly from the task group leader with special responsibility for the patient concerned.

However, the importance of individual 'disorder'-related differences was also noted. Whilst there was a significant difference in 'talking' between the two wards, there was also a significant difference across four patient diagnostic groups. Non-psychotic patients

Figure 10 Percent of 'Location Activity Inventory' Observations Showing Talking Behaviour for each Treatment Programme.

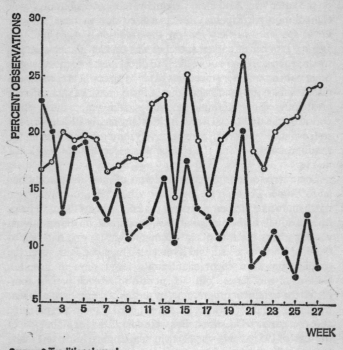

●━━━● Traditional ward
○━━━○ Small group ward

(Taken from Fairweather, 1964, p. 73, Figure 4.8)

talked most, and psychotic patients with periods of hospitalization totalling more than four years talked least. Nonetheless for each diagnostic group the incidence of talking was greater on the small-group ward.

There were also major inter-ward differences in behaviour during large-group ward meetings. There was a great deal of silence during these meetings on the traditional ward but scarcely any silence at all on the small-group ward. Two or more patients were much more likely to be observed speaking at once during groups on the latter ward, and there were many more occasions on which eight or more participants joined in a discussion on the same topic. Fewer patients participated on the traditional ward and the average number of patient speeches was smaller. Patients on the small-group ward were more likely to direct their speeches towards other patients and were much less likely to direct them towards the discussion leader. Staff behaviour in these meetings was different also; both sets of staff found themselves talking more during their period on the traditional ward. Incidentally nearly all categories of staff evaluated their role more positively during their period on the small-group ward, and the change was especially noticeable for nurses.

There were other differences in terms of patients' perceptions and attitudes. For example, patients on the small-group ward were much more likely to perceive other patients as being the most helpful individuals in their hospital lives. In contrast, on the traditional ward, patients more frequently thought that no one had helped them, or if someone had, that it was a staff member. Patients on the small-group ward spent significantly fewer days in hospital. Follow-up was carried out, six months after each patient completed the treatment programme, by means of a questionnaire sent to an individual with whom the patient lived (usually the patient's wife or a parent). Questionnaires were completed for all but five of the total of 195 patients who participated. Comparisons were made in terms of a number of factors. In comparison with the dramatic differences in in-hospital behaviour, differences in community adjustment, assessed by questionnaire returns, were disappointingly slight. However, nearly all differences were in favour of patients who had experienced the small-group ward and differences were larger in terms of some criteria than others. There was a significant difference, for example, in terms of 'verbal communication with others', small-group patients being more likely to be rated as 'often talks'. Small-group patients were also more likely to be rated as getting together with friends regularly and were significantly more likely to be employed (54 per cent of small-group patients versus 38 per cent of traditional ward patients). Other differences were insignificant and particularly disappointing were the almost identical figures for 'appraisal of illness'. Slightly less than half of both groups of patients (43 per cent small-group versus 46 per cent traditional group) were rated as being 'well most of the time'.

Conclusions

Just as parents have different attitudes towards the caretaking of their children so staff of institutions with responsibilities for caring for psychologically disordered people vary in their attitudes. Humanistic and democratic attitudes are likely to be conveyed to patients, perhaps via the same general types of behaviour shown to be facilitative in a family context, and result in patients holding corresponding opinions about members of staff. As in other institutions, processes almost certainly occur whereby there is a greater degree of similarity amongst members of one institution, or part of an institution, than exists across institutions.

Ideologies and styles of staff–patient interaction can be modified by social engineering, sometimes with the help of new concepts (e.g. 'the therapeutic community') and such changes may well have a profound influence upon the overall atmosphere and the behaviour of all concerned. On the other hand, whether these changes make very much difference to the behaviour of individuals once they leave that setting is doubtful.

Other material presented in this chapter shows how much room there is for further study of interactions between patients, and between members of staff. Relationships amongst members of staff are complicated by the existence of different groups with different training and status and the conflicts which frequently occur can have implications for patient care. It has also been shown that relationships within the patient group can affect 'symptomatic' behaviour.

This chapter has illustrated an important general theme, namely the importance of both individual and system factors. The social life of a communal treatment setting is influenced by the characteristic behaviours of its members as well as by its own planned or unplanned milieu.

General Conclusions

For a book which has taken such a rapid and broad sweep, and which had as its purpose the stimulating of interest, no summary as such is in order. It has either succeeded in stimulating interest, or has failed to do so. Nonetheless, two major conclusions may perhaps be drawn.

The first conclusion concerns the state of the science. Clearly it is very early days yet. The same perhaps can be said about social psychology in general. Nothing much is known that isn't open to dispute. There are at least two identifiable reasons for this: one concerns assumptions which have been made about the nature of social events, the other has to do with the availability of useful descriptive techniques.

Much of the research covered rests on the assumption that it is possible, by careful observation or reconstruction of past events, or by the application of sophisticated statistical techniques, to unravel the contributions to current events made by each of several social participants. Mostly such studies set out with one-sided hypotheses: for example, that parental warmth is responsible for child mental health, that husband subordination of wife is responsible for her relapse, or that schizophrenia is responsible for apathy on a mental hospital ward. Mere lip service is paid to the interactional, or reciprocally contingent nature, of social events. We have a sort of *individual* social psychology. Strangely enough, the simplicity of these assumptions leads to the mounting of research which attempts to answer huge questions which are quite beyond its scope. Research has too often tried to isolate causes, sometimes supposing that causes can be found even in events quite remote in time from the events which they are supposed to have caused. Effort would be better spent in taking the pains to make careful observations of current events. Or, if it is required that something be said about cause and effect, then the careful monitoring of current social action, preferably carried out within an experimental design, is what is required. The results may be salutary, as in Fairweather's (1964) experiment. Despite dramatic effects, of social engineering on a hospital ward (in terms of immediate social behaviour), long-term effects were minimal.

Even if, with due modesty, we settle for descriptive study, we may still find that the necessary work to develop the basic tools of the trade has not been done. The establishment of a science often rests very heavily upon the development of techniques. This field has very few techniques of any great power, and serious questions remain about the capacity of the few techniques we do have, such as the adjective check lists, repertory grid, and revealed differences methods.

A second major conclusion concerns the fragmentation of the overall area. On the whole, up to now, research workers have been specialists; interested in child development, marriage, psychotherapy or the hospital milieu, but rarely contributing to more than one of these 'problem' areas. As Heller (1972) has put it:

> In the past, researchers concerned with dyadic interactions tended to emphasize differences between situations rather than highlighting possible commonalities ... [researchers] ... have been notorious for their emphasis on the uniqueness of the phenomena they have been investigating. But this parochial orientation is now changing (Heller, 1972, p. 11).

A variety of themes can be seen to cut across the topics discussed in different chapters of this book. The two-dimensional or circular structure of ratings of interpersonal behaviour (whether of parents, patients or psychotherapists); the importance of non-verbal aspects of interpersonal behaviour for establishing relationships; conflict in social organizations (families with children, marriages, hospitals, halfway houses); construct systems and assumptions (as part of a general 'implicit personality theory', in the perception of a spouse's deviant behaviour, a professional helper's way of looking at the behaviour of his/her charges); modelling as a means of social influence (from parent to child, spouse to spouse, therapist to patient, patient to fellow patient) – these are amongst the general themes which offer some hope of a coherent, systematic, application of social psychology to the problems of mental disorder.

References

ADLER, A., (1929) *The Practice and Theory of Individual Psychology*, Tr. by P. Radin (1946), Kegan Paul.

AINSWORTH, M. D., (1962) 'The Effects of Maternal Deprivation: A Review of Findings and Controversy in the Context of Research Strategy', *Deprivation of Maternal Care: A Reassessment of its Effects*, World Health Organization.

ALANEN, Y. O., (1966) 'The Family in the Pathogenesis of Schizophrenic and Neurotic Disorders', *Acta Psychiatrica Scandinavia*, supplement, vol. 42, no. 189.

AMDUR, M. J., TUCKER, G. J., DETRE, T., and MARKHUS, K., (1969) 'Anorexia Nervosa: an Interactional Study', *Journal of Nervous and Mental Disease*, vol. 148, pp. 559–66.

ARGYLE, M., (1969) *Social Interaction*, Methuen.

ARGYLE, M., ALKEMA, F., and GILMOUR, R., (1971) 'The Communication of Friendly and Hostile Attitudes by Verbal and Non-Verbal Signals', *European Journal of Social Psychology*, vol. 1, pp. 385–402.

ARGYLE, M., and KENDON, A., (1967) 'The Experimental Analysis of Social Performance', in L. Berkowitz (ed.), *Advances in Experimental Social Psychology*, vol. 2, Academic Press.

ARGYLE, M., and MCHENRY, R., (1971) 'Do Spectacles Really Affect Judgements of Intelligence?', *British Journal of Social and Clinical Psychology*, vol. 10, pp. 27–9.

ARGYLE, M., SALTER, V., NICHOLSON, H., WILLIAMS, M., and BURGESS, P., (1970) 'The Communication of Inferior and Superior Attitudes by Verbal and Non-Verbal Signals', *British Journal of Social and Clinical Psychology*, vol. 9, pp. 222–31.

ARGYLE, M., and WILLIAMS, M., (1969) 'Observer or Observed?: A Reversible Perspective in Person Perception', *Sociometry*, vol. 32, pp. 396–412.

ARONSON, E., and CARLSMITH, J. M., (1962) 'Performance Expectancy as a Determinant of Actual Performance', *Journal of Abnormal and Social Psychology*, vol. 65, pp. 178–82.

ARONSON, J., and POLGAR, S., (1962) 'Pathogenic Relationships in Schizophrenia', *American Journal of Psychiatry*, vol. 119, pp. 222–7.

ASCH, S. E., (1946) 'Forming Impressions of Personality', *Journal of Social Psychology*, vol. 41, pp. 258–90.

AUERBACH, A. H., (1963) 'An Application of Strupp's Method of Content Analysis to Psychotherapy', *Psychiatry*, vol. 26, pp. 137–48.

BAGLEY, C., and EVAN-WONG, L., (1970) 'Psychiatric Disorder and Adult and Peer Group Rejection of the Child's Name', *Journal of Child Psychology and Psychiatry*, vol. 11, pp. 19–27.

BANDURA, A., (1970) *Principles of Behaviour Modification*, Holt, Rinehart & Winston; (1971) 'Analysis of Modeling Processes', in A. Bandura (ed.), *Psychological Modeling: Conflicting Theories*, Aldine-Atherton.

BANDURA, A., and WALTERS, R. H., (1959) *Adolescent Aggression*, Ronald Press.

BANNISTER, D., (1965) 'The Genesis of Schizophrenic Thought Disorder: Retest of the Serial Invalidation Hypothesis', *British Journal of Psychiatry*, vol. 111, pp. 377–81.

BANNISTER, D., and FRANSELLA, F., (1966) 'A Grid Test of Schizophrenic Thought Disorder', *British Journal of Social and Clinical Psychology*, vol. 5, pp. 95–102.

BANNISTER, D., and MAIR, J. M. N., (1968) *The Evaluation of Personal Constructs*, Academic Press.

BATESON, G., JACKSON, D., HALEY, J., and WEAKLAND, J., (1956) 'Toward a Theory of Schizophrenia', *Behavioural Science*, vol. 1, pp. 251–64.

BAUMRIND, D., and BLACK, A. E., (1967) 'Socialization Practices Associated with Dimensions of Competence in Preschool Boys and Girls', *Child Development*, vol. 38, pp. 291–327.

BEAKEL, N. G., and MEHRABIAN, A., (1969) 'Inconsistent Communications and Psychopathology', *Journal of Abnormal Psychology*, vol. 74, pp. 126–30.

BELL, R. Q., (1968) 'A Reinterpretation of the Direction of Effects in Studies of Socialization', *Psychological Review*, vol. 75, pp. 81–95.

BERKOWITZ, L., (1969) 'Resistance to Improper Dependency Relationships', *Journal of Experimental Social Psychology*, vol. 5, pp. 283–94.

BERNE, E., (1968) *Games People Play*, Penguin.

BERZINS, J. I., BARNES, D. F., COHEN, D. I., and ROSS, W. F., (1971) 'Reappraisal of the A–B Therapist Type Distinction in Terms of the Personality Research Form', *Journal of Consulting and Clinical Psychology*, vol. 36, pp. 360–69.

BETZ, B. J., (1967) 'Studies of the Therapist's Role in the Treatment of the Schizophrenic Patient', *American Journal of Psychiatry*, vol. 123, pp. 963–71.

BHAGAT, M., and FRASER, W. I., (1970) 'Young Offenders' Images of Self and Surroundings: a Semantic Enquiry', *British Journal of Psychiatry*, vol. 117, pp. 381–7.

BIRTCHNELL, J., (1970) 'Early Parental Death and Mental Illness', *British Journal of Psychiatry*, vol. 116, pp. 281–313.

BLANE, H. T., and BARRY, H., (1973) 'Birth Order and Alcoholism: a Review', *Quarterly Journal of Studies on Alcohol*, vol. 34, pp. 837–52.

BLOCK, J., (1962) 'Some Differences between the Concepts of Social Desirability and Adjustment', *Journal of Consulting Psychology*, vol. 26, pp. 527–30.

BLOCK, J., and THOMAS, H., (1955) 'Is Satisfaction with Self a Measure of Adjustment?', *Journal of Abnormal and Social Psychology*, vol. 51, pp. 254–9.

BLOOD, R. W., and WOLFE, D. M., (1965) *Husbands and Wives: the Dynamics of Married Living*, Collier-Macmillan.

BOWLBY, J., (1961) 'Childhood Mourning and its Implications for Psychiatry', *American Journal of Psychiatry*, vol. 118, pp. 481–8.

BRAGINSKY, B. M., BRAGINSKY, D. D., and RING, K., (1969) *Methods of Madness: the Mental Hospital as a Last Resort*, Holt, Rinehart & Winston.

BRAMEL, D., (1969) 'Interpersonal Attraction, Hostility, and Perception', J. Mills (ed.), *Experimental Social Psychology*, Collier-Macmillan.

BRIM, O. G., (1958) 'Family Structure and Sex-Role Learning by Children', *Sociometry*, vol. 21, pp. 1–16.

BROWN, G. W., BIRLEY, J. L. T., and WING, J. K., (1972) 'Influence of Family Life on the Course of Schizophrenic Disorders: a Replication', *British Journal of Psychiatry*, vol. 121, pp. 241–58.

BROWN, G. W., MONCK, E. M., CARSTAIRS, G. M., and WING, J. K., (1962) 'Influence of Family Life on the Course of Schizophrenic Illness', *British Journal of Preventive and Social Medicine*, vol. 16, pp. 55–68.

BROWN, J. A. C., (1954) *The Social Psychology of Industry*, Penguin.

BROWN, J. S., (1965) 'Sociometric Choices of Patients in a Therapeutic Community', *Human Relations*, vol. 18, pp. 241–51.

BUCK, C. W., and LADD, K. L., (1965) 'Psychoneurosis in Marital Partners', *British Journal of Psychiatry*, vol. 111, pp. 587–90.

BUGENTAL, D. E., LOVE, L. R., KASWAN, J. W., and APRIL, C., (1971) 'Verbal–Nonverbal Conflict in Parental Messages to Normal and Disturbed Children', *Journal of Abnormal Psychology*, vol. 77, pp. 6–10.

BULLOCK, R. C., SIEGEL, R., WEISSMAN, M., and PAYKEL, E. S., (1972) 'The Weeping Wife: Marital Relations of Depressed Women', *Journal of Marriage and the Family*, vol. 34, pp. 488–95.

BURGESS, E. W., and WALLIN, P., (1953) *Engagement and Marriage*, Lippincott.

CAINE, Y. M., and SMAIL, D. J., (1969) *The Treatment of Mental Illness: Science, Faith and the Therapeutic Personality*, University of London Press.

CAMERON, N., (1943) 'The Paranoid Pseudocommunity', *American Journal of Sociology*, vol. 46, pp. 33–8.

CARLIN, A. S., and ARMSTRONG, H. E., (1968) 'Aversive Conditioning: Learning or Dissonance Reduction?', *Journal of Consulting and Clinical Psychology*, vol. 32, pp. 674–8.

CARSON, R. C., (1969) *Interaction Concepts of Personality*, Allen & Unwin.

CATTELL, R. B., and NESSELROADE, J. R., (1967) 'Likeness and Completeness Theories Examined by Sixteen Personality Factor Measures on Stably and Unstably Married Couples', *Journal of Personality and Social Psychology*, vol. 7, pp. 351–61.

CAUDILL, W., (1958) *The Psychiatric Hospital as a Small Society*, Harvard University Press.

CAUDILL, W., REDLICH, F. C., GILMORE, H. R., and BRODY, E. B., (1952) 'Social Structure and Interaction Processes on a Psychiatric Ward', *American Journal of Orthopsychiatry*, vol. 22, pp. 314–34.

CHRISTIE, R., and GEIS, F., (1968) 'Some Consequences of Taking Machiavelli Seriously', in E. F. Borgatta and W. W. Lambert (eds.), *Handbook of Personality Theory and Research*, Rand McNally.

CLAUSEN, J. A., (1966) 'Family Structure, Socialization and Personality', in L. W. Hoffman and M. L. Hoffman (eds.), *Review of Child Development Research*, vol. 2, Russell Sage Foundation, pp. 1–54.

CLAUSEN, J. A., and YARROW, M. R., (1955) 'The Impact of Mental Illness on the Family', *Journal of Social Issues*, vol. 11, pp. 3–65.

CLEVELAND, E. J., and LONGAKER, W. D., (1957) 'Neurotic Patterns in the Family', in A. Leighton, J. A. Clausen and R. N. Wilson (eds.), *Explorations in Social Psychiatry*, Basic Books, pp. 167–200.

COHEN, J., and STRUENING, E. L., (1964) 'Opinions about Mental

Illness: Hospital Social Atmosphere and Patient Time in Hospital',
Journal of Consulting Psychology, vol. 28, pp. 291–8.

COLLINS, J., KREITMAN, N., NELSON, B., and TROOP, J., (1971)
'Neurosis and Marital Interaction: III Family Roles and Function',
British Journal of Psychiatry, vol. 119, pp. 233–42.

COOPERSMITH, S., (1967) *The Antecedents of Self-Esteem*, Freeman
and Freeman.

CORSINI, R. J., (1966) *Roleplaying in Psychotherapy: a Manual*,
Aldine.

COWEN, E. L., (1973) 'Social and Community Interventions', *Annual
Review of Psychology*, vol. 24, pp. 423–72.

CRONBACH, L. J., (1955) 'Processes Affecting Scores on Understanding
of Others and Assumed Similarity', *Psychological Bulletin*, vol. 52,
pp. 177–93.

CULBERTSON, F. M., (1957) 'Modification of an Emotionally Held
Attitude Through Role Playing', *Journal of Abnormal and Social
Psychology*, vol. 54, pp. 230–33.

CUMMING, J., and CUMMING, E., (1956) 'Affective Symbolism, Social
Norms, and Mental Illness', *Psychiatry*, vol. 19, pp. 77–85.

DEUTSCH, M., and SOLOMON, L., (1959) 'Reactions to Evaluations
by Others as Influenced by Self-Evaluations', *Sociometry*, vol. 22,
pp. 93–112.

DREWERY, J., and RAE, J. B., (1969) 'A Group Comparison of
Alcoholic and Non-Alcoholic Marriages Using the Interpersonal
Perception Technique', *British Journal of Psychiatry*, vol. 115,
pp. 287–300.

DUROJAIYE, M. O., (1970) 'The Relationship between Controlled
Projection Responses and Sociometric Status', *Journal of Child
Psychology and Psychiatry*, vol. 11, pp. 143–8.

EHRENWALD, J., (1963) *Neurosis in the Family and Patterns of
Psychosocial Defense: a Study of Psychiatric Epidemiology*,
Hoeber.

EKMAN, P., and FRIESEN, W. V., (1968) 'Nonverbal Behaviour in
Psychotherapy Research', in J. M. Shlienn (ed.), *Research in
Psychotherapy*, vol. III, American Psychological Association.

ELLSWORTH, R. B., (1965) 'A Behavioural Study of Staff Attitudes
toward Mental Illness', *Journal of Abnormal Psychology*, vol. 70,
pp. 194–200.

ERIKSON, E. H., (1956) 'The Problem of Ego Identity', *American
Journal of Psychoanalysis*, vol. 4, pp. 56–121.

ERIKSON, K. T., (1957) 'Patient Role and Social Uncertainty – a
Dilemma of the Mentally Ill', *Psychiatry*, vol. 20, pp. 263–74.

EYSENCK, H. J., (1960) 'The Effects of Psychotherapy', in H. J. Eysenck (ed.), *Handbook of Abnormal Psychology*, First Edition, Pitman; (1967) *The Biological Basis of Personality*, Thomas.

EYSENCK, H. J., and WILSON, G. D., (1973) *The Experimental Study of Freudian Theories*, Methuen.

FAIRWEATHER, G. W. (ed.), (1964) *Social Psychology in Treating Mental Illness*, Wiley.

FAIRWEATHER, G. W., SANDERS, D. H., CRESSLER, D. L., and MAYNARD, H., (1969) *Community Life for the Mentally Ill: an Alternative to Institutional Care*, Aldine.

FARINA, A., HOLLAND, C. H., and RING, K., (1966) 'Role of Stigma and Set in Interpersonal Interaction', *Journal of Abnormal Psychology*, vol. 71, pp. 421–8.

FARINA, A., and HOLZBERG, J. D., (1967) 'Attitudes and Behaviours of Fathers and Mothers of Male Schizophrenic Patients', *Journal of Abnormal Psychology*, vol. 72, pp. 381–7; (1968) 'Interaction Patterns of Parents and Hospitalized Sons Diagnosed as Schizophrenic or Non-Schizophrenic', *Journal of Abnormal Psychology*, vol. 73, pp. 114–18.

FARINA, A., and RING, K., (1965) 'The Influence of Perceived Mental Illness on Interpersonal Relations', *Journal of Abnormal Psychology*, vol. 70, pp. 47–51.

FARINA, A., GLIHA, D., BOUDREAU, L. A., ALLEN, J. G., and SHERMAN, M., (1971) 'Mental Illness and the Impact of Believing Others Know about It', *Journal of Abnormal Psychology*, vol. 77, pp. 1–5.

FELDMAN, M. P., and MACCULLOCH, M. J. (1971) *Homosexual Behaviour, Therapy and Assessment*, Pergamon.

FERGUSON, R. S., and CARNEY, M. W., (1970) 'Interpersonal Considerations and Judgements in a Day Hospital', *British Journal of Psychiatry*, vol. 117, pp. 397–403.

FERREIRA, A. J., and WINTER, W. D., (1965) 'Family Interaction and Decision-Making', *Archives of General Psychiatry*, vol. 13, pp. 214–23; (1968) 'Decision-Making in Normal and Abnormal Two-Child Families', *Family Process*, vol. 7, pp. 17–36.

FERREIRA, A. J., WINTER, W. D., and POINDEXTER, E., (1966) 'Some Interactional Variables in Normal and Abnormal Families', *Family Process*, vol. 5, pp. 60–75.

FESHBACH, S., (1970) 'Aggression', in P. H. Mussen (ed.), *Carmichael's Manual of Child Psychology*, vol. 2, Wiley.

FESTINGER, L., (1957) *A Theory of Cognitive Dissonance*, Row, Peterson.

FESTINGER, L., and CARLSMITH, J. M., (1959) 'Cognitive Consequences of Forced Compliance', *Journal of Abnormal and Social Psychology*, vol. 58, pp. 203–10.

FIEDLER, F. E., (1950a) 'The Concept of the Ideal Therapeutic Relationship', *Journal of Consulting Psychology*, vol. 14, pp. 239–45; (1950b) 'A Comparison of Therapeutic Relationships in Psychoanalytic Nondirective and Adlerian Therapy', *Journal of Consulting Psychology*, vol. 14, pp. 436–45.

FISHER, S., and MENDELL, B., (1956) 'The Communication of Neurotic Patterns over Two and Three Generations', *Psychiatry*, vol. 10, pp. 41–6.

FLETCHER, C. R., (1969) 'Measuring Community Mental Health Attitudes by Means of Hypothetical Case Descriptions', *Social Psychiatry*, vol. 4, pp. 152–6.

FONTANA, A. F., (1966) 'Familial Etiology of Schizophrenia: is a Scientific Methodology Possible?', *Psychological Bulletin*, vol. 66, pp. 214–27; (1971) 'Machiavellianism and Manipulation in the Mental Patient Role', *Journal of Personality*, vol. 39, pp. 252–63.

FOULDS, G. A., (1965) *Personality and Personal Illness*, Tavistock.

FRANK, J. D., (1961) *Persuasion and Healing*, Oxford University Press; (1971) 'Therapeutic Factors in Psychotherapy', *American Journal of Psychotherapy*, vol. 25, pp. 350–61.

FRANK, G. H., (1965) 'The Role of the Family in the Development of Psychopathology', *Psychological Bulletin*, vol. 64, pp. 191–205.

FRANSELLA, F., (1972) *Personal Change and Reconstruction: Research on a Treatment of Stuttering*, Academic Press.

FRANSELLA, F., and ADAMS, B., (1966) 'An Illustration of the Use of the Repertory Grid Technique in a Clinical Setting', *British Journal of Social and Clinical Psychology*, vol. 5, pp. 51–62.

FRASER, N., (1973) *Children in Conflict*, Secker & Warburg.

FREEMAN, H. E., and GIOVANNI, J. M., (1969) 'Social Psychology of Mental Health', in G. Lindzey and E. Aronson (eds.), *The Handbook of Social Psychology*, 2nd edition, vol. 5, Addison-Wesley.

FREEMAN, H. E., and SIMMONS, O. G., (1963) *The Mental Patient Comes Home*, Wiley.

FRENKEL-BRUNSWIK, E., (1939) 'Mechanisms of Self-Deception', *Journal of Social Psychology*, vol. 10, pp. 409–20.

FREUD, A., and BURLINGHAM, D., (1943) *War and Children*, Medical War Books.

FRIEDMAN, I., (1955) 'Phenomenal, Ideal, and Projected Conceptions of Self', *Journal of Abnormal and Social Psychology*, vol. 51, pp. 611–15.

GALLAGHER, E. B., SHARAF, M. R., and LEVINSON, D. J., (1965) 'The Influence of Patient and Therapist in Determining the Use of Psychotherapy in a Hospital Setting', *Psychiatry*, vol. 28, pp. 297–310.

GERGEN, K. J., and JONES, E. E., (1963) 'Mental Illness, Predictability, and Affective Consequences as Stimulus Factors in Person Perception', *Journal of Abnormal and Social Psychology*, vol. 67, pp. 95–104.

GERSHON, E. S., CROMER, M., and KLERMAN, G. L., (1968) 'Hostility and Depression', *Psychiatry*, vol. 31, pp. 224–35.

GEWIRTZ, J. L., (1969) 'Mechanisms of Social Learning: Some Roles of Stimulation and Behaviour in Early Human Development', in D. A. Goslin (ed.), *Handbook of Socialisation Theory and Research*, Rand McNally.

GILBERT, D. C., and LEVINSON, D. J., (1956) 'Ideology, Personality, and Institutional Policy in the Mental Hospital', *Journal of Abnormal and Social Psychology*, vol. 53, pp. 263–71.

GOFFMAN, E., (1959) *The Presentation of Self in Everyday Life*, Doubleday-Anchor; (1964) *Stigma: Notes on the Management of Spoiled Identity*, Penguin; (1968) *Asylums; Essays on the Social Situation of Mental Patients and Other Inmates*, Penguin.

GOLDIN, T. C., (1969) 'A Review of Children's Reports of Parent Behaviours', *Psychological Bulletin*, vol. 71, pp. 222–36.

GOLDMAN-EISLER, F., (1951) 'The Problem of "Orality" and of its Origins in Early Childhood', *Journal of Mental Science*, vol. 97, pp. 765–82.

GOLDSTEIN, A. P., (1971) *Psychotherapeutic Attraction*, Pergamon.

GOVE, W. R., (1970) 'Societal Reaction as an Explanation of Mental Illness: an Evaluation', *American Sociological Review*, vol. 35, pp. 873–84.

GREGORY, I., (1959) 'Husbands and Wives Admitted to Mental Hospitals', *Journal of Mental Science*, vol. 105, pp. 457–62.

GURIN, G., VEROFF, J., and FELDS, S., (1967) 'People Who Have Gone for Help', in S. K. Weinberg (ed.), *The Sociology of Mental Disorders: Analyses and Readings in Psychiatric Sociology*, Staples Press.

GUTRIDE, M. E., *et al.*, (1973) 'The Use of Modeling and Role Playing to Increase Social Interaction among Asocial Psychiatric Patients', *Journal of Consulting and Clinical Psychology*, vol. 40, pp. 408–15.

HAEFNER, H., (1967) 'Psychosocial Changes Following Racial and Political Persecution', in *Social Psychiatry*, proceedings of the Association for Research in Nervous Mental Disease, vol. 47, Chapter 7.

HALEY, J., (1964) 'Research on Family Patterns: an Instruments Research', *Family Process*, vol. 3, pp. 41–65.

HANDEL, G. (ed.), (1968) *The Psychosocial Interior of the Family*, Allen & Unwin.

HARBURG, E., KASL, S. V., TABOR, J., and COBB, S., (1969) 'Recalled Parent Child Relations by Rheumatoid Arthritics and Controls', *Journal of Chronic Disorders*, vol. 22, pp. 223–38.

HARE, E. H., and SHAW, G. K., (1965) 'A Study in Family Health: II A Comparison of the Health of Fathers, Mothers and Children', *British Journal of Psychiatry*, vol. 111, pp. 467–71.

HARLOW, H. F., HARLOW, M. K., DODSWORTH, R. O., and ARLING, G. L., (1966) 'Maternal Behaviour of Rhesus Monkeys Deprived of Mothering and Peer Associations in Infancy', *Proceedings of the American Philosophical Society*, vol. 110, pp. 58–66.

HAY, G., (1970a) 'Psychiatric Aspects of Cosmetic Nasal Operations', *British Journal of Psychiatry*, vol. 116, pp. 85–97; (1970b) 'Dysmorphophobia', *British Journal of Psychiatry*, vol. 116, pp. 399–406.

HEARN, C. B., and SEEMAN, J., (1971) 'Personality Integration and Perception of Interpersonal Relationships', *Journal of Personality and Social Psychology*, vol. 18, pp. 138–43.

HEIDER, F., (1944) 'Social Perception and Phenomenal Causality', *Psychological Review*, vol. 51, pp. 358–74; (1958) *The Psychology of Interpersonal Relations*, Wiley.

HEILBRUN, A. B., (1964) 'Parent Model Attributes, Nurturant Reinforcement and Consistency of Behaviour in Adolescents', *Child Development*, vol. 35, pp. 151–67; (1968) 'Cognitive Sensitivity to Aversive Maternal Stimulation in Late-Adolescent Males', *Journal of Consulting and Clinical Psychology*, vol. 32, pp. 326–32; (1970) 'Perceived Maternal Child-Rearing Experience and the Effects of Vicarious and Direct Reinforcement on Males', *Child Development*, vol. 41, pp. 253–62.

HEILBRUN, A. B., HARRELL, S. N., and GILLARD, B. J., (1967a) 'Perceived Child-Rearing Attitudes of Fathers and Cognitive Control in Daughters', *Journal of Genetic Psychology*, vol. 111, pp. 29–40; (1967b) 'Perceived Maternal Child-Rearing Patterns and the Effects of Social Non-Reaction upon Achievement Motivation', *Child Development*, vol. 38, pp. 267–81.

HELLER, K., (1969) 'Effects of Modeling Procedures in Helping Relationships', *Journal of Consulting and Clinical Psychology*, vol. 33, pp. 522–6; (1972) 'Interview Structure and Interviewer Style in Initial Interviews', in A. W. Siegman and B. Pope (eds.), *Studies in Dyadic Communication*, Pergamon.

HELLER, K., MYERS, R. A., and KLINE, L. V., (1963) 'Interviewer Behaviour as a Function of Standardised Client Role', *Journal of Consulting Psychology*, vol. 27, pp. 117–22.

HERBST, P. G., (1954) 'Conceptual Framework for Studying the Family', in O. A. Oeser and S. B. Hammond (eds.), *Social Structure and Personality in a City*, Routledge & Kegan Paul.

HESTON, L. L., and DENNEY, D., (1968) 'Interactions between Early Life Experiences and Biological Factors in Schizophrenia', in D. Rosenthal and S. S. Kety (eds.), *The Transmission of Schizophrenia*, Pergamon.

HETHERINGTON, E. M., STOUWIE, R. J., and RIDBERG, E. H., (1971) 'Patterns of Family Interaction and Child-Rearing Attitudes Related to Three Dimensions of Juvenile Delinquency', *Journal of Abnormal Psychology*, vol. 78, pp. 160–76.

HEWITT, L. E., and JENKINS, R. L., (1946) *Fundamental Patterns of Maladjustment – the Dynamics of Their Origin*, Michigan Child Guidance Institute, Illinois.

HICKS, M. W., and PLATT, N., (1970) 'Marital Happiness and Stability: A Review of the Research in the Sixties', *Journal of Marriage and the Family*, vol. 32, pp. 553–74.

HILLSON, J. S., and WORCHEL, P., (1957) 'Self-Concept and Defensive Behaviour in the Maladjusted', *Journal of Consulting Psychology*, vol. 21, pp. 83–8.

HINCHLIFFE, M., LANCASHIRE, M., and ROBERTS, F. J., (1970) 'Eye-Contact and Depression: a Preliminary Report', *British Journal of Psychiatry*, vol. 117, pp. 571–2.

HINDE, R. A., and SPENCER-BOOTH, Y., (1970) 'Individual Differences in the Responses of Rhesus Monkeys to a Period of Separation from Their Mothers', *Journal of Child Psychology and Psychiatry*, vol. 11, pp. 159–76.

HIRSCH, S., and LEFF, J. P., (1975) *Abnormality in Parents of Schizophrenics: a Review of the Literature and an Investigation of Communication Defects and Deviances*, Oxford University Press.

HOFFMAN, M. L., (1960) 'Power Assertion by the Parent and its Impact on the Child', *Child Development*, vol. 31, pp. 129–43.

HOFFMAN, L. W., and LIPPITT, R., (1960) 'The Measurement of Family Life Variables', in P. H. Mussen (ed.), *Handbook of*

Research Methods in Child Development, Wiley.

HOMANS, G. C., (1961) *Social Behaviour: its Elementary Forms*, Harcourt, Brace.

HORNEY, K., (1951) *Neurosis and Human Growth*, Routledge & Kegan Paul.

HOWARD, R., and BERKOWITZ, L., (1958) 'Reactions to the Evaluation of One's Performance', *Journal of Personality*, vol. 26, pp. 494–507.

HUTT, S. J., and HUTT, C., (1970) *Direct Observation and Measurement of Behaviour*, Thomas.

HUTT, C., and OUNSTED, C., (1966) 'The Biological Significance of Gaze Aversion with Particular Reference to the Syndrome of Infantile Autism', *Behavioural Science*, vol. 11, pp. 346–56.

INGERSOLL, H., (1948) 'Study of Transmission of Authority Patterns in the Family', *Genetic Psychology Monographs*, vol. 38, pp. 225–99.

JACKSON, D. D., (1957) 'The Question of Family Homeostasis', *Psychiatric Quarterly*, Supplement 31, pp. 79–90.

JACKSON, J. K., (1954) 'The Adjustment of the Family to the Crisis of Alcoholism', *Quarterly Journal of Studies on Alcohol*, vol. 15, pp. 562–86.

JAHODA, M., (1958) *Current Concepts of Positive Mental Health*, Basic Books.

JANIS, I. L., and KING, B. T., (1954) 'The Influence of Role Playing on Opinion Change', *Journal of Abnormal and Social Psychology*, vol. 49, pp. 211–18.

JANIS, I. L., and MANN, L., (1965) 'Effectiveness of Emotional Role Playing in Modifying Smoking Habits and Attitudes', *Journal of Experimental Research in Personality*, vol. 1, pp. 84–90.

JONES, E. E., and DAVIS, K. E., (1965) 'From Acts to Dispositions: The Attribution Process in Person Perception', in L. Berkowitz (ed.), *Advances in Experimental Social Psychology*, vol. 2, pp. 219–66.

JONES, E. E., DAVIS, K. E., and GERGEN, K. J., (1961) 'Role Playing Variations and Their Informational Value for Person Perception', *Journal of Abnormal and Social Psychology*, vol. 63, pp. 302–10.

JONES, E. E., HESTER, S. L., FARINA, A., and DAVIS, K. E., (1959) 'Reactions to Unfavourable Personal Evaluations as a Function of the Evaluater's Perceived Adjustment', *Journal of Abnormal and Social Psychology*, vol. 59, pp. 363–70.

JONES, E. E., and THIBAUT, J. W., (1958) 'Interaction Goals as Bases of Inference in Interpersonal Perception', in R. Tagiuri and

L. Petrullo (eds.), *Person Perception and Interpersonal Behaviour*, Stanford University Press.

JOURARD, S. M., (1959) 'Self-Disclosure and Other-Cathexis', *Journal of Abnormal and Social Psychology*, vol. 59, pp. 428–31.

JOURARD, S. M., and LASAKOW, P., (1958) 'Some factors in Self-Disclosure', *Journal of Abnormal and Social Psychology*, vol. 56, pp. 91–8.

KELLAM, S. G., and CHASSAN, J. B., (1962) 'Social Context and Symptom Fluctuations', *Psychiatry*, vol. 25, pp. 370–81.

KELLER, O. J., and ALPER, B. S., (1970) *Halfway Houses: Community Centred Correction and Treatment*, Heath and Co.

KELLEY, H. H., (1950) 'The Warm–Cold Variable in First Impressions of Persons', *Journal of Personality*, vol. 18, pp. 431–9.

KELLEY, H. H., and STAHELSKI, A. J., (1970) 'Social Interaction Basis of Cooperators' and Competitors' Beliefs about Others', *Journal of Personality and Social Psychology*, vol. 16, pp. 66–91.

KELLY, E. L., (1941) 'Marital Compatibility as Related to Personality Traits of Husbands and Wives as Rated by Self and Spouse', *Journal of Social Psychology*, vol. 13, pp. 193–8.

KELLY, G. A., (1955) *The Psychology of Personal Constructs*, vol. 1, *A Theory of Personality*, Norton.

KENDELL, R. E., COOPER, J. E., GOURLAY, A. J., COPELAND, J. R. M., SHARPE, L., and GURLAND, B. J., (1971) 'The Diagnostic Criteria of American and British Psychiatrists', *Archives of General Psychiatry*, vol. 25, pp. 123–30.

KENDON, A., (1967) 'Some Functions of Gaze Direction in Social Interaction', *Acta Psychologica*, vol. 26, pp. 22–63.

KERCKHOFF, A., and DAVIS, K. A., (1962) 'Value Concensus and Need Complementarity in Mate Selection', *American Sociological Review*, vol. 27, pp. 295–303.

KING, G. F., ARMITAGE, S. G., and TILTON, J. R., (1960) 'A Therapeutic Approach to Schizophrenics of Extreme Pathology: an Operant-Interpersonal Method', *Journal of Abnormal and Social Psychology*, vol. 61, pp. 276–86.

KLEINER, R. J., and PARKER, S., (1963) 'Goal-Striving, Social Status, and Mental Disorder: a Research Review', *American Sociological Review*, vol. 28, pp. 169–203.

KLERMAN, G. L., SHARAF, M. R., HOLZMAN, M., and LEVINSON, D. J., (1960) 'Sociopsychological Characteristics of Resident Psychiatrists and Their Use of Drug Therapy', *American Journal of Psychiatry*, vol. 117, pp. 111–17.

KLINE, P., (1972) *Fact and Fantasy in Freudian Theory*, Methuen.

KOCH, H. L., (1956) 'Some Emotional Attitudes of the Young Child in Relation to the Characteristics of his Siblings', *Child Development*, vol. 27, pp. 393–426.

KOLLER, K. M., and CASTANOS, J. N., (1970), 'Family Background in Prison Groups: a Comparative Study of Parental Deprivation', *British Journal of Psychiatry*, vol. 117, pp. 371–80.

KORNHAUSER, A., (1965) *Mental Health of the Industrial Worker: a Detroit Study*, Wiley.

KREITMAN, N., (1964) 'The Patient's Spouse', *British Journal of Psychiatry*, vol. 110, pp. 159–73; (1968) 'Married Couples Admitted to Mental Hospital', *British Journal of Psychiatry*, vol. 114, pp. 699–718.

KREITMAN, N., COLLINS, J., NELSON, B., and TROOP, J., (1970) 'Neurosis and Marital Interaction: I Personality and Symptoms', *British Journal of Psychiatry*, vol. 117, pp. 33–46; (1971) 'Neurosis and Marital Interaction: IV Manifest Psychological Interaction', *British Journal of Psychiatry*, vol. 119, pp. 243–52.

LAFORGE, R., and SUCZEK, R. F., (1955) 'The Interpersonal Dimensions of Personality: an Interpersonal Check-List', *Journal of Personality*, vol. 24, p. 94ff.

LAING, R. D., PHILLIPSON, H., and LEE, A. R., (1966) *Interpersonal Perception: a Theory and a Method of Research*, Tavistock.

LEARY, T., (1957) *Interpersonal Diagnoses of Personality: a Functional Theory and Methodology for Personality Evaluation*, Ronald.

LEMERT, E. M., (1962) 'Paranoia and the Dynamics of Exclusion', *Sociometry*, vol. 25, pp. 2–20.

LENNARD, H. L., and BERNSTEIN, A., (1969) *Patterns in Human Interaction*, Jossey-Bass.

LERNER, P. M., (1965) 'Resolution of Intrafamilial Conflict in Families of Schizophrenic Patients: I Thought Disturbance', *Journal of Nervous and Mental Disease*, vol. 141, pp. 342–51.

LEVY, D. M., (1970) 'The Concept of Maternal Over-Protection', in E. J. Anthony and T. Benedek (eds.), *Parenthood: its Psychology and Psychopathology*, Little, Brown.

LEWIN, K., LIPPITT, R., and WHITE, R. K., (1939) 'Patterns of Aggressive Behaviour in Experimentally Created Social Climates', *Journal of Social Psychology*, vol. 10, pp. 271–99.

LEWIN, K. K., (1965) 'Non-Verbal Cues and Transference', *Archives of General Psychiatry*, vol. 12, pp. 391–4.

LEWIS, H., (1954) *Deprived Children: the Mersham Experiment: a Social and Clinical Study*, Oxford University Press.

LIDZ, T., CORNELISON, A., FLECK, S., and TERRY, D., (1957) 'The

Intrafamily Environment of Schizophrenic Patients: II Marital Schism and Marital Skew', *American Journal of Psychiatry*, vol. 114, pp. 241–8.

LIDZ, T., CORNELISON, A., TERRY, D., and FLECK, S., (1958) 'The Intrafamily Environment of Schizophrenic Patients: VI Transmission of Irrationality', *Archives of Neurology and Psychiatry*, vol. 79, pp. 305–16.

LONG, B. H., ZILLER, R. C., and BANKES, J., (1970) 'Self-Other Orientation of Institutionalized Behaviour Problem Adolescents', *Journal of Consulting and Clinical Psychology*, vol. 34, pp. 43–7.

LORR, M., and MCNAIR, D. M., (1965) 'Expansion of the Interpersonal Behaviour Circle', *Journal of Personality and Social Psychology*, vol. 2, pp. 823–30.

LUBORSKY, L., CHANDLER, M., AUERBACH, A. H., and COHEN, J., (1971) 'Factors Influencing the Outcome of Psychotherapy: a Review of Quantitative Research', *Psychological Bulletin*, vol. 75, pp. 145–85.

LUCKEY, E. B., (1960) 'Marital Satisfaction and its Association with Congruence of Perception', *Marriage and Family Living*, vol. 22, pp. 49–54; (1964) 'Marital Satisfaction and its Concomitant Perceptions of Self and Spouse', *Journal of Counseling Psychology*, vol. 11, pp. 136–45.

MACCOBY, E. E., and MASTERS, J. C., (1970) 'Attachment and Dependency', in P. H. Mussen, (ed.), *Carmichael's Manual of Child Psychology*, 3rd Edition, vol. 2, Wiley.

MANIS, M., HOUTS, P. S., and BLAKE, J. B., (1963) 'Beliefs about Mental Illness as a Function of Psychiatric Status and Psychiatric Hospitalization', *Journal of Abnormal and Social Psychology*, vol. 67, pp. 226–33.

MARCIA, J. E., (1967) 'Ego-Identity Status: Relationship to Change in Self-Esteem, General Maladjustment, and Authoritarianism', *Journal of Personality*, vol. 35, pp. 118–33.

MARK, J. C., (1953) 'The Attitudes of the Mothers of Schizophrenics towards Child Behaviour', *Journal of Abnormal and Social Psychology*, vol. 48, pp. 185–9.

MARKS, I., (1969) *Fears and Phobias*, Heinemann; (1970) 'The Classification of Phobic Disorders', *British Journal of Psychiatry*, vol. 116, pp. 377–86.

MARLOWE, D., and GERGEN, K. L., (1969) 'Personality and Social Interaction', in G. Lindzey and E. Aronson (eds.), *Handbook of Social Psychology*, 2nd edition, vol. 3, Addison-Wesley.

MATTSSON, A., and GROSS, S., (1966) 'Adaptational and Defensive

Behaviour in Young Hemophiliacs and Their Parents', *American Journal of Psychiatry*, vol. 122, pp. 1349–56.

MAXWELL JONES, (1953) *The Therapeutic Community*, Basic Books.

MAYO, P. R., (1968) 'Self-Disclosure and Neurosis', *British Journal of Social and Clinical Psychology*, vol. 2, pp. 140–48.

MCCARRON, L. T., and APPEL, V. H., (1971) 'Categories of Therapist Verbalizations and Patient-Therapist Autonomic Response', *Journal of Consulting and Clinical Psychology*, vol. 37, pp. 123–34.

MCFALL, R. M., and LILLESAND, D. D., (1971) 'Behaviour Rehearsal with Modeling and Coaching in Assertion Training', *Journal of Abnormal Psychology*, vol. 77, pp. 313–23.

MCFALL, R. M., and MARSTON, A. R., (1970) 'An Experimental Investigation of Behaviour Rehearsal in Assertive Training', *Journal of Abnormal Psychology*, vol. 76, pp. 295–330.

MCGHEE, A., (1961) 'A Comparative Study of the Mother–Child Relationship in Schizophrenia: I The Interview', *British Journal of Medical Psychology*, vol. 34, pp. 195–208,

MCMILLAN, J. J., and SILVERBERG, J., (1955) 'Sociometric Choice Patterns in Hospital Ward Groups with Varying Degrees of Interpersonal Disturbances', *Journal of Abnormal and Social Psychology*, vol. 50, pp. 168–72.

MCNAIR, D. M., CALLAHAN, D. M., and LORR, M., (1962) 'Therapist Type and Patient Response to Psychotherapy', *Journal of Consulting Psychology*, vol. 26, pp. 425–9.

MECHANIC, D., (1966) 'Response Factors in Illness: the Study of Illness Behaviour', *Social Psychiatry*, vol. 1, pp. 11–20.

MEHRABIAN, A., (1971) 'Non-Verbal Communication', in J. K. Cole (ed.), *Nebraska Symposium on Motivation*, vol. 19, pp. 107–61, University of Nebraska Press.

MILLER, D. R., (1970) 'Optimal Psychological Adjustment: a Relativistic Interpretation', *Journal of Consulting and Clinical Psychology*, vol. 35, pp. 290–95.

MINTZ, J., LUBORKSY, L., and AUERBACH, A. H., (1971) 'Dimensions of Psychotherapy; a Factor-Analytic Study of Ratings of Psychotherapy Sessions', *Journal of Consulting and Clinical Psychology*, vol. 36, pp. 106–20.

MISCHEL, W., (1968) *Personality and Assessment*, Wiley.

MISKIMINS, R. W., WILSON, L. T., BRAUCHT, G. N., and BERRY, K. L., (1971) 'Self-Concept and Psychiatric Symptomatology', *Journal of Clinical Psychology*, vol. 27, pp. 185–7.

MOOS, R., and HOUTS, P., (1968) 'Assessment of the Social Atmospheres of Psychiatric Wards', *Journal of Abnormal*

Psychology, vol. 73, pp. 595–604.

MORENO, J. L., (1946) *Psychodrama*, Beacon Press.

MORGAN, R., and CUSHING, D., (1966) 'The Personal Possessions of Long-Stay Patients in Mental Hospitals', *Social Psychiatry*, vol. 1, pp. 151–7.

MORRISON, A., and MCINTYRE, D., (1971) *Schools and Socialization*, Penguin.

MORROW, W. R., and ROBINS, A. J., (1964) 'Family Relations and Social Recovery of Psychotic Mothers', *Journal of Health and Human Behaviour*, vol. 5, pp. 14–24.

MOSHER, L., POLLIN, W., and STABENAU, J. R., (1971) 'Families with Identical Twins Discordant for Schizophrenia: Some Relationships between Identification, Thinking Styles, Psychopathology and Dominance-Submissiveness', *British Journal of Psychiatry*, vol. 118, pp. 29–42.

MUNRO, A., (1969) 'Parent–Child Separation: Is It Really a Cause of Psychiatric Illness in Adult Life?', *Archives of General Psychiatry*, vol. 20, pp. 598–604.

MUNTZ, H. J., and POWER, R. P., (1970) 'Thought Disorder in Parents of Thought Disordered Schizophrenics', *British Journal of Psychiatry*, vol. 117, pp. 707–8.

MURRAY, E. J., and COHEN, M., (1959) 'Mental Illness, Milieu Therapy, and Social Organization in Ward Groups', *Journal of Abnormal and Social Psychology*, vol. 58, pp. 48–54.

MURSTEIN, B. I., (1970) 'Stimulus-Value-Role: a Theory of Marital Choice', *Journal of Marriage and the Family*, vol. 32, pp. 465–81.

MURSTEIN, B. I., and GLAUDIN, V., (1966) 'The Relationship of Marital Adjustment to Personality: a Factor Analysis of the Interpersonal Check List', *Journal of Marriage and the Family*, vol. 28, pp. 37–43.

MYERS, J. K., and ROBERTS, B. H., (1959) *Family and Class Dynamics in Mental Illness*, Wiley.

NELSON, B., COLLINS, J., KREITMAN, N., and TROOP, J., (1970) 'Neurosis and Marital Interaction: II Time Sharing and Social Activity', *British Journal of Psychiatry*, vol. 117, pp. 47–58.

NIELSEN, J., (1964) 'Mental Disorders in Married Couples (Assortative Mating)', *British Journal of Psychiatry*, vol. 110, pp. 683–97.

NORRIS, F. M., JONES, H. G., and NORRIS, H., (1970) 'Articulation of the Conceptual Structure in Obsessional Neurosis', *British Journal of Social and Clinical Psychology*, vol. 9, pp. 264–74.

NUNNALLY, J. C., (1961) *Popular Conceptions of Mental Health*, Holt, Rinehart & Winston.

O'CONNOR, N., and FRANKS, C. M., (1960) 'Childhood Upbringing and Other Environmental Factors', in H. J. Eysenck (ed.), *Handbook of Abnormal Psychology*, 1st edition, Pitman.

OFFER, D., and SABSHIN, M., (1966) *Normality: Theoretical and Clinical Concepts of Mental Health*, Basic Books.

ORFORD, J., HAWKER, A., and NICHOLLS, P., (1975) 'An Investigation of an Alcoholism Rehabilitation Halfway House: III Reciprocal Staff–Resident Evaluation', *British Journal of the Addictions*, vol. 70, pp. 23–32.

ORFORD, J., (1974) 'Simplistic Thinking about Other People as a Predictor of Early Drop-Out at an Alcoholism Halfway House', *British Journal of Medical Psychology*, vol. 47, pp. 53–62.

OTTO, S., and ORFORD, J., (1976) *Community Houses for Alcoholics*, in preparation.

PARSONS, T., and BALES, R. F., (1955) *Family, Socialization and Interaction Process*, Free Press.

PEARLIN, L. I., and ROSENBERG, M., (1962) 'Nurse–Patient Social Distance and the Structural Context of a Mental Hospital', *American Sociological Review*, vol. 27, pp. 56–65.

PERRUCCI, R., (1963) 'Social Distance Strategies and Intra-Organisational Stratification: a Study of the Status System on a Psychiatric Ward', *American Sociological Review*, vol. 28, pp. 951–62.

PHARES, E. J., (1972) 'A Social Learning Theory Approach to Psychopathology', in J. B. Rotter (ed.), *Applications of a Social Learning Theory of Personality*, Holt, Rinehart & Winston.

PHILIP, A. E., and MCCULLOCH, J. W., (1968) 'Personal Construct Theory and Social Work Practice', *British Journal of Social and Clinical Psychology*, vol. 7, pp. 115–21.

PHILLIPS, D. L., (1963) 'Rejection: a Possible Consequence of Seeking Help for Mental Disorders', *American Sociological Review*, vol. 28, pp. 963–72.

PHILLIPS, L. and RABINOVITCH, M. S., (1958) 'Social Role and Patterns of Symptomatic Behaviours', *Journal of Abnormal and Social Psychology*, vol. 57, pp. 181–6.

PINE, F., and LEVINSON, D. J., (1961) 'A Sociopsychological Conception of Patienthood', *International Journal of Social Psychiatry*, vol. 7, pp. 106–22.

POLAK, P. R., (1967) 'The Crisis of Admission', *Social Psychiatry*, vol. 2, pp. 150–57.

POLLIN, W., STABENAU, J. R., and TUPIN, J., (1965) 'Family Studies with Identical Twins Discordant for Schizophrenia', *Psychiatry*, vol. 28, pp. 60–78.

RACHMAN, S., (1971) *The Effects of Psychotherapy*, Pergamon; (1972) 'Clinical Applications of Observational Learning, Imitation and Modeling', *Behaviour Therapy*, vol. 3, pp. 379–97.

RAPHAEL, E. E., HOWARD, K. I., and VERNON, D. T. A., (1967) 'Social Process and Readmission to the Mental Hospital', in S. K. Weinberg (ed.), *The Sociology of Mental Disorder: Analyses and Readings in Psychiatric Sociology*, Staples Press.

RAPOPORT, R. N., (1960) *Community as Doctor: New Perspectives on a Therapeutic Community*, Tavistock.

RAUSH, H. L., (1965) 'Interaction Sequences', *Journal of Personality and Social Psychology*, vol. 2, pp. 487–99.

RAUSH, H. L., and RAUSH, C. L., (1968) *The Halfway House Movement: a Search for Sanity*, Appleton, Century, Crofts.

RAZIN, A. M., (1971) 'A–B Variable in Psychotherapy: a Critical Review', *Psychological Bulletin*, vol. 75, pp. 1–21.

RENSON, G. J., SCHAEFER, E. S., and LEVY, B. I., (1968) 'Cross National Validity of a Spherical Conceptual Model of Parent Behaviour', *Child Development*, vol. 39, pp. 1229–35.

RINGUETTE, E. L., and KENNEDY, T., (1966) 'An Experimental Study of the Double Bind Hypothesis', *Journal of Abnormal and Social Psychology*, vol. 71, pp. 136–41.

ROGERS, C. R., (1959) 'A Theory of Therapy, Personality and Interpersonal Relationships, as Developed in the Client-Centred Framework', in S. Koch (ed.), *Psychology: The Study of a Science*, vol. 3, McGraw Hill.

ROSENBERG, M., (1962) 'The Association between Self-Esteem and Anxiety', *Psychiatric Research*, vol. 1, pp. 135–52.

ROSENBERG, S., and SEDLAK, A., (1972) 'Structural Representations of Implicit Personality Theory', in L. Berkowitz (ed.), *Advances in Experimental Social Psychology*, vol. 6, Academic Press.

ROSENTHAL, D., (ed.), (1963) *The Genain Quadruplets: a Case Study and Theoretical Analysis of Heredity and Environment in Schizophrenia*, Basic Books.

ROTHAUS, P., HANSON, P. G., CLEVELAND, S. E., and JOHNSON, D. L., (1963) 'Describing Psychiatric Hospitalization: a Dilemma', *American Psychologist*, vol. 18, pp. 85–9.

ROTTER, J. B., (1966) 'Generalized Expectancies for Internal Versus External Control of Reinforcement', *Psychological Monographs*, vol. 80, whole number 609; (1967) 'A New Scale for the Measurement of Interpersonal Trust', *Journal of Personality*, vol. 35, pp. 651–65.

ROUSELL, C. H., and EDWARDS, C. N., (1971) 'Some Developmental Antecedents of Psychopathology', *Journal of Personality*, vol. 39, pp. 362–77.

RUTTER, D. R., and STEPHENSON, G. M., (1972) 'Visual Interaction in a Group of Schizophrenic and Depressive Patients', *British Journal of Social and Clinical Psychology*, vol. 11, pp. 57–65.

RUTTER, M., (1966) *Children of Sick Parents: an Environmental and Psychiatric Study*, Oxford University Press; (1972) *Maternal Deprivation Reassessed*, Penguin.

RUTTER, M., TIZARD, J., and WHITMORE, K., (1970) *Education, Health and Behaviour*, Longman.

RYLE, A., and BREEN, D., (1972) 'A Comparison of Adjusted and Maladjusted Couples Using the Double Dyad Grid', *British Journal of Medical Psychology*, vol. 45, pp. 375–82.

RYLE, A., and HAMILTON, M., (1962) 'Neurosis in Fifty Married Couples', *Journal of Mental Science*, vol. 108, pp. 265–73.

RYLE, A., and LUNGHI, M., (1970) 'The Dyad Grid: a Modification of Repertory Grid Technique', *British Journal of Psychiatry*, vol. 117, pp. 323–7.

SAPOLSKY, A., (1965) 'Relationship between Patient–Doctor Compatibility, Mutual Perception, and Outcome of Treatment', *Journal of Abnormal Psychology*, vol. 70, pp. 70–76.

SCHAEFER, E. S., (1959) 'A Circumplex Model for Maternal Behaviour', *Journal of Abnormal and Social Psychology*, vol. 59, pp. 226–35.

SCHAEFER, E. S., and BELL, R. G., (1958) 'Development of a Parent Attitude Research Instrument', *Child Development*, vol. 29, pp. 339–61.

SCHEFF, T., (1964) 'Preferred Errors in Diagnosis', *Medical Care*, vol. 2, pp. 166–72; (1966) *Being mentally Ill*, Aldine; (1968) 'Negotiating Reality: Notes on Power in the Assessment of Responsibility', *Social Problems*, vol. 16, pp. 3–17.

SCHEFLEN, A. E., (1963) 'Communication and Regulation in Psychotherapy', *Psychiatry*, vol. 26, pp. 126–36.

SCHNEIDER, K., (1958) *Psychopathic Personalities*, tr. by M. W. Hamilton, Cassell.

SCHOFIELD, W., (1964) *Psychotherapy: the Purchase of Friendship*, Prentice-Hall.

SCHOTTSTRAEDT, W. W., JACKMAN, N. R., MCPHAIL, C. S., and WOLF, S. G., (1963) 'Social Interaction on a Metobolic Ward – the

Relation of Problems of Status to Chemical Balance', *Journal of Psychosomatic Research*, vol. 7, pp. 83–95.

SCHUHAM, A., (1967) 'The Double Bind Hypothesis a Decade Later', *Psychological Bulletin*, vol. 68, pp. 409–16.

SCHUTZ, W. C., (1958) *FIRO: a Three-Dimensional Theory of Interpersonal Behaviour*, Holt, Rinehart & Winston.

SCHWARTZ, A. N., and HAWKINS, H. L., (1965) 'Patient Models and Affect Statements in Group Therapy', in *Proceedings of the 73rd Annual Convention of the American Psychological Association*, American Psychological Association.

SCHWARTZ, C. G., (1957) 'Perspectives on Deviance – Wives' Definitions of Their Husbands' Mental Illness', *Psychiatry*, vol. 20, pp. 275–91.

SCOTT, R. D., and ASHWORTH, P. L., (1965) 'The Axis Value and the Transfer of Psychosis: a Scored Analysis of the Interaction in the Families of Schizophrenic Patients', *British Journal of Medical Psychology*, vol. 38, pp. 97–116.

SEARS, R. R., (1936) 'Experimental Studies in Projection: I Attribution of Traits', *Journal of Social Psychology*, vol. 7, pp. 151–63; (1970) 'Relation of Early Socialization Experiences to Self – Concepts and Gender Role in Middle Childhood', *Child Development*, vol. 41, pp. 267–90.

SEARS, R. R., MACCOBY, E. E., and LEVIN, H., (1957) *Patterns of Child Rearing*, Row, Peterson.

SECORD, P. F., and BACKMAN, C. W., (1961) 'Personality Theory and the Problem of Stability and Change in Individual Behaviour: an Interpersonal Approach', *Psychological Review*, vol. 68, pp. 21–32; (1964) *Social Psychology*, McGraw-Hill.

SHABAN, J., and JECKER, J., (1968) 'Risk Preference in Choosing an Evaluator: an Extension of Atkinson's Achievement Motivation Model', *Journal of Experimental Social Psychology*, vol. 4, pp. 35–45.

SHANNON, J., and GUERNEY, B., (1973) 'Interpersonal Effects of Interpersonal Behaviour', *Journal of Personality and Social Psychology*, vol. 26, pp. 142–50.

SHAPIRO, D. A., (1969) 'Empathy, Warmth and Genuineness in Psychotherapy', *British Journal of Social and Clinical Psychology*, vol. 8, pp. 350–61.

SHAPIRO, J. G., (1968) 'Relationships between Visual and Auditory Cues of Therapeutic Effectiveness', *Journal of Clinical Psychology*, vol. 24, pp. 236–9.

SHAPIRO, J. G., FOSTER, C. P., and POWELL, T., (1968) 'Facial and

Bodily Cues of Genuineness, Empathy and Warmth', *Journal of Clinical Psychology*, vol. 24, pp. 233–6.

SHAW, M. E., and REITAN, H. T., (1969) 'Attribution of Responsibility as a Basis for Sanctioning Behaviour', *British Journal of Social and Clinical Psychology*, vol. 8, pp. 217–26.

SHRAUGER, S., and ALTROCCHI, J., (1964) 'The Personality of the Perceiver as a Factor in Person Perception', *Psychological Bulletin*, vol. 62, pp. 289–308.

SIEGELMAN, E., BLOCK, J., BLOCK, J. H., and VON DER LIPPE, A., (1970) 'Antecedents of Optimal Psychological Adjustment', *Journal of Consulting and Clinical Psychology*, volume 35, pp. 283–9.

SIEGLER, M., and OSMOND, H., (1966) 'Models of Madness', *British Journal of Psychiatry*, vol. 112, pp. 1193–1203.

SILBER, E., and TIPPETT, J. S., (1965) 'Self-Esteem: Clinical Assessment and Measurement Validation', *Psychological Reports*, vol. 16, pp. 1017–71.

SINNETT, E. R., and HANFORD, D. B., (1962) 'The Effects of Patients' Relationships with Peers and Staff on Their Psychiatric Treatment Programmes', *Journal of Abnormal and Social Psychology*, vol. 64, pp. 151–4.

SLATER, E., and WOODSIDE, M., (1951) *Patterns of Marriage; a Study of Marriage Relationships in the Urban Working Classes*, Cassell.

SMITH, M. B., (1972) 'Normality: for an Abnormal Age', in D. Offer and D. X. Freedman (eds.), *Modern Psychiatry and Clinical Research: Essays in Honour of Roy R. Grinker*, Basic Books.

SODDY, K. and AHRENFELDT, R. H. (eds.), (1967) *Mental Health and Contemporary Thought*, Tavistock.

SOMMER, R., and OSMOND, H., (1962) 'The Schizophrenic No Society', *Psychiatry*, vol. 25, pp. 244–55.

STANTON, A. H., and SCHWARTZ, M. S., (1954) *The Mental Hospital: A Study of Institutional Participation in Psychiatric Illness and Treatment*, Tavistock.

STAR, S., (1955) 'The Public's Ideas about Mental Illness', paper presented at the annual meeting of the *National Association for Mental Health*, Indianapolis, Indiana.

STEELE, B. F., (1970) 'Parental Abuse of Infants and Small Children', in E. J. Anthony and T. Benedek (eds.), *Parenthood: its Psychology and Psychopathology*, Little, Brown.

STEINER, C. M., (1969) 'The Alcoholic Game', *Quarterly Journal of Studies on Alcohol*, vol. 30, pp. 920–56.

STRODTBECK, F. S., (1954) 'The Family as a Three-Person Group', *American Sociological Review*, vol. 19, pp. 23–9.

STRUPP, H. H., and BERGIN, A. E., (1969) 'Some Empirical and Conceptual Bases for Coordinated Research in Psychotherapy', *International Journal of Psychiatry*, vol. 7, pp. 18–90.

SULLIVAN, C. E., GRANT, N. Q., and GRANT, J. E., (1957) 'The Development of Interpersonal Maturity: Application to Delinquency', *Psychiatry*, vol. 20, pp. 373–86.

SULLIVAN, H. S., (1953) *The Interpersonal Theory of Psychiatry*, Norton.

SUOMI, S. J., HARLOW, H. S., and DOMEK, C. J., (1970) 'Effect of Repetitive Infant–Infant Separation of Young Monkeys', *Journal of Abnormal Psychology*, vol. 76, pp. 161–72.

SUTTON-SMITH, B., and ROSENBERG, B. G., (1970) *The Sibling*, Holt, Rinehart & Winston.

SZASZ, T. S., (1957) 'Committment of the Mentally Ill: Treatment or Social Restraint?'; *Journal of Nervous and Mental Disease*, vol. 125, pp. 293–307; (1961) *The Myth of Mental Illness*, Hoeber-Harper; (1971) 'The Sane Slave: an Historical Note on the Use of Medical Diagnosis as Justificatory Rhetoric', *American Journal of Psychotherapy*, vol. 25, pp. 228–39.

TAYLOR, D. A., and ALTMAN, I., (1966) 'Intimacy-Scaled Stimuli for Use in Studies of Interpersonal Relations', *Psychological Reports*, vol. 19, pp. 729–30.

TAYLOR, S. D., WILBUR, M., and OSNOS, R., (1966) 'The Wives of Drug Addicts', *American Journal of Psychiatry*, vol. 123, pp. 585–91.

TEASDALE, J., SEGRAVES, R. T., and ZACUNE, J., (1971) 'Psychoticism in Drug Users', *British Journal of Social and Clinical Psychology*, vol. 10, pp. 160–71.

TERMAN, L. M., (1938) *Psychological Factors in Marital Happiness*, McGraw-Hill.

TERMAN, L. M., and ODEN, M. H., (1947) *The Gifted Child Grown Up: Twenty-five Years' Follow-up of a Superior Group*, Stanford University Press.

THARP, R. J., (1963) 'Psychological Patterning in Marriage', *Psychological Bulletin*, vol. 60, pp. 97–117.

THIBAUT, J. W., and KELLEY, H. H., (1959) *The Social Psychology of Groups*, Wiley.

THIBAUT, J. W., and RIECKEN, H. W., (1955) 'Some Determinants and Consequences of the Perception of Social Causality', *Journal of Personality*, vol. 24, pp. 113ff.

THORNE, F., (1957) 'Epidemiological Studies of Chronic Frustration–Hostility–Aggression States', *American Journal of Psychiatry*, vol. 113, pp. 717–21.

TIENARI, P., (1963) 'Psychiatric Illness in Identical Twins', *Acta Psychiatrica Scandinavia*, supplement 171.

TRUAX, C. B., (1966) 'Influence of Patient Statements on Judgements of Therapist Statements during Psychotherapy', *Journal of Clinical Psychology*, vol. 22, pp. 335–7.

TRUAX, C. B., and CARKHUFF, R. R., (1967) *Toward Effective Counseling and Psychotherapy*, Aldine.

TUDDENHAM, R. D., (1959) 'The Constancy of Personality Ratings over Two Decades', *Genetic Psychology Monographs*, vol. 60, pp. 3–30.

VITALO, R. L., (1971) 'Teaching Improved Interpersonal Functioning as a Preferred Mode of Treatment', *Journal of Clinical Psychology*, vol. 27, pp. 166–71.

VON BERTALANFFY, L., (1966) 'General System Theory and Psychiatry', in S. Arieti (ed.), *American Handbook of Psychiatry*, vol. 3, Basic Books.

WALTERS, J., and STINNETT, N., (1971) 'Parent–Child Relationships: a Decade Review of Research', *Journal of Marriage and the Family*, vol. 33, pp. 70–111.

WALTZER, H., (1963) 'A Psychotic Family – *Folie à Douze*', *Journal of Nervous and Mental Disease*, vol. 137, pp. 67–75.

WARR, P. B., and KNAPPER, C., (1968) *The Perception of People and Events*, Wiley.

WATSON, J. P., (1970) 'A Repertory Grid Method of Studying Groups', *British Journal of Psychiatry*, vol. 117, pp. 309–18.

WATZLAWICK, P., BEAVIN, J. H., and JACKSON, B. D., (1968) *Pragmatics of Human Communication: a Study of Interactional Patterns, Pathologies and Paradoxies*, Faber.

WEINSTEIN. E. A., (1969) 'The Development of Interpersonal Competence', in D. A. Goslin (ed.), *Handbook of Socialization Theory and Research*, Rand-McNally.

WHALEN, C., (1969) 'Effects of a Model and Instructions on Group Verbal Behaviours', *Journal of Consulting and Clinical Psychology*, vol. 33, pp. 509–21.

WHITE, R. W., (1964) *The Abnormal Personality*, 3rd edition, Ronald Press.

WILLIAMS, E., (1971) 'The Effect of Varying the Elements in the Bannister–Fransella Grid Test of Thought Disorder', *British Journal of Psychiatry*, vol. 119, pp. 207–12.

WINCH, R. S., (1958) *Mate Selection: a Study of Complementary Needs*, Harper.

WING, J. K., (1967) 'Institutionalism in Mental Hospitals', in T. Scheff (ed.), *Mental Illness and Social Processes*, Harper.

WINTER, W. D., and FERREIRA, J. (eds.), (1969) *Research in Family Interaction*, Science and Behaviour Books.

WOOTTON, B., (1959) *Social Science and Social Pathology*, Allen & Unwin.

WORTHY, M., GAREY, A. L., and KAHN, G. M., (1969) 'Self-Disclosure as an Exchange Process', *Journal of Personality and Social Psychology*, vol. 13, pp. 59–63.

WRIGHT, P. H., (1968) 'Need Similarity, Need Complementarity and the Place of Personality in Interpersonal Attraction', *Journal of Experimental Research in Personality*, vol. 3, pp. 126–35.

WYNNE, L., RYCKOFF, I., DAY, J., and HIRSCH, S., (1958) 'Pseudo-Mutuality in the Family Relations of Schizophrenics', *Psychiatry*, vol. 21, pp. 205–20.

YARROW, M. R., CAMPBELL, J. D., and BURTON, R. V., (1968) *Child Rearing: an Inquiry into Research and Methods*, Jossey-Bass.

ZEITLYN, B. B., (1967) 'The Therapeutic Community – Fact or Fantasy?' *British Journal of Psychiatry*, vol. 113, pp. 1083–6.

ZIGLER, E., and PHILLIPS, L., (1960) 'Social Effectiveness and Symptomatic Behaviours', *Journal of Abnormal and Social Psychology*, vol. 61, pp. 231–8.

Index

Subject Index

A–B therapist variable, 173–4

Acceptance, *see* Affection, Empathy, Warmth

Adlerian school of psychotherapy, 166, 176

Adjustment, 46, 53, 57, 61, 76, 83, 86–7, 108–9, 118, 122, 137–9, 142–5, 162, 164, 174

Adolescents, 16, 19, 25, 28, 48, 50, 53–4, 56, 58–9, 61, 88–9, 147, 150

Affection, 20, 31–2, 38–9, 42, 48, 50–51, 53, 60, 61, 67, 71, 75, 81–2, 89, 95, 103, 117–18, 122–3, 172, 191, 195, 200; *see also* Empathy, Warmth

Aggression, aggressiveness, 23, 34, 40, 44, 58, 66–7, 76, 88–9, 110, 126, 133, 136, 144, 150, 155, 187, 207, 215; *see also* Criticality, Hostility, Rejection

Alcoholism, alcohol use, 15, 40, 43, 47, 72, 83, 90, 95, 105–7, 113, 126, 128, 175, 185, 193, 217

Alienation, 61

Anti-social behaviour, disorder, *see* delinquency

Anxiety, 54, 56, 59, 64, 78, 92, 110, 141, 143, 145, 153, 157, 180, 183, 206

Arson, 78

Artefacts, *see* Methodological problems

Assertiveness, *see* Dominance

Assertive training, 190–92

Atmosphere
  in the home, 14–15, 20, 22–3, 27, 46
  in the hospital, 203–4, 215–16, 218–19, 225

Attitude change, 160–61, 192–3

Attitudes
  in families, 12, 23, 33, 37–8, 40, 47–8, 65, 225
  towards mental illness, 149–56, 209, 212
  towards others, 60–63, 74–85, 88–9, 92, 108
  towards race, 192, 214–15
  towards self, 53–9, 85–8, 90
  towards smoking, 192–3
  in treatment settings, 176, 197–203, 210–12, 215–16, 218–19, 224–5

Attraction, 62, 65–6, 68, 71, 81–2, 89, 92, 96, 141–2, 184–6, 188, 195

Attribution theory, 134–7, 145, 162

Authoritarian, authoritarianism, 34, 75, 196, 198–9, 202

Autonomy, *see* Control of others' behaviour

Battered children, 41

Biological explanations, 11–12, 46–8, 51, 53–4

Birth order, 13, 15–16, 37, 39, 45, 50

Broken home, *see* Loss of parents

Causation, 12–13, 16, 21, 27, 43–50, 52, 64–5, 70–71, 88, 110, 117–23, 131, 136–7, 181, 184–5, 226–7

Childhood disorder, maladjustment, 15–16, 28, 35–6, 39–40, 61, 64, 75–6, 88–90, 187–8

Child-caretaking, child-rearing, 12, 14, 24–5, 27, 31–2, 34–9, 44–6, 50, 104, 111–13, 122, 134

Circumplex ordering of behaviour, 30–32, 66–9, 184, 227

Climate, *see* Atmosphere

Cognitive complexity, 83

Cognitive dissonance, 89, 192–3

Communication, 17–19, 29–30, 45, 129–30, 132, 134, 150, 167–8, 177, 186, 190, 204, 213, 216, 218, 224

Communicational analysis, 174–5

Complementarity, complementariness, 71–3, 89, 95–6, 100, 172, 195

Conflict
  in families, 25–8, 44, 50, 227
  in hospital, 209–17, 225, 227
  over hospital admission, 133
  between individuals, 75–6, 132
  between levels of communication, 17–19
  in marriage, 12, 20, 46, 50, 97, 122, 227
  response to, 46

between roles, 148–9, 162, 179

Confrontation, 183–4, 195, 218

Consistency theories, 85–7, 89, 192

Contact with family, 20, 23–4, 32–3, 100, 112, 114–16, 122

Contagion, 22–3, 98–100, 122, 214–15

Control of others' behaviour, 30–34, 36–41, 47–9, 51, 53, 62, 95–6, 122, 130, 143, 172, 196, 200–203

Control of own behaviour, 127, 134–5, 149–50, 155, 179

Criticality, criticism, 116, 122, 176, 180, 195, 201, 206–8

Custodialism, 198–200, 217

Decision-making, 27–9, 43, 50, 59, 95, 110–14, 117, 145–6, 208, 218

Defensiveness, defence mechanism, 57, 59–60, 92, 112, 143, 169, 179–80, 215

Delinquency, 14–17, 28–9, 34–6, 61–2, 170

Delusions, 23, 40, 42, 52, 56, 88, 132–3, 145, 152

Depression, 13, 15, 22, 56, 64, 91, 110, 112, 130, 139–40, 144–5, 153–5, 180

Deprivation, 14, 98

Diagnosis, 17, 34–6, 64, 72, 95, 97, 122, 124, 144–6, 148, 162, 185, 198, 210–11

Directiveness, 176, 178, 180–82, 195

Discipline, *see* Child-caretaking

Discord, *see* Conflict

Disorder in other family members, 20–21, 120

Author Index

More about Penguins and Pelicans

Penguinews, which appears every month, contains details of all the new books issued by Penguins as they are published. From time to time it is supplemented by *Penguins in Print*, which is our complete list of almost 5,000 titles.

A specimen copy of *Penguinews* will be sent to you free on request. Please write to Dept EP, Penguin Books Ltd, Harmondsworth, Middlesex, for your copy.

In the U.S.A.: For a complete list of books available from Penguins in the United States write to Dept CS, Penguin Books, 625 Madison Avenue, New York, New York 10022.

In Canada: For a complete list of books available from Penguins in Canada write to Penguin Books Canada Ltd, 41 Steelcase Road West, Markham, Ontario.

Some books on Psychology and Psychiatry
published by Penguin Books

Some books on Psychology and Psychiatry published by Penguin Books

Some books on Psychology and Psychiatry
published by Penguin Books

Some books on Psychology and Psychiatry
published by Penguin Books